CW00665341

THE LAST KNIGHT OF MALTA

Fighting against the ruin of an Order

THOMAS FRELLER
GABRIELE VON TRAUCHBURG

midsea BOOKS

Published by Midsea Books Ltd.
Carmelites Street, Sta Venera HMR 11, Malta
Tel: 2149 7046   Fax: 2149 6904
sales@midseabooks.com

Copyright © Literary, Thomas Freller 2010
Copyright © Editorial, Midsea Books Ltd 2010

No part of this publication may be reproduced,
stored in a retrieval system or transmitted
in any form by any means, electronic, mechanical,
photocopying, recording or otherwise,
without the previous written permission
of the authors.

First published in 2010

Produced by Mizzi Design and Graphic Services Ltd.
Printed at Gutenberg Press Ltd, Malta

ISBN: 978-99932-7-330-1

CONTENTS

Introduction – A knight and his principles v

Chapter 1

A youth in the shadow of the Cross of Malta 1

Chapter 2

A page in Malta – and a tense atmosphere 13

Chapter 3

In the limelight of history – The campaign of Algiers 23

Chapter 4

Bavarian Officer and member of the Order of Malta 61

Chapter 5

A dangerous mission and the last days

of Hospitaller Malta 85

Chapter 6

Fighting until the end 101

Chapter 7

Immersed in the Order's struggle for survival 125

Chapter 8

Back in the Mediterranean – Bavarian envoy and

spy in Catania 169

Chapter 9

A hero of the Napoleonic Wars and the closing

of a circle 185

Sources and further reading referring

to the respective chapters... 205

Bibliography

1) Archival manuscript sources 219

2) Single manuscript sources 221

3) Printed works 223

    a) Sources 223

    b) Literature 225

ACKNOWLEDGMENTS

Besides Louis J. Scerri, MA,
for his essential help, the authors would like to thank:
Ms Maroma Camilleri, MA;
Albert, Graf von Rechberg;
Bernhard, Graf von Rechberg;
Albrecht, Graf von Rechberg;
Mgr John Azzopardi;
Ms Nataliya Gurevich;
Dr Albert Friggieri;
Mr Michael Galea;
Mr Walter Ziegler;

and the staffs of
the National Library of Malta;
the Bayerisches Hauptstaatsarchiv, Munich;
the Landesbibliothek Wiesbaden (Hesse);
the Stadt- und Universitätsbibliothek Frankfurt a. M.;
the Bayerische Staatsbibliothek, Munich;
Kreisarchiv Göppingen; and
Gräflich Rechbergsches Familienarchiv Donzdorf

INTRODUCTION –
A KNIGHT AND HIS PRINCIPLES

The protagonist of this book was, of course, not the last knight of the famous Order of Malta (Sovereign Military Hospitaller Order of St John of Jerusalem, of Rhodes, and of Malta). The Order still exists and its members (volunteers, doctors, nurses, and knights – whether professed knights of justice, knights of devotion, or knights of grace) still give most valuable services to the poor, the sick, and persons in need all over the world. However, the title of this book is correct in a way as Josef Maria von Rechberg was one of the last knights of the Order who embodied and lived the millennial virtues of the institution, especially loyalty to its zeals and commands. Although Hospitaller Malta at the end of the eighteenth century is very often described as a place of corroded virtues and declining spirit, there were knights with strong principles and real dedication. Joseph Maria von Rechberg was one of them. This fact would not necessarily be enough to make him the protagonist of a monograph. It is his remarkable military career, his direct participation in many of the spectacular events of the late eighteenth and early nineteenth century which makes him worth studying and a subject of interest for the general public.

Joseph Maria von Rechberg was truly an eyewitness of the upheavals at the turn of the nineteenth century. It was the time when an entire epoch, the *Ancien Régime*, came to an end. In many of these events Rechberg stood in the front line. He fought in the last big battle of the Order against Muslim forces – the notorious Algiers campaign of 1784 – and he carried out a most risky mission to Malta in the spring of 1798 to warn the Order of an oncoming French attack. He was the commander of Fort Tigné and fought prominently against the French invasion of Malta in June 1798 and he was the last knight who gave up his arms to the superior French forces; he participated as colonel, later as general, in the Napoleonic wars; and he acted as Bavarian envoy and spy for the Order during its exile in Catania. Owing to a twist of political opportunism of his lord, the Bavarian king, Rechberg then for many years marched with his old enemies, the French, and participated in Napoleon's disastrous Russian campaign. He also witnessed when the fall of the star of Napoleon descended on European battlefields after 1813.

On a more global level, the background of the events described in this book is the epoch when new thoughts, new political systems, and secularism shook many European societies from the roots. Joseph Maria von Rechberg lived through all these new movements: enlightened absolutism, Freemasonry, secularization, and the rise of bourgeois concepts of society. He also witnessed how the Order of Malta, seen by many then as a strange sort of a centennial institution, rooted in the spirit of medieval Christianity, clashed with the rather materialistic plans of enlightened princes. Rechberg was also present when the Order was expelled from Malta, an event which can serve as a symbol of the end of a whole period of European history and culture. It was also a watershed in Mediterranean history, signalling the end of the smaller powers and the beginning of a movement which came to be labelled as French or British imperialism.

Rechberg's notes and observations serve to make us understand better a period of transition when the Order was desperately trying to protect its status and prerogatives and trying to establish a network of spies, intelligence, and lobbies which have not yet been fully understood and very often wrongly interpreted by historians. Rechberg's brave resistance against the French in the fateful June of 1798 was mentioned by various contemporary authors and eyewitnesses like Louis de Boisgelin de Kerdu, Charles Joseph

Joseph Maria von Rechberg

Meyer de Knonau, Joseph de Maisonneuve, and Fortunato Panzavecchia. Starting from Panzavecchia's *L'ultimo periodo della Storia di Malta* (1835), his name was, however, misspelt as *Reichberg* which created some confusion amongst later scholars and authors. This wrong spelling ('*Le Baron de Reichberg*') already appears in the '*Note des Prieurs Commandeurs et Chevaliers designés par S.A.S.E. pour former la nouvelle Langue*

Coat of arms of the Rechberg family

Anglo Bavaroise' which was drawn up early in 1783. That is what Cannon Panzavecchio reported about Rechberg's brave resistance against the French: '*Fort Tigné era presiditiato da una porzione del reggimento di cacciatori sotto il commando del leale e coraggioso Reichberg* (sic), *della lingua di Baviera. Furono quei bravi in quod giorno ben per tre volte assaliti dai repubblicani, i quali però furono altrettante volte costretti a ritirarsi con qualche perdita.*' Rechberg's military deeds subsequently went not unnoticed by modern historians like Carmel Testa, Michael Galea, Alison Hoppen, and Stephen C. Spiteri. Testa, in his authoritative book on *The French in Malta. 1798–1800*, noted: '*On the other side of Valletta, the Bavarian Knight-commander Reichberg* (sic) *was in charge of Fort Tigné which was garrisoned by a company of* Cacciatori Maltesi.'

This book brings together and interprets the various documentary fragments of Rechberg's chequered and adventurous life and career spread in various archives and libraries in Europe. Besides the archives of the Rechberg family in Donzdorf (Baden-Wuerttemberg, Germany), the core of this material lies in the Archives of the Order of Malta housed in the National Library of Malta at Valletta; the Archives of the Grand Magistry, Palazzo di Malta, Rome; and the Bayerisches Hauptstaatsarchiv in Munich. An important contribution was Rechberg's own letters and the diary he kept during the Algiers campaign of 1784. Some of Rechberg's diary notes were published by Emil Gemeinder, a clerk in the service of the counts of Rechberg. He translated parts of the French manuscript into German and published it in 1971. The diary is today preserved in the archives of the Rechberg family in Donzdorf.

CHAPTER 1
A YOUTH IN THE SHADOW
OF THE CROSS OF MALTA

Joseph Maria Johann Nepomuk Hyazinth Franz Xaver Kasimir Franz de Paula, to give the full name of the protagonist of this book, was born on 8 March 1769 in the Swabian village of Donzdorf. Joseph Maria's parents were Maximilian Emanuel, Baron (from 1810 Count) von Rechberg und Rothenloewen zu Hohenrechberg (1736–1810) and Walburga Maria Baroness von Sandizell (1744–1818). One of his several brothers and sisters, his elder brother Aloys Franz Xaver Maximilian Franz de Paula (1766–1849), later became a highly reputed Bavarian diplomat, chamberlain, and minister and also became involved in the affairs of the Order of Malta when he was chosen to calm down Czar and Grand Master Paul I after the Bavarians had sequestrated the Order of St John's possessions. Other brothers were Franz Xaver Johann Nepomuk Alois Hyacinth Norbert (1770–1841), Bavarian secret councillor and member of the cathedral chapters of Passau and Ratisbon, and Johann Nepomuk Joseph Maria Karl Johann vom Kreuz (1773–1817), Knight of Malta, Bavarian secret councillor and general director of the forests.

Joseph Maria von Rechberg was born in the last years of the *Ancien Régime*. The nobility of France, the lands of Germany, Italy, and Eastern Europe was then still a cosmopolitan class very much opposed to the atmosphere of the national states. The education of the offspring of these nobles was an international affair. The leading European language was French, and even in the lands of Germany the private teachers and tutors very often came from France or Italy. In the case of the young Rechberg it was a private tutor

Count Maximilian
Emanuel von Rechberg
und Rothenlöwen

The castle of Hohenrechberg (Swabia), the old residence of the Family of
Rechberg (engraving c.1830 by Louis Mayer)

from Luxembourg who took care of his early training and education, namely in French, mathematics, and geography. From his parents' comments, it appears that he was an intelligent and hard-working pupil.

Besides French, Rechberg knew Latin fluently and, during his time in Malta, he also came to learn Italian very well. This sort of education and training produced people who did not think in terms of national boundaries and frontiers. According to the concept of the type of *honnête homme* – now also influenced by the ideas of enlightenment – good and appropriate behaviour had to be orientated by nature and based on reason and knowledge. The absolutistic rulers of the seventeenth century had managed to integrate the nobility in their courts and to tame them by absorbing them into their systems of administration. Nobles served in the high offices of administration, diplomacy, military, and also the clergy. To cope with these duties and tasks, it was necessary to possess a *nobilitas erudita*, a basic knowledge of common law, state law, diplomacy, administration, military sciences, geography, and a general *conduite*. The Enlightenment had left a massive stamp of utilitarianism and centralism in the concept of princely administrations. The evolving process of secularization in the mid-eighteenth century would find its eruptive results after the French Revolution.

Still in this period of increasing regulation and rational utility, there were possible careers which did not follow the straight road and instead opted for exceptional alternatives. The life of Joseph Maria von Rechberg is one example. The Order of St John, then still based on the rocky island of Malta in the central Mediterranean, offered such careers. The reason why a noble family should enrol their offspring in this centennial Order – or other such military or religious Orders – was, however, very often extremely pragmatic and prosaic. For many second- or third-born male children of nobles, enrolment in a religious or military Order meant a good option of being provided with income, titles, power,

3

benefices, sinecures, and prebends. From the rational point of view, the structures, rich possessions, and activities of many of these Orders went against the concept of the Enlightened State, and in fact – as documented in Prussia under Frederick II and in Austria under Emperor Joseph II – many princes tried their best to reduce these institutions' power and riches.

Considering these circumstances and the cultural milieu, hardly any religious zeal could be expected from these young men. There were many German families who enrolled their children in the Teutonic Order – which, by the eighteenth century, had long lost its former territories in the Baltic States and had declined into an institution without any military tasks – not for national or religious motives but to secure their sons income, titles, and prestige. In case of the Order of St John, there was a slight difference as the knights had kept their headquarters at the fringe of Christian Europe and claimed a role as a bulwark against Ottoman expansion and a sort of 'Christian Police' in the Mediterranean. However, with the new network of treaties of the Ottomans and beys of North Africa with the Christian powers, this function as a bulwark had ceased to be relevant. It is true that the Order officially kept carrying out its famous caravans against Muslim corsairs but, as we will observe later, they had become merely a sort of a façade.

It must have presumably been rather materialistic thoughts which motivated Baron Maximilian Emanuel von Rechberg und Rothenlöwen to send his second eldest son at the tender age of 14 as a page to Grand Master Rohan Polduc and to pay the *passagio* (entrance fee) to have him received as a novice into the Order. The usual age of profession was 18, with the caravans at Malta being normally deferred to the twentieth year. Some families, however, were allowed to send their boys at the age of 12 or 13 years as pages to the grand master. There were sixteen of them at a time and selection was a greatly coveted honour. Enrolment at such an early age also favoured a promising career, as the Order had established the concept of seniority – the *droit d'ancienneté* – which meant that the more years a member served, the more he was entitled to good positions and commanderies. In a letter dated 23 May 1786 sent to conventual chaplain Johann Felix Eisele, priest-commander of Altöttingen, in Malta Maximilian Emanuel von Rechberg explained his thoughts and projects: '*I love my children very much and wish for them the best on earth. But this happiness should not come from riches and possessions but from an inner satisfaction, inner calmness, and from a harmony with the principles of their class and status.*' Only a few months later Joseph Maria's younger brother Johann Nepomuk also was sent as page to the grand master's court at Malta.

The knights of justice were still the backbone of the Order. This position was longed for when the young Rechberg joined the Order. Only knights of justice were qualified to advance to the dignities of grand prior, *bali*, or grand master. Although he was expected to devote himself to the interests of the Order, he was permitted to take employment in the service of kings or princes. Thus – especially in the eighteenth century – many of these knights were 'seconded' for special appointments in foreign courts, for naval or military duty or on diplomatic missions. Besides Rechberg, many such will be encountered in this book. The page and aspirant to the grade of a knight of justice had to present himself in the grand priory in his home country. Because of the special family connections with Bavaria, the young Rechberg did not go to Heitersheim in Baden the seat of the grand priory of Germany – but to Munich where the new Bavarian grand priory was being set up. We will soon come back to this special case.

That the Swabian Baron Maximilian Emanuel von Rechberg und Rothenlöwen did not opt for the Teutonic Order – although it had some rich commanderies not far from the family headquarters at the castle of Rechberg and the village of Donzdorf in Swabia – but for the knights of St John had certainly much to do with contemporary events. For young Joseph Maria and also for his younger brother Johann Nepomuk these developments would decisively form his future life and career. In the early 1780s Bavarian Duke Elector Karl Theodor was working hard to establish a grand priory of the Order in his territory, efforts which would later lead to the erection of the Anglo-Bavarian langue. Joseph Maria's and Johann Nepomuk's father must have known about this affair at a very early stage and he must have immediately taken an initiative. Several members of the Rechberg-Family had served as *Oberhofmeisters* at the court of the dukes of Bavaria. Baron von Rechberg himself was *Oberhofmeister* of Duchess Anna Maria. The Rechbergs lived in Munich in winter, but moved to their castle at Donzdorf in summer.

The direct contact with the (not yet officially founded) Bavarian grand priory was made by Joseph Maria's uncle Count Joseph von Törring. There was some correspondence between Maximilian Emanuel von Rechberg and the count of Törring in the summer of 1781 discussing the matter. On 26 July 1781 the Rechbergs officially applied for one of their sons for a position in the pagery of the grand master of Malta. Another channel of intelligence between Munich and the Rechbergs and one reason for the close contacts with the Order could have been Joseph Maria's Bavarian mother, Walburga Maria Baroness of Sandizell. Her brother Joseph Maria von Sandizell was then also earmarked as Bavarian knight of St John. Like his nephew, he would also make a good career in Bavarian service by becoming secret councillor and vice-president of the Bavarian court. The documents concerning the proofs of nobility were presented to *Bali* Johann Baptist von Flachslanden, who was earmarked to become the lieutenant of the Bavarian grand prior, and the administrator and *ricevitore Abbé* Casimir Haeffelin. The German langue of the Order – and officially also the new Anglo-Bavarian langue – required 16 quarterings of nobility. The Rechberg family – documented since the twelfth century as important *ministeriales* of the Hohenstaufen dynasty could

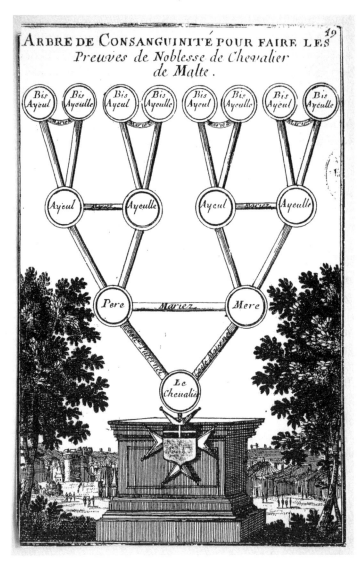

Proofs of nobility of a French knight of the Order of St John, French engraving, c.1700

easily provide them. In Munich, a special commission – presided over by Casimir Haeffelin – investigated the case and found no obstacles for Joseph Maria von Rechberg and later Johann Nepomuk to be sent to Malta as pages of the grand master and as aspirants of knights of justice. On 16 September 1781 the conventual chaplain Giuseppe Massimiliano de Branca informed Maximilian Emanuel von Rechberg that the application had been favourably received.

That explains why in the summer of 1781, when the negotiations to establish the new Bavarian grand priory were still far from being concluded, there appeared 'Le Baron de Reichberg (sic)' in a *Note des Commandeurs et Chevaliers aspirant dans l'Ordre de Malte* compiled by the clerks of the Bavarian court in Munich. The 12-year-old Joseph Maria was listed '*dans la minorité*' as an aspirant to become a Bavarian knight of St John, at a time when the Rechberg family had not even paid the *passagio* to the treasury of the Order.

But let us present the events in their proper context which will also serve to understand the future career and life of Joseph Maria von Rechberg. The background to the creation of the Bavarian grand priory and subsequently the Anglo-Bavarian langue clearly showed how much the Order had become a passive victim on the chessboard of international politics and also of personal greed and prestige. In fact, the driving forces behind the installation of the new langue was not the Order but Bavarian Duke Elector Karl Theodor who was keen to provide his bastard son Karl August von Bretzenheim with a prestigious post; he was duly assisted by *Abbé* Casimir Haeffelin and the former captain general of the Order's galleys, *Bali* Johann Baptist von Flachslanden who smelled more riches and income. Even before the langue was officially installed and the agreements signed and ratified by Grand Master Rohan and Pope Pius VI, the hardly 12-year-old count of Bretzenheim was nominated grand prior of Bavaria. Still a baby, he had been nominated imperial count on 17 April 1774, while on 12 May 1790 he was invested as a prince of the empire. Flachslanden was nominated as his plenipotentiary with the right of succession. The governor of the Palatinate, Count Franz Albert Leopold von Oberndorff, was nominated as the *balí* of Neuburg.

In all 28 commanderies were created in Bavaria, including four commanderies reserved for clerics. By 9 April 1782, the Order's ordinary council had accepted the project. The title 'langue of England' was officially changed into 'Anglo-Bavarian langue'. On 13 April 1782 Rohan informed the pope in detail about the new decrees. According to the bulls of 1782, the Anglo-Bavarian langue was to consist of the grand priory of Ebersberg, the bailiwick of Neuburg, together with, in theory, the grand priories of England, Ireland, and the bailiwick of Eagle. Most of the first commanders were granted dispensation from the vow of celibacy. The Order insisted that no change should be made in the composition of the councils, which meant no increase in the number of conventual *balís*, and so it was decided to derive the titles and functions from those of the dormant English langue. Duke Elector Karl Theodor kept the right to appoint the first commanders and to dispense them from the obligation to undertake their caravans in Malta. In future, however, the members of the new langue had to follow the common statutes of the Order. An aspirant for membership had to be already in the military or civil service of the duke elector. But – as in the case of young Joseph Maria – there were exceptions. Like all other clerical possessions, the possessions of the Bavarian grand priory were also subject to government taxes which had to be paid by the commanders to the provincial chapter which then handed the money over to the Bavarian minister of finance. The swift Haeffelin was made *ricevitore* of the new langue, entrusted with the collection of the responsions and other dues and taxes for the common treasury.

Rohan's interest in maintaining good relations with the Bavarians is shown by the fact that one of the six pensions of magistral grace he was allowed to bestow went to Flachslanden.

9

The Jesuit possessions in Ebersberg with a revenue of 20,000 guilders passed to the grand prior of Bavaria. The bailiwick of Neuburg had an annual revenue of 10,000 guilders while the rest of the possessions amounted to 141,000 guilders. On 22 July 1782, a rescript by the duke elector fixed the jurisdictional position of the new lands of the Order in Bavaria. The future grand prior, who was equal in status to a prelate, had the lower jurisdiction over the lands directly granted to him while the commanders were to be considered members of the estates of the country. By a decree of 5 August 1782, all former possessions of the Jesuits in Bavaria, Palatinate-Neuburg, and Palatinate-Sulzbach were officially transferred to the new langue. On 16 January 1783 the duke elector officially announced the list of the knights and their commanderies, which included Baron Joseph Maria von Sandizell, the previously mentioned uncle of young Joseph Maria. In the same '*Note des Prieurs Commandeurs et Chevaliers designés par S.A.S.E. pour former la nouvelle Langue Anglo Bavaroise*' the young Joseph Maria ('Le Baron de Reichberg (sic)') was also included. A few months later (5 August 1783) this list – including the name of Baron von Rechberg – was confirmed by the authorities in Malta. Presumably this refers to Joseph Maria and not to Johann Nepomuk, who was then only ten years old.

The pope's *Vidimus* of the decrees of the Order's council for the Anglo-Bavarian langue had been given on 18 September 1782 at S. Maria Maggiore. In early November 1782 the papal bull of the new langue arrived in Malta, with the final ratification by Pius VI coming on 19 May 1783. Although the *Installation Solemnelle de l'Ordre de Malte en Bavière* had been announced in Bavaria on 14 October 1782, the installation of the langue took place in Munich on 10 and 11 December 1782 with great pomp. In the church of St Michael, Flachslanden introduced all the new knights to Karl Theodor who decorated each one with the insignia of the Order. To commemorate the foundation of the langue, the duke elector struck a medal. In the church of St Michael a monument was erected, and cordial congratulations were received from the king of France and the German emperor. The Bavarian commanderies and documents of membership and investitures were officially handed over to their holders on 1 March 1784. Joseph Maria was not present at this ceremony because he already had departed for Malta the previous year. A rescript of 22 October 1784 confirmed the aspirants and holders of the commanderies in Bavaria. Johann Nepomuk is listed as holder of the commandery of Mindelheim St Johannes.

In the meantime the young Joseph Maria's training and formative years continued. In 1780 and 1781 he attended the princely academy for cadets *(Marianische Landakademie)*. In the autumn of 1781 he was enrolled in the highly reputed Benedictine school in the French town of Metz. On his travels from Eastern Swabia to Metz, he was accompanied by his parents, his brothers Franz Xaver, Johann Nepomuk, Carl, and Anton, and his sister Elisabeth. The family stopped in Strasbourg where one daughter, Maximiliane, lived in a convent. From there they travelled via Sarrebourg, Lunéville and Nancy, reaching Metz on 26 November. Despite its clerical character, the Benedictine school in Metz was then an institution very much influenced by the principles of enlightened studies and modern approaches to the teaching of the sciences. In the next one and a half years the young sons of the Rechberg family were trained by the Benedictine fathers in Latin, French, religion, philosophy, mathematics, and other natural sciences. For Joseph Maria, this period of education stopped in March 1783. According to the documents in the Rechberg family archive he had returned to Donzdorf by late March of that year.

In the meantime in the headquarters of the Bavarian grand priory in Munich and at the Order's seat in Valletta, everything had been prepared for Joseph Maria's voyage to Malta. On 17 February 1783 Duke Elector Karl Theodor had informed Joseph Maria's father that his son should prepare himself to travel to Malta in April and take up service in the pagery of Grand Master Rohan. The same letter contained instructions about acquiring a uniform of the Order, to prepare again the documents of the proofs of nobility to take to Malta, and to collect the sum of 675 guilders for the passage. Joseph Maria was still in Germany when, on 22 February 1783, he was appointed *supernumeraire* second lieutenant in the regiment of the heir of the elector. Until the last preparations for the journey to Malta were completed, the Rechbergs invested the princely sum of 1772 guilders to provide Joseph Maria with the suitable uniforms, arms, the passage money, and other necessities.

CHAPTER 2
A PAGE IN MALTA –
AND A TENSE ATMOSPHERE

Joseph Maria von Rechberg must have arrived in Munich by early May 1783. There he met another young Bavarian nobleman who was also aiming for a career in the Order, Count Guido von Taufkirchen, who was then going to Malta to fill the post of an acting lieutenant-turcopilier. Taufkirchen would act as a sort of tutor for the younger Joseph Maria. Together they arranged the last preparations for their tour to Malta. On 13 May they left Munich accompanied by Taufkirchen's servants.

According to Joseph Maria's letters, the crossing of the Alps went by without any problems. By 26 May they had arrived in Venice. The Venetian Count Rambaldi – apparently the father of a student friend of one of Joseph Maria's brothers at the academy of Metz – had been prepared by means of letters about the coming of the young German noblemen. Rambaldi received them in his residence and over the following days showed them around the sites of the city. He also introduced them to members of the Venetian upper class. In a letter from Venice, dated 28 May 1783, Joseph Maria informed his brother Franz Xaver in Metz in detail about the most interesting places of the *Serenissima* and advised him to address the subsequent letters to 'Monsieur le baron de Rechberg, Lieutenant du regiment de Churprince, Chevalier de l'ordre de Malthe de la langue angloise-bavaroise, et page de son Eminence le Grand Maitre'.

On 23 June Rechberg and Taufkirchen boarded a Venetian merchant vessel bound for Malta. To fight the notorious North African pirates and corsairs, the ship was equipped with eight large-calibre guns. The passage down the Adriatic Sea and along the south-western Italian coast was rather uneventful. The ship sailed into Malta's famous *Porto Grande* after eighteen days.

During most of his stay on the island, the young Rechberg was accommodated in the palace of Gaspart Corneiro *Balí* of Acre facing Marsamxett which had been built in 1696 by the Maltese architect of Syrian descent Carlo Gimach; it was purchased in 1783 by the representatives of the Bavarian langue for 24,000 *scudí* to be converted into the auberge of the new langue and soon became known as the *Auberge de Baviere*. On 22 October 1784, 6,000 *scudí* were voted for the maintenance of the auberge and the seat of the chapter. The regulations of the daily life in the auberge and the appointment of a secretary and an archivist were also stipulated. The upkeep of the auberge and the provision of the resident members of the langue finally came to cost annually 10,000 guilders. The Anglo-Bavarian langue took over the chapel of San Carlo Borromeo *'detta delle reliquie'* in the conventual church of St John's. This chapel had originally been reserved for the langue of England and had later been annexed by that of Germany. On the outside of the *Auberge de Bavière* the flags of Bavaria, England, and (after 1785) Poland were flown.

For the Bavarians, it was soon obvious that they were not welcome in Malta by all. This was for various reasons. The incorporation of the Anglo-Bavarian langue into the normal 'working process' of the Order was not an easy one. In fact the installation of the new langue was not received enthusiastically by all members of the Order. For the more farsighted and 'enlightened' of the knights, the real background of the installation of the new institution was only too clear to see. So all these activities concerning the new langue and the Bavarian delegations to the Order's headquarters in 1782 and 1783 were very carefully and sceptically observed by Chevalier Caumont-Seystres, French *chargé d'affaires* in Malta, by the *Balí* Des Pennes, and the various other French knights who reported to the French foreign minister Vergennes on the matter. Obviously it was feared that the 'newcomers' would take away privileges and revenues which had been held before by knights of the three French langues. The new situation brought Rohan in conflict with the priory of France which in their provincial chapters, criticized and opposed this new arrangement and even went to the extent of bringing a case against their grand master to the courts of Rome.

The political 'modern' members of the French langue like Deodat de Dolomieu, *Balí* Des Pennes, and treasurer Bosredon de Ransijat, especially strongly opposed the seemingly obscure and sinister motives of the Bavarians, particularly of their representatives Haeffelin and Flachslanden. The members of the new langue who arrived in Malta were cold-shouldered by this party. The critical rebellious French knights who gathered in the so-called 'Auvergnat Club' had various points to make. Certainly there was considerable envy of the *Balí* Flachslanden who had landed a pension of 12,000 *livres* a year and of the newcomer and mysterious Haeffelin who had obtained another considerable pension. One of the main points of discussion was that in 1782 Flachslanden had also been appointed to the traditional office of the pilier of England, that of turcopilier. Since the possessions of the English langue had been sequestrated by King Henry VIII in 1540, this post had traditionally been held by a knight of the langue of Provence. The French *chargé d'affaires* Caumont-Seystres and the *Balí* Des Pennes protested as soon as they learned of these developments. As Flachslanden was not in Malta, Des Pennes '*alla testa di tutta quasi la lingua di Provencia*' mainly concentrated his confrontation against the new Lieutenant-Turcopilier Count Friedrich von Vieregg. The situation threatened to become violent.

But Flachslanden's and Haeffelin's friends were more powerful and the Bavarian court must have contacted the French court on the matter. On 12 July 1784 the council

15

Grand Master Rohan
Polduc with pages

of the Order met to discuss the affair. To calm the French knights down, soon after the French foreign minister Comte de Vergennes ordered Des Pennes to stop his agitations against the Bavarians. In October 1784 an instruction of the French king via Vergennes finally settled the affair. But the resentments against the Anglo-Bavarian langue in Bavaria as well abroad lingered for long. On losing their case, the French priories continued the insubordination. Grand Master Rohan was forced to take disciplinary actions, degrading some knights and expelling some from the island. Various – mostly anonymous – publications in the 1780s and 1790s harshly criticized the creation of the new institution 'created solely to satisfy the hunger for revenues and prestige of noblemen'.

Protected by Count Taufkirchen and Grand Master Rohan, these tensions did not concern young Joseph Maria too much when, in mid-July 1783, he officially entered the grand master's service as a page. Most of the time he was based at the grand master's palace in Valletta. In the hot summer months, he also had to accompany the French grand master to his customary visits to his summer residence at San Anton. The old summer resort of the grand masters, the palace of Verdala, was rarely visited. During his time as page and novice in Malta, his family still sent regular sums of money to pay their son's expenses and maintenance. In a letter dated 2 August to his brother Franz Xaver, the young page summarized some of his first impressions of Malta. The climate he found unbearably hot, and he seemed to have suffered from a sort of allergy. He described Valletta as a beautiful city built in a very unique style. The whole conurbation of the Porto Grande appeared as an impregnable fortress. The coast of the island was protected by numerous watchtowers. The same letter has some interesting details about the life of a page: *'You might be surprised that even the pages here have to pay everything out of their own pocket. Only the meals – which are exceptionally good – are free of charge. Normally we dine together with the officers of the magisterial palace.'* For the cleaning, washing, and repairing of his clothes and uniforms, Joseph Maria had to pay. He also employed a servant.

During his service Joseph Maria was allowed to wear the uniform of a Bavarian second lieutenant. Besides their service at the grand master's table and in the palace, the pages also had study sessions and Joseph Maria praised the local professor of mathematics and the drawing master as excellent teachers and experts. He lists mathematics, drawing, the study of arms and fortifications, and dancing as the main subjects of study. For these and also for his cello lessons, Rechberg had to pay for. There must have been a tight schedule for the pages as he laments about his restricted freedom. With some relief, he got to know that his term as a page would only last just over six months. Then he could undertake the famous caravans of the Order's navy.

The general custody of the pages was in the hands of the grand prior of St John's, Raymond Albino Menville, the former auditor of the grand master. Rechberg, who was not yet familiar with the hierarchy of the Order, in his first letter calls him '*commandeur ecclesiastique*' and describes him as a very polite and nice man. In his letter of 2 August, he also dedicates some words to the latest naval exploits of the Order. Only a few days earlier, the sailing squadron of the Order had captured a North African corsair vessel and freed the Christian slaves on board which had been freshly captured from a seized Christian merchantman. The young Swabian nobleman is rather vague about the background of the events and he is certainly wrong to label the corsair as a Turkish ship. The documents in the archive of the Order do not mention any captured or attacked Turkish vessel for all of 1783. It was most likely an Algerian vessel.

What came as a great surprise for the young Rechberg and surely excited his interest was the extent of the contacts between Hospitaller Malta – officially the archenemy of the Muslim world – and the North African principalities. During his time as a page and his service in the palace of the grand master, he witnessed the visits of several dignitaries and envoys dressed in Oriental fashion. Rechberg soon got to know more about the background of the Maltese policies towards the beys of North Africa, especially those of Tunis and Algiers. In these relations, slavery stood out as a very important aspect of business as well as of disturbance. The young German nobleman could see slaves everywhere, employed in private households and by the Order as well as working in construction, cleaning, shipbuilding, and agriculture. Although it did not have the importance it had in the sixteenth or seventeenth centuries, the slave trade was still a major source of income. For states like Malta and the Barbary regencies, slaves were of the utmost importance in keeping society in motion and for everyday life. They were employed on the ships, in fortress- and house-building, in private households, and as servants of the rich and mighty.

In the age of enlightenment and the discussion of human values, slavery was regarded by European intellectuals as a relic of the 'gothic' past and a symbol of cruelty and suppression. Various authors now started criticizing heavily the once-so-admired knights of St John for their *corso* and their involvement in the slave trade. In addition to the human aspect, the activities of the Order's navy and the Maltese corsairs were attacked for the disturbance and damage they caused to Mediterranean trade. Still the slave business remained a fact on the Christian and Muslim sides of the Mediterranean, including Malta. But in the eighteenth century the decline of the Maltese *corso* had reduced the number of slaves being brought to the island. In 1716 the Venetian Giacomo Capello had reported 6,000 slaves living on the island, but this number fell to 3,000 and even fewer in the second half of the century. Especially as a result of French pressure, the Order and the Maltese had to stop their anti-Ottoman corsairing and privateering operations in the Levant and some other parts of the Mediterranean. In the second half of the eighteenth century many European states, such as France, the Netherlands, Denmark, and England, had concluded peace treaties with the Barbary regencies and Morocco. Venice had made considerable progress in peace treaties with North African beys: in 1763 it had concluded linepeace treaties with Algiers, in 1764 with Tripoli, and in 1765 with Morocco. Subsequently even the North Africans downsized their corsairing fleets. In general even the number of slaves in the Barbary States went down. In Algiers there were 7,000 slaves in 1749; in 1767 this number was reduced to 2,662; and in 1787 there were only around 500 left. At Tunis it was estimated there were between 6,000 and 12,000 slaves in the seventeenth century; in 1780 only 200 were left.

What Rechberg witnessed was the especially lively contacts between Morocco and the Order. Up to the mid-eighteenth century, the sultans of Morocco and the beylerbeys of Tunis, Tripoli, and Algiers had been more or less in permanent conflict with Spain and Malta. Spanish relations with Morocco had improved since the 1760s when envoys had been exchanged. There was certainly an area of some economic interest to Spain and a useful source of grain for Andalusia in times of dearth. Malta ruled by the Order – although officially still at war with the infidel countries – in reality had since long found a convenient and profitable *modus vivendi* with the North African states. The kingdom of the Two Sicilies – since the early eighteenth century a viable state, overtly sovereign, but in practice a satellite of Spain – closely followed Spanish policies and was certainly interested in relieving the local sea trade of the fear of North African corsair attacks. During Rechberg's service in the palace, there was still very much talk of the day the previous year when the Moroccan diplomat Muhammad Ibn Uthmān al-Miknasi had been sent by the sultan as his special envoy to Malta, to negotiate the ransom of all the Muslim slaves on the island. Muhammad Ibn Uthmān al-Miknasi had come with a large and colourful entourage of interpreters, servants, and women. Little did Rechberg know that in less than a year he would himself be fighting the Muslims at the North African coast.

In his meeting with Grand Master Rohan in June 1782, the Moroccan envoy had put forward Sultan Sayyidā Muhammad Ibn Abdallāh's wish of a perpetual peace between the two states. If such an agreement were to be concluded, the sultan promised to impose peace on the other Barbary States, especially Algiers. Algiers was then the most thriving corsairing and piracy centre. That such a peace would contribute considerably to the prosperity of Mediterranean trade did not need to be emphasized. Ibn Uthmān gave the example of Tunis whose friendship with the European states and with Malta had resulted in a prosperous trade relationship. A good insight into these friendly relations had also been given in the summer of 1782 when the son-in-law of the bey of Tunis had stopped in Malta on his return voyage from Mecca. In the future, so the envoy hoped, the exchange of slaves and captives would become more easy and could be carried out 'one by one, as is the custom in the Christian states'. That Rohan was not completely enthusiastic about the Tunisian *laissez faire* was because of the huge contraband trade between North Africa and Malta.

Although Rohan saw the utility of friendship with Morocco, he did not intend to commit himself to talks about a perpetual peace. He only would enter into such a matter if a similar agreement or treaty were concluded before by Morocco with other European states, preferably Naples. So things lingered on. When Rechberg was serving as a page in the summer and autumn of 1783, he witnessed a lively correspondence between Morocco and Malta regarding the ransom of slaves and peace treaties. Most of this correspondence went through the hands of the Spanish minister Floridablanca who acted as the intermediary. There had been some complications before when the Moroccan envoy Ibn Uthmān claimed to have paid the sum of $271,358\frac{1}{2}$ *pesos* to ransom all the Muslim slaves in Malta. The money was deposited in Spain. At first Grand Master Rohan refused to negotiate further but a few months later he declared that the Order was willing to agree to ransom all Muslim slaves who had been in Malta during Ibn Uthmān's visit. The grand master announced that he would send two frigates to Cadiz to collect the money, but there seemed to have been some misunderstanding and postal delays as some other North African envoys and agents informed the sultan that the Maltese were again not keeping their promises according to the agreement reached with Ibn Uthmān. Still the sultan expressed his wish to continue with his policy of ransoming slaves, but requested the Spanish King Carlos III not to hand the money over to Malta. In another letter he gave more details to the Spanish king of what he had heard from Malta,

21

namely that the grand master had never intended nor would he allow the slaves to be ransomed as a good part of them – at least 300 – were needed as cheap labour in the quarries, the building of houses, and on the galleys. As a result the sultan finally decided to donate the money to the holy shrines of Mecca and he informed Carlos III that the money should be handed over to the Turkish Sultan Abd al-Hamīd I who would pass it over to the authorities at Mecca.

For another time Carlos III was now trying to mediate between the sultan and the grand master to bring the negotiations to a good end. In October 1783 he recommended the grand master that the sultan's secretary – then still in Malta – should draw up a new list of all Muslim slaves and compile a paper to clarify the whole matter of the ransom. This was to be signed by the grand master and sent to Carlos III who would hand it over to the sultan for his – hopeful – confirmation. This manoeuvre, however, came too late as Sultan Abdallāh could not wait any longer for a reply from Malta. In subsequent letters to the Spanish court, the sultan left the door open for future initiatives for ransoming the slaves. Indeed in 1785 negotiations were resumed between Morocco, Spain, and Malta regarding on the matter. Again Carlos III – with the help of Ferdinand IV of Naples – acted as an intermediary. After long negotiations, in 1788 the ransom of more than 300 of the Order's slaves and 230 belonging to private owners in Malta was agreed to. In total 600 slaves were liberated for about 1,000 *scudi* each which earned the treasury of the Order over 548,680 *scudi*. The money was transferred from Morocco via Spain. Some of the money had been handed over in May 1788 when some slaves had been transported on the Order's galleys to Cadiz.

CHAPTER 3
IN THE LIMELIGHT OF HISTORY –
THE CAMPAIGN OF ALGIERS

Joseph Maria had begun his duties as a page at the relatively advanced age of 14 – normally pages began their service at the age of 12 – and he therefore stayed in the pagery only just over six months. In early March 1784 his time as page ended and the young Swabian nobleman opted to start his spell on board of the Order's navy immediately although even the expenses on board had to be paid for by the young noble caravanists. To participate in these caravans at the tender age of 15 was no exception. Even the newly founded *Reggimento di Malta*, consisting of soldiers and officers hailing from Spain, Piedmont, Corsica, Germany, Tuscany, France, Milan, Genoa, and the Papal States included – among its total number of 1,130 men – 89 boys under 16 years of age.

To sort of document his training and progress, the adolescent began penning down his observations in a diary. What shines through these notes is his deep interest in everything naval. The fleet was still the backbone of the *raison d'être* of the Order in the late eighteenth century. Between 1779 and 1783 the *Arsenale delle Galere* (galley dockyard) had alone cost the Order the considerable sum of nearly 50,000 *scudi*. The yearly upkeep (inclusive of the costs of the crews) of the three men-of-war, the *San Zaccaria*, *Sant'Elisabetta*, and *Santa Maria del Pilar*, amounted approximately to 190,000 *scudi*. On the other hand, the treasury of the Order earned the sum of 500 *scudi* as fees from every locally registered corsair vessel for the privilege of flying the Order's flag.

Joseph Maria von Rechberg's preparations for this naval service must have been extremely short as already in the morning of 10 March he boarded the frigate *Santa Maria del*

The galley arsenal at Vittoriosa (*c*.1780)

The men-of-war arsenal at Senglea (*c*.1780)

Pilar (40 guns; commanded by Pierre Annibale de Soubiras; first lieutenant Joseph de Roquefort). Rechberg in his diary misspells the name as Sobirast. The *Santa Maria del Pilar*, one of the longest surviving frigates of the Order, had been built in 1765. In June 1798 it was seized by the French and renamed *Ateniese*. The frigate was later broken up by the French for fuel during the siege of Valletta. Directly next to the *Santa Maria del Pilar* Rechberg could observe the impressive *San Zaccaria*. The *San Zaccaria* belonged to the squadron of the so-called third rates of the Order of St John, introduced by Grand Master Perellos at the beginning of the eighteenth century to adapt to the changing naval tactics and demands. Until 1781, the

The naval arsenal by Charles Frederick Brocktorff (*c*.1820)

Order had possessed two more third rates, the *San Gioacchino* and the *San Giovanni*, but in that year they were sold to the king of Naples for 117,000 *scudí*. The *San Zaccaria* was built in 1765 and carried 64 guns. Together with the newly built frigate *Sant'Elisabetta* (40 guns) commanded by Paul Julian de Suffren de Saint Tropez (the first lieutenant was Chevalier de Campion), the *San Zaccaria* and the older *Santa Maria del Pilar* sailed out of Malta's *Porto Grande* at noon of 10 March.

Several modern maritime historians have claimed that the *Sant'Elisabetta* then was commanded by Pierre André de Suffren de Saint Tropez who was certainly one of the most prominent naval officers of the Order in the eighteenth century and French admirals. In the early 1780s he had fought several famous battles against the British navy in the West Indies. In 1784, however, it was not him who commanded the *Sant'Elisabetta* but his younger brother *Balí* Paul Julian Suffren de Saint Tropez who also had an impressive naval career and later became lieutenant-general in the Order's fleet.

25

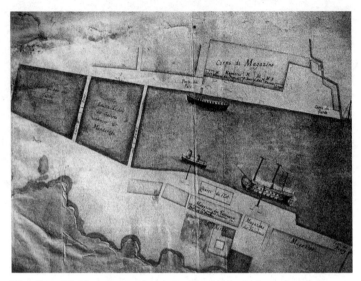

The *Parco delle Navi*; picture shows the shipyard gate, the main warehouses, and the soldiers' barracks (*c.*1750)

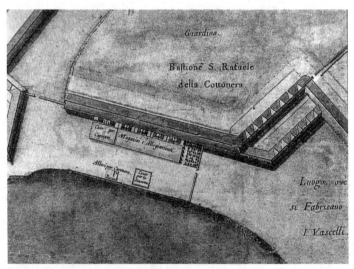

Plan of the Senglea ship arsenal (NLM, Libr. MS 156)

Grand Master Perellos y Roccaful, founder of the sailing ship squadron of the Order of St John

The building of another new frigate, the *Santa Catarina* because of some delays had not been completed yet and therefore this ship could not participate. There were also two chebecs, the *San Pietro* and *San Paolo* but they then were engaged in escorting the transport vessels supplying Malta with grain and other foodstuff from Sicily.

The squadron was commanded by Lieutenant-General (*Luogotenente Generale dei Vascelli*) Giovanni Battista Tommasi, a rather experienced seaman who had already held the post of captain of the third rate *San Antonio* in 1776. He was then acting lieutenant-general of the Order's sailing ships as it was only in 31 March 1784 that he was officially promoted to this post, which was at the time held by the Portuguese Rodrigo Gorjao. In early March Tommasi had received command to chase some North African corsairs sailing off Sicily. Little did young Joseph Maria von Rechberg know that this encounter with the lieutenant-general would be the beginning of a very long acquaintance in good and in bad times.

27

Marine Battalion Sergeant-Major (*c.*1790); *Agozzino*, Slave warden (*c.*1790); *Comito*, boatswain (*c.*1790); Captain-General of the galleys (*c.*1790); Captain of a galley (*c.*1790); Captain of a man-of-war (*c.*1790)

'With a rather moderate wind', so the young Swabian caravanist wrote, 'we sailed out of the harbour of Malta'. The exact route and destination of the ships was then not yet known to the minor officers and the crew. The amount of foodstuff and munitions carried on board the ships pointed to a longer excursion. The wind blew favourably and the

Lieutenant-
General Giovanni
Battista Tommasi

ships moved north with full sails. Already on the following day (11 March), with the coastline of Sicily on the horizon, the Maltese could observe a North African corsair vessel approaching a Sicilian merchantman. When the corsair noticed the squadron of the Order, he set full sail to escape. Tommasi gave command to chase the corsair from various sides and therewith restrict his possibilities of escaping. The chase continued for four full days but in the end the swift corsair ship proved too fast and its crew too experienced in taking profit of the wind. The hunt was then called off and the Maltese squadron joined again off the south-eastern coast of Sicily. From there Rechberg could see the promontory of Capo Passero some distance away.

The squadron then continued to sail west. The wind blew very strongly and most favourably from the east and so

A Maltese third rate; detail of a *veduta* of Valletta (c.1750)

the ships could move on very fast. Already on the 18th, they were in sight of Pantelleria. Rechberg described the island as a place without a good port and with just a few miserable villages. It was then owned by some Sicilian noblemen. The Maltese ships kept away from the island, most presumably to avoid intelligence of their presence. From the waters of Pantelleria the ships headed north and in fact it soon appeared that this time the secrecy had worked. On the passage from the western tip of Sicily to Sardinia, they encountered some suspicious ships. This time the Maltese proved too fast for the other ships to escape. The *Sant'Elisabetta*, the fastest ship of the squadron, caught up with them in less than half an-hour. On approaching the foreign vessels, it was discovered that they were not North African corsairs but Swedish merchant vessels which had loaded salt in Cagliari. Interrogated about the North African corsairs, the Swedes replied that they did not know anything.

The very windy conditions on the rest of the passage to Sardinia caused a mast on the *Sant'Elisabetta* to break and

Tommasi ordered the squadron to proceed to the Golfo di Pálmas in Sardinia and to anchor in the sheltered waters near the town of San Pietro to repair it. This was soon carried out and by 22 March the squadron was again on the open sea. Rechberg described the Sardinian coast as dry, not fertile, and full of dangerous reefs and rocks. While waiting for the repair of the *Sant'Elisabetta*, the crews had killed time by hunting some animals. Not too far south of Sardinia, they encountered a convoy of French merchant vessels on their way from Tunis to Marseille and who informed them that some corsair ships in Tunis were preparing for an expedition against Christian shipping. After a short council on board of the *San Zaccaria*, Tommasi and the other captains agreed to proceed immediately to Tunis to prevent these ships from getting into action. Unfavourable weather conditions, however, prevented a direct south-easterly course. Rechberg writes about a 'very ugly and cold wind' and also reports that they encountered two French, two Austrian, and a Danish vessel. The bad weather finally forced the Maltese squadron to give up their plans – at least for the moment – and to return to the Golfo di Pálmas and to seek shelter in the port of San Pietro where they arrived on 29 March. The bad weather lasted for eight full days and young Rechberg reports how the crew and knights lamented about the extraordinary cold and the apparently endless showers of hail and rain.

Some further problems cropped up when it was discovered that not enough water could be taken on at San Pietro. A few days later – on 6 April – the storm became so intense that it appeared too dangerous to stay in the Golfo di Pálmas. The wind had even caused the ships to drag their anchors. A few hours later the ships were back on the open sea sailing for Porto Conte in the north-west of Sardinia to fetch the lacking water from there. Because the strong opposing winds, it was impossible to land at Porto Conte and Tommasi decided to head farther west to fetch water and more provisions from Las Palmas at Majorca. On 9 April the unpredictable weather conditions played another trick on the Maltese squadron. All of a sudden the wind died down and halted the ships completely. Things became difficult and worrying as the potable water was nearly all used up. Fortunately the following day a fresh breeze made it possible for the voyage to be continued.

The squadron reached Las Palmas on 14 April and took on the necessary barrels with water and provisions. Rechberg described Las Palmas as a well-built and equipped port with safe quays and moles. The city itself he found rather small and full of old shabby houses. Still many noble families lived there. The language spoken was not Spanish but Catalan and Rechberg pointed out that the locals dressed very differently from people of other regions of the Mediterranean.

For the ordinary crew and officers and also for the novices like Rechberg, it only now became clear that Tommasi's decision to proceed to Majorca was not only motivated to load provisions. Rechberg and his comrades wondered

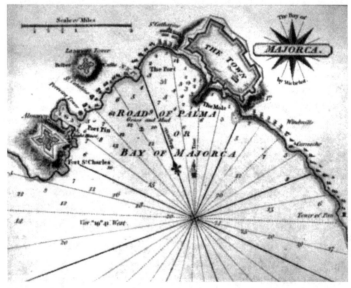

Majorca Bay (British engraving, *c.*1810)

why the ships did not sail out again after all necessities had been taken on board but remained in the port as if waiting for something. This waiting had a special reason. While at anchor in Palmas at Sardinia, Tommasi had received secret intelligence from the admiral of the Order Giovanni Battista Amalfitano that he should sail to Majorca and to join his squadron with the small Spanish fleet under the count of Gravina, an Italian. This, of course, was not known to the crew, ordinary soldiers, and officers on board of the Maltese ships. The authorities of the Order had decided that the Maltese squadron should accompany the Spanish ships on their passage to Algiers and to investigate the situation there. This expedition was part of a bigger scheme to prepare for a future huge attack by Spanish, Portuguese, Neapolitan, and Maltese forces against this North African city. Of course, this spying expedition was intended to be carried out under a low profile and as secretly as possible. For the moment all this was known only to Lieutenant-General Tommasi and the captains of the frigates *Sant'Elisabetta* (*Balí* Suffren de St Tropez) and *Santa Maria* (Commander Soubiras).

After one week of waiting, the Spanish fleet finally arrived. It consisted of a frigate, five chebecs, and a balander. The latter was a flat ship with two masts which could sail in shallow waters and channels. After an exchange of greetings, formalities, and news, on 22 April the united fleets left Las Palmas, passed the islands of Ibiza and Formentera, and headed south. Thanks to favourable winds, the ships were already in sight of the gulf of Algiers on the evening of 27 April. The ships approached the land 'until the distance of half-an-hour'. With binoculars and telescopes and a clear sky, the crew could observe the skyline of Algiers and even the movements in the port. Rechberg notes in his diary 'that we could see that many new batteries had been built and some of us even reported that there was a lot of movement, excitement, and noise in the city ...' This, of course, was provoked by the arrival of the Spanish-Maltese fleet. On 29

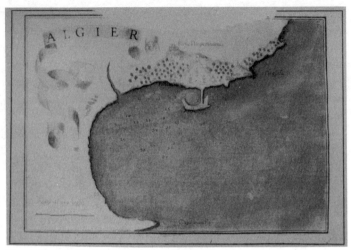

Plan of the Gulf of Algiers (18th century)

April, because of a strong northerly wind, the Christian fleet had to stop their observations and it sailed west. After three more days of waiting for favourable winds, the Christian squadrons separated, with the Spanish sailing west to Alicante and the Maltese heading towards Pantelleria.

It was then that the young Rechberg first experienced the dangers and hardships of life at sea. In the afternoon of 4 May, the sky grew dark and a heavy rain set in. By eight it was completely dark and the crew of the *Santa Maria del Pilar* had lost sight of the other ships. The sea started to make huge waves although there was not a strong wind as yet. Shortly afterwards Rechberg heard gunshots which, he was told, were signals from the *Sant'Elisabetta*. Experienced sailors assumed that the frigate had been hit by lightning. After a pitch-dark night, the following morning showed that this assumption had been correct. Tommasi's flagship, the *San Zaccaria* and the *Santa Maria del Pilar*, moved alongside the *Sant'Elisabetta* to help and Rechberg could see a frightening scene: '*One mast had been completely destroyed, another was partly damaged, and several sails and ropes were torn. When we inquired further, we got to know that the lightning had killed three men and injured three others ...*' It was a hard job to carry out provisional repairs on the frigate and to put her in a position to resume sailing. The plan to sail towards Pantelleria was given up. After a discussion, it was decided to sail to Majorca. With no little effort, the Maltese squadron finally reached Las Palmas again on 8 May where the damage on the *Sant'Elisabetta* could be repaired in a relatively short time. For some unknown reason, Tommasi ordered that only the *Sant'Elisabetta* should anchor in the port while the other two ships had to wait outside. The repair work was relatively soon done and, three days later, the ships could leave again.

The crews and soldiers – and also Rechberg – expected that this was the start of the return voyage to Malta but they

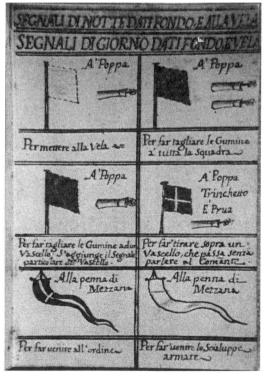

A collection of naval signals effected by flags and pennants (*c.* 1710)

soon observed that the squadron was not sailing south-east but west towards the Spanish coast. It was then announced that their destination was the port of Alicante on Spain's south-east coast. During their voyage, they encountered a huge Dutch ship-of-the-line, the *Admiral Tromp*, a brand-new 74-gun warship, which greatly impressed the young Rechberg who thought it was the finest ship of this type he had seen until then. The Dutch captain greeted the Maltese with 15 blank gunshots and the ships of the Order responded with the same number of gunshots.

Alicante was reached on 13 May. When the *Santa Maria del Pilar* glided into the huge harbour, Rechberg could observe an impressive scene which he describes in his diary as a 'nice town with a labyrinth of small alleys and passages and impressive palaces'. Rechberg and the ships' crew and soldiers were still not informed that they had to wait there to join the galley squadron of the Order. When the galleys did not show up after two days of waiting, Tommasi gave order to set sail. The vessels left port in the evening of 15 May but, because of a calm, they hardly could move at all. Early the following morning, only a few hours' out of

The *capitana* of the Order's fleet (18th century)

Alicante they saw four ships with lateen sails some distance away. At first they believed these were Turkish galleots but it was soon discovered that these were the galleys of the Order accompanied by a Maltese *tartana*. The officers and crew on board the *San Zaccaria*, the *Sant'Elisabetta*, and the *Santa Maria del Pilar* burst out in shouts of joy and Tommasi ordered the galleys' captain general – his superior in the hierarchy of the Order – to be greeted with 19 blank gunshots. The galleys responded by firing their main guns.

The Maltese galley squadron then stood under the command of the young Captain General Alexandre Ludovic de Freslon de la Freslonnière about whom there had been some nasty rumours going round. He was accused of being a protégé of his famous uncle *Balí* and Grand Cross Jean-Baptiste-Gabriel de Freslon, the colonel of the Regiment of Malta and Grand Master Rohan's master of the horse. Resisting *Balí* Freslon's wishes and intrigues seemed to have been rather difficult. Rechberg had been told about his several duels with other knights and officers, including the major of the Regiment of Malta Ferret and his successor Fresinet. The galley squadron of the Order then consisted of the flagship (*capitana*) with 28 banks or oars on her port quarter and 29 on her starboard side and armed with one 24-pounder bronze corsier gun, two 18-pounder bronze guns, and 16 guns of minor calibre together with the *Padrona*, the newly built *Magistrale*, and the *San Luigi*.

From this moment on, we have a complementary eyewitness account of the coming events to that described by Rechberg. This other account was written by another novice in the service of the Order, the young nobleman from Normandy François Gabriel de Bray. De Bray was 18 years old when he arrived in Malta in 1783 and during the Algiers campaign he served on board the *capitana* – the flagship of Captain General Freslon. The captain of the *capitana* was Antonio de Ligondez. The *San Luigi* was commanded by Charles Ludovic de Mesguigny, while the *Magistrale* was commanded by another interesting character, the Milanese nobleman Giulio Renato Litta who would later make an illustrious career at the Russian court. Another source for the coming events is a 'Relazione del Bombardamento di Algere dalla flotta Spagnola, Napoletana, Portoghesa, e Maltese', preserved in the Archives of the Order in Rome. Like Rechberg, de Bray had come to Malta in 1783 at the age of 18 and had immediately started his caravans. We do not have knowledge at all that Rechberg and de Bray were acquaintances but, considering the smallness of Valletta and the restricted society of the knights, it is most probable that they knew each other. It is a fact that later de Bray was very much helped in his career in the Bavarian service by Joseph Maria's older brother Aloys von Rechberg. After he had left Malta de Bray served with a French delegation at the Diet of Ratisbon in 1789. Following the overthrow of the French monarchy in August 1792, he abandoned French service and, after extensive travels in Germany, Switzerland, Holland, England, and Austria, he served as a counsellor and representative of the Order of Malta at the Congress of Rastatt between 1797 and 1799. There he collaborated with Joseph Maria's brother Aloys who then represented the Palatinate and Bavarian Duke Elector Karl Theodor. In 1799 the Bavarian grand priory sent de Bray and *Balì* Flachslanden on an important mission to Czar Paul I in St Petersburg who had been just elected grand master of the Order. We will come back to this later on. After a similar mission to London, he served as the Bavarian ambassador in Berlin from 1801 to 1808, where he married the daughter of the Livonian Count Löwenstern. De Bray was then appointed Bavarian ambassador to St Petersburg, a post he held from 1809 to 1812. This connection between the de Bray and Rechberg families continued when a daughter of François Gabriel de Bray later married a son of Johann Nepomuk von Rechberg.

After the salutes were fired, the caique of the *San Zaccaria* was lowered in the water and Tommasi and some other officers proceeded in it to the *capitana*. His arrival and departure were again saluted with four gunshots. A few hours later the captain general came on board of the *San Zaccaria* and was greeted with 19 rounds. It was only when Tommasi's squadron and the galleys were united that the crews and soldiers on the *San Zaccaria* and the other ships were told about the mission of the fleet which was to join Spanish, Neapolitan, and Portuguese contingents to attack and destroy corsair-infested Algiers. Rechberg and the knights knew that this was not the first such attempt to subdue the bey of Algiers and to put a stop to the permanent Algerian threat of Spanish, Portuguese, and Neapolitan trade. These campaigns against Algiers have to be understood in their political context. In the 1780s Spain was following a policy of appeasement with several North African beys and states, especially Morocco. In the mid-1780s there had even been efforts to sign a peace treaty with the Ottoman Empire, for long the inveterate enemy of Spain. The effects of this appeasement policy was not very favourable for Malta because the Spanish did not want to allow Maltese corsairs to sail into certain areas of Levantine waters which was a great set-back for the local corsairing business. In fact many Maltese patrons and sailors on these corsair ships had lamented to Grand Master Rohan that, as a result, their families were falling into great penury, reducing them to beggars.

This Spanish appeasement policy, however, suffered several setbacks. When in 1782 – during the Spanish campaign against the English to regain the island of Minorca – the bey of Algiers had sided with the British, it became improvident for Spain to solicit a peace on her own term. The subsequent campaigns and bombardments of Algiers were basically meant to prove that Spain had sufficient force to impede the depredations of the corsairs of Algiers. In many modern history books the campaign is described as an effort to conquer the city; this, however, was not the case.

The commander-in-chief, the Spanish Lieutenant-Admiral Antonio Barceló, was an experienced man. Born of a modest family from Majorca and nicknamed 'Capitàn Toni' on his home island, he achieved some fame as a commander of small vessels against Barbary corsairs in the 1740s and 1750s. Between 1760 and 1769, he had gained further fame by sinking around 20 corsair vessels, taking 1,600 prisoners and freeing over 1,000 Christian slaves. Between 1779 and 1783 he was in charge of the bombardment of the British possessions of Gibraltar. Barceló was no stranger to Algiers: he had commanded the vanguard forces in the first Spanish campaign against the North African town in 1775.

Young Rechberg and de Bray and their comrades were told what had happened then. The general command of this first Spanish effort to conquer Algiers had been in the hands of Lieutenant-General Pedro González de Castejón. It ended in a total disaster. Overall the Spanish forces consisted of seven ships-of-the-line with 70 cannon each, 12 frigates with 27 cannon, four urcas of 40 cannon, nine chebecs of 32 cannon, and several more light ships like galleots, transport ships, gunboats, and bombardiers, in total 46 ships and 1,364 cannon. On board of the ships there was a contingent of over 18,000 troops under General Alexander O'Reilly. After the Spanish fleet was joined by a frigate of the Order of Malta and two frigates from Tuscany, the operations started on 8 July. Things were badly prepared and the troops were put ashore in the wrong places and the landing was conducted in such disorderly fashion that the enemy forces, namely their 12,000 troops cavalry (*jinetes*) did not have many problems to strike deadly at the Spanish troops. At the end of the day the Spanish lost 5,000 soldiers (including five generals) and abandoned 15 cannon and over 9,000 muskets.

Barceló also participated in the second campaign against Algiers in July 1783, in which campaign the Spanish fleet was again assisted by the Order of Malta, which sent the two frigates *Sant'Elisabetta* and *Santa Maria del Pilar*. The Spanish fleet consisted of four ships-of-the-line with 70 cannon each, four frigates, nine chebecs, and several light ships and special vessels for bombarding and landing manoeuvres, in total a force of 1,250 cannon. In the port town of Cartagena, the fleet took on 14,500 troops and sailed away on 1 July but unfavourable winds prevented it from reaching Algiers before 26 July. Bad winds again delayed the attack which finally started on 1 August with intensive fire from the 19 gunboats. These were moved back when they had used up nearly all their munitions and when nine Algerian galleots and several other small ships appeared to try to seize the gunboats. The Spanish gunfire had indeed caused some damage and parts of the city were set on fire. In the following seven days the Spanish continued their bombardments, firing almost 4,000 bombs and cannonballs of large calibre. According to the French consul then residing in Algiers this destroyed 10 per cent of the houses and greatly damaged the fortifications. Recalling the disaster of the 1775 campaign, no attempt was made to land troops and so the Christian side only lost some 20 soldiers. After some more days of observations, the Spanish called it a day and retreated to Cartagena. This bombardment had its effect as the bey of Tripoli – threatened by an attack on his city – signed a peace treaty with Carlos III and interdicted the local corsairs from molesting Spanish shipping. The government of Algiers, however, were not ready to show any signs of appeasement.

Backed by their successful resistance and by British support the bey of Algiers continued his anti-Spanish actions and it caused some anger at the Spanish Court of Carlos III when in September 1783 it was heard that five corsair ships from Algiers had near Palamós taken two Spanish polaccas as prizes. In the winter of 1783/84, the fortifications of Algiers were strengthened by French specialists, new batteries added, and, in expectation of a new Spanish attack, 4,000 Ottoman voluntary troops and 50 new cannon were brought over. Another effective weapon was the preparation of 70 fire-ships to prevent the enemy from landing troops.

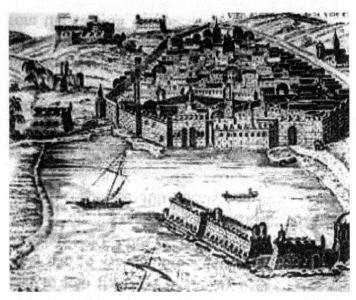

Algiers and its port in the 18th century

In the meantime the Spanish government had decided on a new attack on Algiers. This time the command of the whole expedition was laid in the hands of Antonio Barceló who was appointed to lieutenant-general (*Teniente General*). By May

1784, he had gathered in Cartagena a fleet of four ships-of-the-line with 80 cannon each, four frigates, 12 chebecs, three brigantines, and several smaller units including some specialized vessels for bombardment: there were 24 special ships with 24-pounder guns, eight with 18-pounder guns, and 24 vessel carriers of mortars. Barceló sailed on the flagship, the 84-gun *El Rayo*.

There was intense communication between Spain and its allies and this time the allies promised to contribute stronger forces while the Papal State offered financial help. The kingdom of Naples promised to send two ships-of-the-line, three frigates, two chebecs, and two brigantines under Admiral Bologna while Portugal sent two ships-of-the-line and two frigates under Admiral Ramírez de Esquivel. Grand Master Rohan agreed to send the fleet on which Rechberg was sailing, composed of the *vascello San Zaccaria*, the two frigates *Sant'Elisabetta* and *Santa Maria del Pilar*, and the galley squadron, then consisting of the *Vittoria*, the *Padrona*, the *Magistrale*, and the *San Luigi*.

It was during this campaign against Algiers that Rechberg got to know another member of the newly founded Anglo-Bavarian langue whose ways he would cross several times in future: Anton Friedrich von Vieregg. Born in December 1755 to the Bavarian chamberlain Wolfgang Heinrich Thaddaeus Baron von Vieregg, Anton joined the army of the Bavarian duke elector in 1774. In August 1776 he was promoted lieutenant in the cavalry regiment 'Count la Rosee'. Together with his father, he became involved in the complicated genesis of the Anglo-Bavarian langue. Early in 1782, he accompanied Flachslanden, Haeffelin, and his father from Munich to Malta to conclude the establishment of the new langue. In early 1784 Vieregg prepared to return to Malta. There were then still some outstanding questions regarding the exact structure of the leadership of the Anglo-Bavarian langue. Although he belonged to the German langue, *Balí* Flachslanden had been accepted in the Anglo-

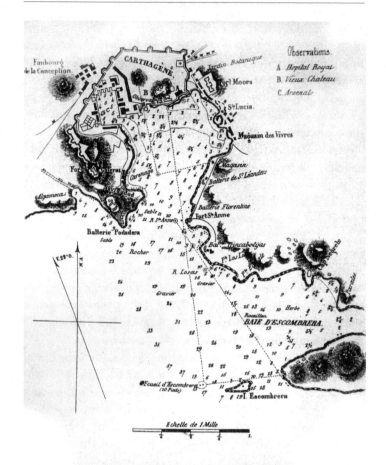

PORT & RADE DE CARTHAGÈNE.

Map of the Spanish port of Cartagena

Bavarian langue and in 1782 he had been officially appointed turcopilier. He was also nominated as the plenipotentiary and coadjutor of the grand prior of Bavaria with the right of succession and minister of the Order at the court at Munich which entitled him to supervise the setting-up of the new langue and the incorporation of the Polish grand priory within it. Since, because of his several businesses and functions in Bavaria and Germany, Flachslanden did not want to reside in Malta, he sent the young Count Guido von Taufkirchen as his lieutenant instead who later was replaced as lieutenant of the turcopilier by Count Friedrich von Vieregg in 1784. When the troops for the new Algiers campaign were gathered in Malta in April and early May 1784, Vieregg was amongst them. He sailed as officer on board of the *capitana* – Captain General Alexandre de Freslon de la Freslonnière's flagship. Like Rechberg, he aimed to complete the programme of his caravans to be received into the Order as a knight of justice.

But let us turn back to the events of the summer of 1784. De Bray reported that the squadron of four galleys and a *tartana* under Captain General Freslon had left Malta's *Porto Grande* on 4 May 1784. Freslon received the order from the council to sail to Alicante and to join his forces with Tommasi's squadron. The galleys stopped at some Sicilian ports to load water and provisions and to obtain more intelligence before crossing over to Alicante. As already mentioned by Rechberg, they joined Tommasi a few miles off Alicante on 16 May. There are some inconsistencies regarding these dates in the diaries of Rechberg and de Bray. In general Rechberg's diary appears more reliable and tallies better with the general sequence of the campaign. So his chronological sequence is followed here. After an exchange of news, the unified Maltese fleet sailed to Cartagena, then one of the major bases of the Spanish navy, to join the Spanish, Portuguese, and Neapolitan ships. On their way south the Maltese encountered two British squadrons with two ships-of-the-line and eight frigates. For some days a strong north-westerly wind prevented the ships from moving in the direction of Cartagena. On the 22nd they encountered eight Swedish merchant vessels sailing to Leghorn.

While the vessels were waiting for better weather, news arrived that the Spanish fleet had already left Cartagena for Ibiza. So the Maltese changed direction and proceeded there, reaching the main port of the island carrying the same name on 9 June. It was an impressive scene when the Maltese entered the port and saw the Spanish fleet anchored: There were four 80-gun ships-of-the-line, four frigates, 12 chebecs, three brigantines, and a huge variety of smaller units, including some specialized vessels for bombardment. When the Maltese *capitana* entered the harbour, she was saluted by 13 blank gunshots from the Spanish flagship *El Rayo*. After anchoring in the crowded port, Captain General Freslon and Lieutenant-General Tommasi went on board the Spanish flagship to discuss the further proceedings with Don Antonio Barceló.

Young Rechberg observed keenly the Spanish forces and noted that for the direct attack there were 32 bomb vessels that could fire 24-pound cannonball and four that could fire 12-pound ones, in addition to 24 special gunboats, 11 of them equipped with howitzers for long-distance fire, as well as six supporting vessels to transport gunpowder, bombs, cannonballs, and food. The gunboats had crews of 36 men each. The Neapolitan squadron consisted of two ships-of-the-line, three frigates, two chebecs, and two brigantines. The Portuguese had promised to send two ships-of-the-line and two frigates but they arrived late and the departure had to be delayed several times.

Finally the Portuguese Admiral Ramírez de Esquivel and his squadron arrived and, after a long religious ceremony with prayers for a successful outcome of the campaign, the actions could start. Barceló's flagship even carried a precious icon from Cartagena on board. Finally over 100 vessels left Ibiza. There was a strict order of sailing to obey. The vanguard consisted of 4 chebecs, 4 galleys, 1 galleot, and the Spanish flagship *El Rayo* accompanied by a loup. Then followed the large part of the united fleet in four columns with the ship-of-the-line *San Germano* sailing behind and followed by a huge line of transport vessels. Two brigantines and two chebecs

Maltese vascello, 18th century (NLM, Libr. MS 318)

sailed on their sides. The rearguard consisted of one ship-of-the-line, two chebecs, and a balander.

Not the least because of the constant delays in sailing, the bey of Algiers had had ample warning of the oncoming danger. Algiers had time to prepare its defences and to gather troops, munitions, provisions, and water. In the winter of 1783/84, a new and modern fortification provided with 50 guns was hastily added to the city walls.

Because of the weather conditions and the uneven speed of the variety of types of ships, the Christian fleet did not sail all together, with the transport ships and their escorting frigates and chebecs and rearguard staying behind. The Maltese galley squadron sailed with the vanguard. So it was only one part of the Christian fleet that arrived off Algiers on 7 July, with the other part arriving the following day. Some brigantines were sent force close to the shore to observe the situation. Through their binoculars, the crews could see how well the lines of defence and fortifications were kept and that there was a long row of floating platforms with artillery and several gunboats and bomb ketches hidden from view.

On 8 and 9 July the weather was fine and there was a very clear visibility. In the evening of the 9th, however, a strong wind arose which prevented the Christian ships from being brought to a suitable position to attack. Because of the various shallow waters and dangerous reefs in the gulf of Algiers, it took three full days for the proper attack formation to be set up. There was an intense communication between the commanders and Rechberg and de Bray could observe the caiques hectic moving from one flagship to another. This further delay gave the garrisons in Algiers enough time to finish their preparations. Rechberg notes some interesting details; for example, on the 10th a huge number of small Algerian 'lance-boats' appeared in the port. These ships, normally used for the close fighting and for boarding other vessels, were not suitable for modern naval warfare. The Christians interpreted this as a provocation on the part of the bey to show that he was not taking the oncoming attack seriously.

On 12 July a light breeze made it possible for the Christian fleet to launch their attack at 8.30 a.m. The vanguard was composed of the special vessels to bombard the fortifications. De Bray observed how the guns of Algiers answered with heavy fire but all their shots fell into the sea a few meters short of the Christian ships. The bombardment continued until 4 p.m. and was mainly directed on the supposed weak spots of the fortifications and the line of defence at the southern flank of the city. Rechberg reports:

Everything started when Major General Goicoechea moved his four bomb vessels and 7 gunboats with his high calibre howitzers near the southern flank of the fortifications and gave the order to open fire. The right and left flanks of our fleet were composed of 18 bomb vessels and two gunboats with howitzers. These gunboats with howitzers were placed at the very end of each side. The contingent on the right side was supervised by the commander of the bomb vessels, while that on the left side stood under the supervision of the commander of the gunboats. Don Antonio

48

Parcello (sic) and Lieutenant-General Tommasi supervised the movement of the centre of the fleet. ... The vessels with the troops for the landing were spread between the gunboats and bomb vessels. The galleys, balanders, brigantines, and some of the chebecs had set sail to fake an attack and a landing at a different place on the shore and to provoke some action from the enemy....

On the first day the allied forces fired 600 bombs, 1,440 large-calibre cannonballs, and 260 special grenades. According to Rechberg and de Bray, this initial bombardment had a very limited effect. The Spanish sources, giving a different picture, attest that the enemy forces of over 60 small swift units which had tried to stop the specialized vessels, bomb vessels, gunboats, and ships equipped with mortars from being brought into a perfect position were held at bay. In the heavy exchange of gunfire four Algerian vessels were sunk. According to de Bray, more damage could have been done had the huge Neapolitan ships-of-the-line not been equipped only with small-calibre guns which could not be used at a greater distance.

Spanish sources mention that the bombardment had damaged the fortifications and started fires in the inner city. Rechberg reports that the guns from the fortifications and from the floating platforms caused considerable damage on some Christian ships. The Spanish sources, however, speak only of a few losses, six deaths, and nine sailors being injured. Most of these casualties were not caused by enemy fire but by a misguided salvo from a Neapolitan frigate under Captain José Rodriguez.

This first day of attack was marked by a tragic incident among the Christian forces. With all attention being focused on the effects of the bombardment on the fortifications of Algiers, the Christian forces were guilty of some careless handling and actions. An explosion in the early afternoon on a Neapolitan gunboat with a crew of 32 caused great confusion while the crews of nearby ships who were injured by a rain of burning pieces of wood and sail canvas. After a hectic interrogation, it turned out that the explosion had not been caused by the enemy but by the carelessness of a sailor who had started the fire when he lost his lit pipe. The longer the bombardment took, the more difficult the conditions became for the Spanish, Neapolitan, and Maltese gunners. De Bray's notes give a good impression of the events:

> … as the smoke became thicker and thicker, we could not observe any more the effects of our guns. … These conditions were exploited by the enemy. Under the protection of the smoke, they managed to move forward with some gunboats and open fire on us. The Neapolitan ships-of-the-line which lay next to our galleys could not respond to this attack as their guns were too old and weak to hit the enemy at that range. This caused the Captain General [Alexandre de Freslon de la Freslonnière] to order our galleys to retreat to avoid further damage…

Most of the ships kept on firing despite of the unfavourable weather conditions and the limited visibility. It was only when strong winds set in at four in the afternoon that Lieutenant-General Barceló decided to stop the bombardment and to move the Christian ships back out of range of the enemy guns. The joint retreat of such a big fleet was a difficult procedure, especially with the strong winds blowing. A Maltese galley almost came to a tragic end when she was rammed by a Portuguese frigate. The knock was so strong that the planks of the stern of the galley which was much lower than the frigate broke and water started to flow in. Still there was enough time to evacuate the crew, soldiers, and slaves before the galley sank.

Two days later – on 15 July – the unified Christian fleet was again ready to strike. However, the enemy seemed to have had intelligence of Barceló's plans as just before daybreak a part of the still unprepared and anchored fleet was attacked by some Algerian gunboats. Rechberg was already awake and stood on board the *Santa Maria del Pilar* observing the silhouettes of those ships approaching in the distance and he saw the flashes when the enemy ships opened fire. Subsequently the *San Zaccaria* opened fire with its 24 18-pounder guns on the lower deck. For the 26 12-pounder guns on the upper deck and the 12 8-pounder guns on the quarter deck, the enemy was too far away to offer a promising target. The attack lasted less than half-an-hour; before the Christian ships could return the fire and start a counter-attack, the gunboats had returned to their sheltered bases next to the lines of fortifications.

Despite this incident, Barceló did not change his plans and with some delay the lines of the Christian ships moved forward and the bombardment started again. This time the weather conditions were more favourable and the wind blew the smoke away. The visibility allowed the Spanish, Portuguese, Neapolitan, and Maltese gunmen to continue firing until after eight in the evening when darkness set in. Rechberg on board of the *Santa Maria del Pilar* and de Bray on board of the *capitana* give different accounts of what occurred that day. Apparently the three sailings ships of the Order were much better equipped and munitioned than the *capitana* which de Bray described as badly equipped and supplied with munitions. The Maltese *capitana* indeed cut a bad figure that day. When Barceló's command to attack was received, the flagship of the Maltese galley squadron moved forward but after a few minutes it was hit by some Algerian gunshots. As it was also discovered that the gunpowder was running out, Captain General Freslon ordered the galley to retreat.

With their limited firepower, the galleys were anyway not used in the front line of attacks and Rechberg's account is much more precise when it comes to the observation of the enemy lines and the action. Rechberg's *Santa Maria del Pilar*, with her 40 large-calibre guns, was mostly acting in the first line of attack, while de Bray's *capitana* and the other galleys with their limited firepower stayed at the back. Both authors, however, agree that the other crews were not well-trained and very much inexperienced in fighting. Some of the Spanish and Neapolitan ships did not have enough munitions and had to stop firing in the afternoon. At quarter to eight in the evening, Admiral Barceló ordered the bombardment to end, mainly due to the fact that nearly all bomb vessels and gunboats were running out of munitions and powder. The day had a bad ending when, during their retreat, these gunboats and bomb vessels were suddenly attacked by several swift Algerian chebecs and galleots. They caused some considerable damage and it was difficult for the men-of-war which had already retreated further to fire on the Algerians without endangering the own vessels.

The reports by the young Rechberg and de Bray about the following days differ considerably which might be explained by the different positions of their ships during the fighting as well as by the fact that de Bray wrote down his notes much later. De Bray reports that there was heavy fog on 16, 17, and 18 July which made Lieutenant-General Barceló hesitate to order new attacks. Rechberg, on the contrary, writes that on those days the bombardment was continued. He even describes two attacks of the Christian ships on 18 July. It is most likely that de Bray's *capitana* did not take part in the fighting and stayed in a very distant position from the front line. The Spanish reports and the anonymous chronicler of the 'Relazione del Bombardamento di Algere' more or less confirm what Rechberg has written,

That there was fog, however, was true. Protected by fog, on the 18th the Algerians had floated a line of platforms equipped with artillery in front of the most vulnerable parts of the fortifications. These platforms prevented the Spanish gunboats, bomb vessels, and mortar carriers from being moved to the best positions. The commander in charge of these specialized ships, Major General José Lorenzo de Goicoechea, had to consult Barceló as to how to proceed. Barceló himself left his flagship and boarded a caique to move to the frontline to instruct Goicoechea but he nearly lost his life when the small boat was hit by a shot and Barceló

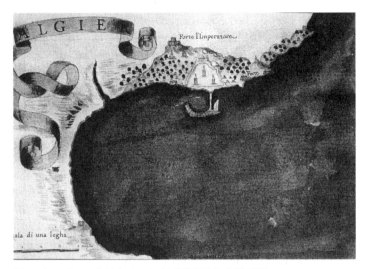

Plan of the Port of Algiers, *c.* 1750 (NLM Lib. MS 317)

fell into the sea. He was soon taken on board of another ship from where he continued to direct the ships during the three hours' assault on that day.

Things took a more dramatic turn on 20 July. In the early morning a Christian slave managed to reach the vanguard of the Spanish ships. He had escaped from the bagnio of Algiers the previous evening and, under cover of darkness, had swam over to the Christian ships. This man, who hailed from Valencia, brought most welcome intelligence and reported that the Algerian naval force was composed of seven chebecs with a firepower of 18 up to 36 guns per ship, and no fewer than 50 other ships with guns with calibres between 18 and 24 pounds, manned with experienced sailors who were also well-trained in close fighting. There were also another nine vessels equipped with howitzers, three bomb vessels, and several galleots. The forts of the city were commanded by four Christian officers. The general command over the batteries and all artillery was in the hands of the Chevalier de Tournon, a brilliant expert in the art of fortification and

53

coastal defences, who had been sent to Algiers by the Chamber of Commerce of Marseilles to support the bey in all things military. During the winter of 1783/84, he had supervised the building of new lines of defence and instructed the Algerians where to install new batteries and gun platforms. The huge number of English, French, Italian and Spanish renegades – most of them experienced sailors and soldiers – in the Algerian forces also contributed to lift the military efficiency of the defenders. Tournon had received further help and equipment from Marseilles in the spring. That the merchants of Marseilles were so keen to help the Algerians does not come as a surprise. For the merchant towns of the Cote d'Azur, Algiers and the other North African cities like Tunis, Tanger, Bizerta, and Tripoli, were important trading partners. The French thought it imperative that the Spanish should be prevented from gaining more influence in North Africa and thus put obstacles to the French trade. In fact a lot of intelligence about Christian actions and intentions went via Marseilles or Toulon to Algiers and Tunis.

On this day the Maltese contingent composed of the *vascello San Zaccaria*, the frigates *Sant'Elisabetta* and *Santa Maria del Pilar,* and the three remaining galleys were posted on the right flank of Barceló's main forces. The advance was conducted as usual and the Maltese captains were still mainly pre-occupied to avoid the shallow waters and reefs in waters that were unknown to them when, all of a sudden, some Algerian galleots and chebecs – whose captains were very familiar with the coast and the waters – approached them from the side and opened fire. This unexpected attack caused some confusion and interrupted communications with Barceló's flagship *El Rayo*. Lieutenant-General Tommasi and the young General Captain Freslon decided not to wait for Barceló's commands and took quick decisions. With some swift moves – thanks to their oars they did not depend on the wind – the Maltese galleys under Freslon counter-attacked. Soon even Tommasi's men-of-war managed to turn and bitter fighting raged for a full hour raged until the light Algerian vessels retreated. The Maltese galleys suffered major damage with Chevalier de Village's galley suffering considerable damage and losing its main mast.

Because of these events, the advance was called off and the main attack postponed for the following day, 21 July, which, however, did not start very promisingly. Moving on the deck of the *Santa Maria del Pilar*, Rechberg found that fog had greatly limited visibility and it was decided to wait until this morning-fog would disappear. But things again took a different turn when this limited visibility was used by Algerian brigantines and frigates to approach forces unseen from the side and suddenly opened fire. The enemy ships had in fact managed to come so close that they could use their muskets on the Maltese and Spanish sailors and soldiers. Even when, after some fighting, the Algerians retreated, Barceló ordered the fleet to stop advancing. According to de Bray, this day was marked by a complete chaos in communication. After more than one week, some of the captains of action had lost their fighting spirit anyway and there was a rumour that, in the limited visibility, a French frigate and four French gunboats had joined the Algerian forces.

When the fog failed to lift, a council was convened on *El Rayo*. After some discussion it was agreed to stop the attack for the day. Another advance under those conditions appeared too risky because, without good visibility, the Algerian forces might launch a new attack. Obviously on such days there was ample time on board the Christian ships to discuss the pros and cons of future plans of attack. This was also done on board the *Santa Maria del Pilar*. Listening to the officers and comrades, Rechberg heard the rumours that a few Algerian prisoners of war – including a Spanish renegade – had been captured when the Spanish guns had sunk an Algerian brigantine that morning. A short while after these rumours were confirmed. The Algerians had been taken on board a Spanish frigate and the Spanish renegade had been immediately interrogated by the captain but with rather disappointing results. The Spaniard told them that until then the Christian bombardment had not produced much damage on the lines of defence and fortifications. Two shots had hit the bey's palace and one the residence of the Swedish consul. This Spanish renegade gave more information about the fabulous French officer Tournon who had contributed so much to modernize and strengthen the fortifications and military of Algiers. Because of problems connected with a marriage contracted with a woman of a lower class, Tournon, a nobleman, had left France and gone to North America and to fight in the War of the Independence before moving to Constantinople and taking up military service with the sultan. There this able engineer had been made most welcome and he had helped the sultan to strengthen the defence of his Black Sea fortresses to hold the Russians at bay. This is confirmed in a letter exchange between the envoy of the newly founded United States in Paris and his home office in North America. In September 1784 he reports about the 'expatriated adventurer' Tournon who conducted the defence of Algiers.

Already then it could be observed that the expedition had not been all too well prepared. It was not only that the strength and defensive qualities of the Algerians – with their French support – had been underrated, but logistic defects in the Christian fleet had caused serious problems. The changeable weather conditions had prevented a more solid planning of the operations. Because of these reasons, Barceló had not ordered a new attack for the following day but instead convened a meeting of the most senior officers on his flagship. Rechberg observed Lieutenant-General Tommasi and the young Freslon going over to *El Rayo*, together with the other captains of the Order's ships, on board caiques. In the discussion which followed most of the participating officers opted to halt the campaign. Captain General Alexandre Ludovic de Freslon de la

Freslonnière – very frankly and honestly – pointed out his youth and naval inexperience and therefore opted to stay neutral. According to de Bray, who apparently was present at this meeting, Tommasi had a rather pragmatic approach. He said:

> It looks like that, through the help of certain foreign nations, the Algerians – who are normally only capable of plundering and corsairing – have managed to organize their fleet and fortifications so much that it appears impossible to continue with the forces at our disposal a successful campaign against the city. I therefore recommend an honourable retreat before things turn against us. This would keep our honour and respect.

This opinion was followed by the Neapolitan Admiral Bologna and many others.

Only Barceló and the Neapolitan Major Fortiguerri opted for another attempt but they were finally talked over by the others and so it was decided to stop the campaign and to retract from the scene. The young and ambitious Rechberg somehow regretted this decision, which meant that he could not earn any more merits. His diary documents his great interest in all maritime aspects and the theatre of war. He painstakingly noted that during this campaign no fewer than '4,665 bombs, 2,580 shells, 13,951 cannonballs of all calibres, and 1,153 special mortar bombs' had been rained on Algiers. He calculated the total Christian casualties were 300 dead and injured. The Spanish sources give a different and more positive picture. In total the allied forces fired no fewer than 20,000 large-calibre cannonballs, grenades, and bombs. Their losses were 53 dead and 64 injured men, most of them caused by accidents and by misguided friendly fire.

The retreat of the united Christian fleet started on 22 July. After some farewell salutes to the Neapolitans, the Maltese squadron sailed together with the Spanish fleet to Cartagena on Spain's east coast. Captain Village's galley did not follow the rest of the fleet but opted to sail directly to Malta as the captain claimed that it was too heavily damaged to undertake a tour of Spain's east coast.

After two days of sailing, a storm came up which caused considerable disorder. Rechberg even reports that some smaller vessels sank. Since the whole fleet could not sail in formation in these conditions, it was decided that the slower vessels and the galleys – including the Maltese *capitana* with de Bray on board – should stay behind in a separate fleet, while the faster ships – including Rechberg's *Santa Maria del Pilar* and the two other Maltese vessels – should sail with the vanguard. The vanguard reached Cartagena on 27 July. Admitting such a huge number of ships in the port turned out to be a most difficult procedure. It was certainly no masterpiece of control and nautical skills and some captains and pilots showed a stunning ignorance. Rechberg observed a nautical disaster: Some of the bigger ships ran aground while entering the narrow mouth of the port. Some chebecks were seriously damaged when some Spanish ships-of-the-line crashed into them. Some frigates even lost their main masts and suffered considerable damage in the hulls. The Maltese frigates *Sant'Elisabetta* and *Santa Maria del Pilar* suffered some minor damage. The precious icon on board of *El Rayo* was later secretly returned to the convent where it was usually venerated.

On 8 August, after some repair work, the Maltese squadron left Cartagena for Alicante where to meet the Order's galley squadron. On 10 August the Maltese fleet – except Captain Village's galley – was re-united. On the 11th while the Maltese ships were loading provisions and water, news came in that a North African corsair ship had been observed near the coast not very far away. Captain General Freslon immediately gave the order to leave port to chase this ship. It was obvious that the Maltese commanders were keen to achieve some nautical success after the disappointing Algiers campaign. But even the chase of the North African corsair vessel proved in vain. When the Maltese reached the place indicated, there was no

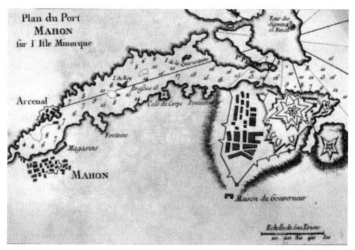

Plan of the port of Mahón on the island of Menorca (French engraving, 1764)

sign of the corsair ship or any news as to where it had gone. The convoy of Spanish chebecs and galleots they met there could not give them any news about the corsair vessel and so it was decided to take up the original plan to return to Malta.

Because of lack of wind, it took until 21 August for the fleet to reach the port of Mahón at the island of Menorca. According to Rechberg, this was the most 'beautiful port in the Mediterranean'. Menorca had been retaken by the Spanish from the British the previous year and Rechberg could still observe the damage done to the city during the siege. Interestingly he could still notice a sort of English atmosphere in Mahón. The place was full of merchants from many different countries. The following six days the Maltese ships stayed in the port to take on provisions and water. For the subsequent passage to Malta, the fleet was divided again. While the swifter *vascello* and the two frigates sailed as a vanguard, the galley squadron followed in a separate group. The galleys made a stop in the small Sicilian port of Serignano, while the Maltese men-of-war continued on their way. After some rather uneventful days at sea, Rechberg's *Santa Maria*

59

del Pilar entered Malta's *Porto Grande* on 8 September. De Bray's *capitana* and the other galleys arrived a day later. This time De Bray's account and dating is confirmed by other contemporaries such as, for example, Louis de Boisgelin's *Ancient and Modern Malta*.

Although this campaign could not be called a military success, in the long run it had some effect. Since the bey of Algiers expected another such bombardment in 1785, he finally decided to open negotiations with Spain. On 14 June 1786, Algiers and Spain finally concluded a peace treaty and the Algiers corsairs stopped – at least for a time – their attacks on Spanish shipping.

CHAPTER 4
BAVARIAN OFFICER AND MEMBER
OF THE ORDER OF MALTA

The disappointing outcome of the Algiers campaign did not harm Joseph Maria von Rechberg's further career within the Order - as we will see subsequently. Unfortunately we do not have archival sources about Rechberg's activities for the later part of 1784 and early 1785. So we do not know if he again joined Lieutenant-General Tommasi and his fleet in the campaign of the Venetian Admiral Emo against Tunis. The winter of 1784/85 Joseph Maria most probably spent in Malta, as the caravans and excursions of the fleet of the Order usually suspended in winter. Life in Valletta was by no means cheap and the expenditure on luxury items, entertainment, and gambling was high with many knights spending exorbitant sums. Young Joseph Maria seems to have fallen in for some of these temptations as, in April 1785, his father sent him a letter complaining his expenditures. His son apparently did not understand – so his father wrote – how much money and effort it had cost his family to support his career and well-being. Maximilian Emanuel von Rechberg reached agreement with the Order's administration that his son himself had to pay for his debts and that only the money which the family had sent should be given to him. The son should not be allowed to take up any more loans. But by the time Maximilan had written this letter the young nobleman already had left Malta.

Together with a new friend, the young Bavarian Count Friedrich von Preysing, Joseph Maria travelled to southern France in March 1785. Sailing to Marseilles, they proceeded to Toulon, then the French navy's main port. In Marseilles and Toulon the two young noblemen visited the local markets and theatres. In June 1785 they were back in Malta with some luxury commodities like coffee, sugar, liquors, and music notes, things which were then difficult to get and expensive in Malta. Apparently Joseph Maria still took a lively interest in music. The fruits of these formative years in different countries and cultural milieus – Swabia, Munich, Metz, and Malta – would show up in various aspects of his life. Besides music, Joseph Maria showed a lifelong interest in the arts and later became a keen collector of paintings. After nearly five years abroad, he asked his brothers in his letters home to write to him in German and to send him German books not to lose contact with his native language and culture.

In the meantime things had taken a positive turn for the Rechbergs in Bavaria. On 22 October 1784 Joseph Maria's younger brother Johann Nepomuk (*Giovanni Nepomiceno Barone de Rechberg*) is listed in the Order's documents as a candidate to the commandery of St Johannes at Mindelheim (*Mündelheim a Scto. Joanne*) in Bavarian Swabia. This position entailed the obligation to undertake all the requested caravans before the age of 24. Indeed the young Johann Nepomuk served in the pagery of the Order in Malta in the late 1780s and later undertook three caravans. We will later see that the checking of the obligation to undertake the full number of four caravans was then not as strict as it had been in previous centuries. In 1797 – aged 24 years – Rechberg had still not carried out all four caravans and he still appears as candidate to the commandery of Mindelheim.

In late October 1784 Duke Elector Karl Theodor confirmed him as candidate for the commandery of Mindelheim. At the same time he is mentioned as commander ('*Dans la Minorité*') in the 'Note des Prieurs, Commandeurs et Chevaliers designés par S.A.E. pour former la nouvelle Langue Anglo-Bavaroise'. The history of the possessions of the Order of St John in the town of Mindelheim in the Swabian part of Bavaria is a special one. In fact, it was the only town in the lands of Germany where the Order held

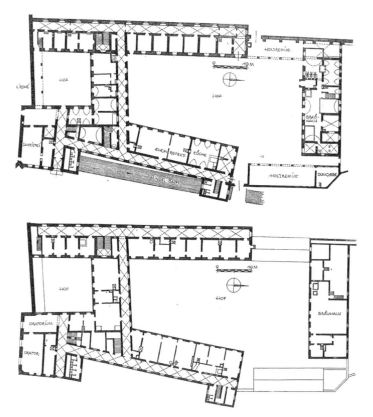

Plan of the Commandery of Mindelheim St Johannes, cross-section, ground floor; Plan of the Commandery of Mindelheim, cross-section, first floor

two commanderies. The territorial possessions of these commanderies were the former possessions of the Jesuits and of some local monasteries which in 1782 had been passed to the newly established Anglo-Bavarian langue. The Jesuits had taken over the huge Benedictine monastery in Mindelheim in 1618 whose old medieval structure had been subsequently altered and augmented. Schools and libraries were established. By 1622 the possession had been raised to the status of a college. In the early 1770s the Bavarian duke elector had sequestrated all Jesuit properties in his lands, and the properties in Mindelheim were passed to the 'Bavarian School funds' which financed the country's educational system. In 1777 parts of the former Jesuit buildings were converted into a hunting lodge for the duke elector. In 1782 the possessions were finally passed over to the Anglo-Bavarian langue.

That same year Johann Baptist von Flachslanden, the lieutenant of Grand Prior Karl August Count of Bretzenheim – then only 13 years old – decided to create two commanderies, called St Johannes and St Martin respectively, out of these rich possessions. Philipp Johann von Lamberg, who had been commander of Enzenried, was eventually promoted commander of St Martin, while the young Johann Nepomuk was installed as commander-candidate of St Johannes. Surely the Rechbergs were aware of their family's old ties with Mindelheim. Their ancestors Bero I von Rechberg (1432–62) and his son Bero II had resided in the town and one of the buildings of the Augustinian monastery was still called *Rechbergtrakt* (Rechberg section). Bero II had been a sort of black sheep of the family and, after his father's death, had quarrelled with the German emperor and the Church. In 1467 he was forced to sell his Mindelheim possessions for 60,000 Rhinian guilders to Ulrich von Frundsberg, the husband of Bero's sister, Barbara. It might well be that these family connections played a role when it was decided to appoint Rechberg as commander of Mindelheim 'St Johannes'.

The audit books of the Order (October 1784) list an income of 5,000 guilders for the commandery of 'Mündelheim a S. Giovanni.' For the first ten years, the holders of the two commanderies of Mindelheim – as all commanders of the Anglo-Bavarian langue – were exempted from paying the responsions in full, but only 2½ percent of the total income. This reduction in the responsions was meant to help set up these new possessions on an economically sound and prosperous basis. Therefore Rechberg's commandery is listed with the sum of 125 guilders to be paid as responsions to Malta. This financial structure was still in existence when the commandery was taken over by Joseph Maria von Rechberg after 1799.

Shortly after his return from France to Malta in the summer of 1785, a new caravan of the sailing-ship squadron of the Order sailed out under the command of Lieutenant-General Giovanni Battista Tommasi. Although Rechberg participated in it, his letters home are very economic about the events. According to the Order's archives, that summer the *San Zaccaria*, *Sant'Elisabetta*, and *Santa Maria del Pilar* sailed along the coast of Algiers chasing North African corsairs. Rechberg just says that he participated in this campaign, most likely again on board the *Santa Maria del Pilar*, then still commanded by Pierre Annibale de Soubiras. Contrary to what had happened the previous year, this campaign was rather uneventful and no prizes were taken. The subsequent journey of the ships of the Order north to Sardinia, Marseilles, and Toulon was marked by strong autumn storms. Joseph Maria spent the winter of 1785/86 again in Malta. Winter, when the naval season was suspended, was traditionally the time when the knights and members of the Order, crammed together in Valletta without having much to do, would often clash among themselves. This often tense atmosphere also shows through in some of Joseph Maria's letters to his brothers and parents. He describes many of his fellow brethren as mean characters, lusty for intrigue. It seems that he was now also on bad terms with his former friend Friedrich von Preysing who had accompanied him on his tour to Southern France the previous year. An exception was Friedrich von Vieregg, his companion in the Algiers campaign whom he describes as '*remplis de bon sens*'.

In his leisure moments Joseph Maria therefore does not seemed to have mixed a lot with other members of the Order but turned to music and the arts. He again asked his brother Aloys to send him music scores for his cello and more German books. In April 1786, the season for the naval campaigns finally commenced again. In the meantime Pierre André de Suffren de St Tropez had replaced Giovanni Battista Tommasi as lieutenant-general in charge of the men-of-war squadron. The young Rechberg again participated in the rather uneventful campaign of 1786. By now he had carried out three caravans and he needed just one to fulfil the obligations to become of professed knight of the Order. Rechberg was now 17 years old and he had to decide which directions he was to follow. The undertaking of the long and sometimes dangerous caravans normally would indicate that the young nobleman intended to seek a career in the Order. Still his father was not yet decided as to what to recommend.

In May 1786 there was an exchange of letters between Maximilian Emanuel von Rechberg and Johann Felix Eisele, the Bavarian chaplain in Malta, about the subject. In the father's eyes, his second oldest son was – despite his intelligence and talents – still not fully mature and still very temperamental in his decisions. The father asked Eisele for advice as he knew the young man very well. It has to be kept in mind that, if the oldest son of the Rechberg family were to die, Joseph Maria would be the legal successor. If by that time Joseph Maria would be a professed knight, he would not be excluded from becoming the official heir but he would not be allowed to marry. In the end it was agreed that the young man should be left to decide for himself. Various comments by the father show how well he was then informed about the internal affairs of the Anglo-Bavarian langue. In his letter to Eisele of May 1786, he mentions the possibility that one day the Bavarian grand priory would be dissolved. Most likely he was informed about what was then going on behind the scenes, namely that if, after the death of ruling Duke Elector Karl Theodor, he would be succeeded by a member of the Zweibrücken branch of the princely family, the property of the priory would be sequestrated. We will later see how well reasoned these fears were.

In the autumn of 1786 there was the most welcome arrival of two novices of the Anglo-Bavarian langue, namely Emanuel von Törring and Vincenz von Minucci. Rechberg's family had used this occasion to send with Count Törring and Count Minucci some music notes and books for Joseph Maria. The year 1787 passed rather calmly in Malta. In summer Rechberg carried out his fourth caravan. His achievements now showed also some monetary results. In June 1787 (*'Per Decreto del Sacro Consiglio die 15 Giugno 1787'*) he started receiving 150 guilders a year from the income of the commandery of Vogach. A few months later another 150 guilders income from the commandery of Schierling was added.

On some unknown date in 1788 Rechberg left Malta to return to Munich where his family had prepared the affairs concerning his future career in the Bavarian army. Maximilian Emanuel von Rechberg had written on behalf of his son to Duke Elector Karl Theodor's wife, to Duke Max von Zweibrücken, and to the prince of Isenburg, then president of the council of war. The handwritten diary of the Algiers campaign and his participation in the caravans of the Order had certainly supported Joseph Maria's case. On 23 February 1788 – when he still was in Malta – Joseph Maria had been appointed first lieutenant in the duke elector's own regiment. That, just one month later, he had received a captain's patent in this regiment was possibly helped by some money from the family – buying a captain's patent was a normal practice then – but certainly also by his experience in the Order's navy.

In the autumn of 1788 Joseph Maria took up his service in the duke elector's own regiment in Munich. Even in Munich Rechberg did not stop pursuing his private and intellectual interests. He now started to learn English and practised the language in his letters to his brother Franz Xaver who was studying this language at the University of Heidelberg. These letters also provide some information about the young officer's circle of friends and acquaintances. Besides some relatives, he spent most of his time with the priest Lechner, Commander Streicher, and the young Baron Reisach who was then a member of the Bavarian grand priory *dans la minorité*.

During his Bavarian military service, Rechberg was witness to the reforms carried out by Benjamin Thompson, count of Rumford who drastically re-structured and modernized the Bavarian army. Training was very much intensified and soldiers were also used for works to repair roads, public buildings, and for police services. To save costs, Count Rumford had issued a decree in May 1791 that there would be no promotion from the rank of captain to major for the following ten years. To avoid this demotivating blockage of his career, Joseph Maria turned again to the 'Maltese' option and tried to take up service as officer in the *Reggimento di Malta* which was composed of soldiers of fortune from various European countries. In 1791 the strength of the regiment totalled 992 men. To keep it in good strength and training, the Order then spent no fewer than 97,200 *scudí* every year in its maintenance. Obviously Rechberg remembered the good pay of the high-ranking officers of this regiment. In his letters to his brothers in the spring of 1791, he had mentioned the pay of 500 guilders yearly for a captain plus an additional 300 guilders as a permanent pension. Rechberg planned to enrol for three years after which he would decide to continue or not. These plans were supported by his uncle and knight of Malta Joseph Theodor Heinrich Topor von Morawitzky who was then a member in the Bavarian council of war.

For some unknown reasons, these plans did not bear fruit. Rechberg instead managed to get a transfer to the prestigious Guards Regiment of the duke elector of Bavaria but, when it turned out that this regiment would not be participating in the ongoing war against the French, he tried again to get a transfer to a regiment which was actually taking part in the defence of the parts of the Palatinate on the western bank of the Rhine. The Palatinate was then part of the territory

The town of Mindelheim (painting, late 18th century)

of the dynasty of the Wittelsbach family which was ruling in Munich. With an active participation in the war, the young and ambitious officer hoped to improve his chances – against Rumford's regulations – for a promotion. His request for such a transfer was, however, at first blocked by Rumford who did not want a constant interchange among the officers of the regiments. In the summer of 1792 the situation, however, looked somewhat more promising as in the meantime some officers in the army of the Palatinate had died or been too seriously wounded to continue serving. But again matters took a long turn until, finally, in the summer of 1793 there arose the possibility of a post as *aide de camp* in the service of the Prince Reuss, a member of the headquarters of Prince Max Joseph von Zweibrücken. To take up this post and equip himself as status demanded meant another heavy financial burden and Joseph Maria had to ask his brothers to act as financial guarantees for these expenditures. The salary of an *aide de camp* was just 60 guilders monthly and did not cover all these expenses. When the preparations for the march to the Palatinate started taking a long time, Rechberg thought of enrolling in the *Reggimento di Malta* even for less salary and at a lower grade. He also considered to take up service in the Order's navy. After he had overcome a sickness in the autumn, things finally started moving and, in early February 1794, he received the order to go to the fortress of Mannheim in the Palatinate.

In Mannheim he was introduced to the commander of this important bulwark against the French, Major General Count Bernhard Erasmus von Deroy who would provide important for Rechberg's further career. He also had the chance to meet personally Duke Max Joseph von Zweibrücken, the future Bavarian duke elector. Mannheim was then only at the periphery of the war and Rechberg merely witnessed only a few short French attacks on the defensive outposts on the river Rhine nearby. Over the following months, he observed the lack of co-ordination among the Bavarian forces and the retreat of the imperial army. In his own letters Rechberg does not give many details about his personal participation in the actions but he concentrates on the more global picture of the theatre of war and questions of strategy. This may be a case of modesty as the writings of his father and some other contemporaries mention the young officer's military talent and cold-bloodedness. When the French launched a massive attack on the defences at the Rhine near Mannheim in the autumn of 1794 and there was an acute emergency Rechberg showed himself a brilliant artillery commander and demonstrated great skills in defending the lines. In the long run, the few German successes did not prevent the negative outcome of the war. In 1795 the fortress of Mannheim surrendered to the French but Rechberg was not present to witness this degrading event. He had been sent to the region of Odenwald to gather some scattered contingents of artillery some weeks before.

In 1796 fighting approached Rechberg's home town and his own family. In the War of the First Coalition the French northern army occupied Belgium and the Netherlands, while the southern army, under the command of young Napoleon Buonaparte, fought very successfully against the Austrians in Northern Italy. The French generals Laroche and Moreau were engaged in fighting the Austrian and German troops north of the Alps. In these campaigns the French moved deep into Bavarian territory, only to retreat when they were in danger of being cut off from their supplies. During these retreats, in July 1796, some of the troops were set to march through Donzdorf, the Swabian hometown of Joseph Maria von Rechberg, who rushed home to help his family and to negotiate with the French commanders to leave the civil population and their possessions untouched. The passing of the military contingents of course did not take place without plundering and sequestrations. The Rechberg family estates were then at the mercy not only of the French enemy but also of roaming Austrian contingents.

Against all odds and the regulations of Count Rumford, Rechberg's military talent and achievements in the war against the French proved too strong not to be rewarded with a promotion. In early January 1797, he was officially promoted major in the third Grenadier-Regiment 'Count Isenburg'. But still this did not satisfy Rechberg's hunger for new achievements and advances. As he was afraid that his regiment would not be involved in the frontline of the action he – with support from his father – opted to change posts with his acquaintance Baron von Stengel as major to the first Fusilier-Regiment of Count-Palatinate Wilhelm von Birkenfeld. Serving in this regiment promised much better chances to participate in the vanguard the army and therewith obtain more experience and to boost his personal reputation.

In the meantime Joseph Maria was keenly following the ups and downs of 'his' Anglo-Bavarian langue and especially his family's involvement in its affairs. In the late 1780s there was, for example, a long-lasting dispute between the commander of Mindelheim St Martin, Philipp Johann von Lamberg, and the representative who administered the commandery of Mindelheim St Johannes on behalf of the minor Johann Nepomuk von Rechberg and the parish of St Martin in the village of Unteregg. The Maltese commanderies in Mindelheim held the right of tithes in the villages of Unteregg and Oberegg. Lamberg and Rechberg's representative finally agreed to use a third of the sum of 3,800 guilders to build a new house for the parish priest and to repair the church. Such sharing of costs was also maintained in later times.

The auditing exercise carried out by Bishop Casimir von Haeffelin, the receiver, and the auditor of the provincial chapter of the Bavarian grand priory provides a good idea of the financial situation of the commandery of Mindelheim St Johannes. In the 1790s, when after ten years the administration and the running of the Bavarian commanderies were fully established and functioning, the commanders had to pay the full responsions to Malta. For Mindelheim St Johannes, which then apparently held bigger properties and a greater income than the neighbouring commandery of Mindelheim St Martin, this was fixed as 250 guilders per year. Commander Philipp Johann von Lamberg only had to pay 125 guilders to the Order's treasury. There seemed to have been some difficulties in 1796 – most likely because of the French revolutionary wars which also hit south-west Germany – as Haeffelin then recorded that Johann Nepomuk von Rechberg still owed 125 guilders to the Order. In April 1798 Haeffelin informed the treasury for the last time before the fall of Malta over the responsions paid. Mindelheim is again listed with 250 guilders.

Although for the moment pursuing his career in the Bavarian army, Rechberg could not avoid from becoming involved in some of the problems of the Anglo-Bavarian langue in the 1780s and 1790s, especially since he still hoped to receive a lucrative commandery and position in the Bavarian grand priory one day. As in the 1790s it could be observed that his younger brother Johann Nepomuk had lost his zeal to be an active member of the Order, Joseph Maria developed the plans to take over his commandery, an issue that shall be addressed later on. Many of the internal problems of the grand priory were home-made and attributable to the personal weaknesses and greed of some of its leading members. The question of money contributed a lot to these internal tensions.

Surely the prestige of the Order gained by the establishment of the Anglo-Bavarian langue superseded the real 'material' benefit. The new langue was endowed with a revenue of 171,000 guilders (= 151,703 Maltese crowns), on which sum the responsions were assessed. It was obvious that the Order could not expect high returns from the Bavarian priory at the beginning. Calculating that 10 per cent of this revenue – without '*passaggi, spogli, mortori*' and '*vacanti*' – had to be paid as responsions to Malta, that would amount to 15,170 Maltese crowns. It was stipulated that the Bavarian knights had to pay the responsions on the same day as and together with the German knights. As the first commanders of the Bavarian grand priory had to pay only $2\frac{1}{2}$ per cent of the proceeds of their commanderies, the mediocre sum of 3,794 Rhinian dollars was remitted to Malta as the first responsions in 1787/88. To put this in perspective: the total income of the Order for 1788 was 1,354,556 Maltese crowns against a total expenditure of 1,172,513 Maltese crowns. The general chapter decided that, from 1776 onwards, the German langue alone was to contribute 467,757 Rhinian dollars. The revenue from the Anglo-Bavarian langue was increased when the Polish grand priory was incorporated within it in 1785. In 1782 the annual responsions of the grand priory of Poland were increased from about 6,000 Rhinian dollars to 7,500. In subsequent years the heterogeneous interests and character of the members of the Anglo-Bavarian langue became more and more visible. There were the hyperactive Flachslanden and Haeffelin, the loyal and hard-working commanders Guido von Tauffkichen, Friedrich von Vieregg, and the count von Törring, Maillot de la Traille, and Vacquier de la Barthe and a great number of commanders who did next to nothing but just lived off the fruits of the work of others. What was common for all members was the hunger for more prestigious posts and revenues. Flachslanden received 31,000 guilders annually from his various posts in the Bavarian grand priory, together with a life pension – one of the so-called *Pensioni utalizie* – for his services in the establishing the Anglo-Bavarian langue. Haeffelin's yearly income from the commandery of Kaltenberg alone was 4,000 German guilders. As a receiver of the Bavarian grand priory, he had an income of 12,000 Maltese crowns. The yearly income of the count of Bretzenheim as grand prior with the two commanderies of Munich and Ebersberg was 25,000 German guilders. Count Minucci as a grand cross of honour received 4,000 *scudí*, while Joseph Maria von Rechberg – at a much lower level – profited from the generosity of the leaders of the institution. From June 1787 onwards, he was granted an additional pension of 150 *scudí* from the income of the commandery of Vogach.

During the 1780s and 1790s some reshuffles took place in the posts and commanderies. In 1794 Emanuel von Törring replaced Rechberg's friend Friedrich von Vieregg as lieutenant-turcopilier whose duties included the visitation of the Bavarian commanderies. Friedrich von Preysing was appointed *Conservatore*. The Anglo-Bavarian langue – or better its revenues – remained an attraction for the Bavarian nobility who kept applying to be received into the Order.

One of the biggest problems was the grand prior of Bavaria himself, the illegitimate son of Duke Elector Karl Theodor. In the spring of 1787 Grand Prior Karl August von Bretzenheim visited Malta and was received with all honours by Grand Master Rohan. After this return on 23 June 1787, Karl Theodor felt obliged to write a letter to Rohan to thank him warmly for the prestigious reception he had given his illegitimate son. In 1788, when the young count of Bretzenheim came of age, he officially started to administer his lands himself. His real activities were more or less concentrated on letters of thanks or polite replies to Grand Master Rohan whenever a member of the Anglo-Bavarian was awarded tokens of honour or crosses of the Order. After two years of negligence, his lazy performance as grand prior provoked *Bali* Flachslanden to become rather harsh with his 'lord'. The recent events of the French Revolution had sharpened Flachslanden's scepticism even more about the performance of some members of the high nobility. In a memoir of December 1790, Flachslanden blamed Karl August for the fact that the grand priory of Bavaria was in a state of lethargy and that its members were most selfish and lacked any real spirit for the Order. Certainly not all holders of commanderies in the lands of Bavaria had visited Malta to undertake their caravans in the fleet of the Order. In fact, many of the Bavarian knights had been dispensed by the grand master from the caravans. Besides Rechberg and Friedrich von Vieregg, one of the few who really distinguished himself in his military service in Malta, was Baron von Wefeld. Others were Count Friedrich von Preysing and Baron von Zedwitz, who both came to Malta with Joseph Maria, Count Gaetano von Spreti, and Count Maximilian von Arco who later travelled to Malta together with Johann Nepomuk von Rechberg. Count Arco later received the commandery of Schierling, while Count Spreti was installed as commander of Randegg. Another one was Count Emanuel von Törring who established himself as an active member of the Order in Malta in the 1790s. In 1790 he was conferred with the bailiwick of Egle and made a member of the council. Others – like the later Bavarian general and minister of war Baron Anton von Gumppenberg – were noted down for service in Malta but, because of the events of 1798, never actually made it to the island.

Besides the laziness of the count of Bretzenheim and the lethargy of some of the Bavarian knights, there was a certain insecurity that was harming the institution – so Flachslanden wrote. Still many Bavarian nobles – and rightly so – were not sure if Duke Elector Karl Theodor's successors would preserve the priory and bailiwick of the Order in Bavaria. There were two reasons why the existence of the Anglo-Bavarian langue could never be completely taken for granted. There was still the unsolved question of the confirmation of the institution by the agnates of the house of Wittelsbach. And there were the policies of Karl Theodor himself which raised several doubts. Throughout the 1780s secret negotiations went on between Karl Theodor and Emperor Joseph II which centred on the so-called 'exchange project'. When Bavaria fell in the hands of Austria, Karl Theodor would be 'refunded' with Belgium (the Austrian Netherlands) and he could move his court to Brussels. It was the Zweibrücken branch of the family, namely the future Duke Elector Max IV Joseph and the minister Hofenfels, which opposed these plans. These developments could not be hidden from the alerted Flachslanden and Haeffelin. One of the answers was to create an 'assurance' in case of Karl Theodor's death.

Bali and Turcopilier Johann Baptist von Flachslanden

We will later see that Flachslanden's worries about the unsolved question of the court of Zweibrücken were entirely justified. Flachslanden was even more active in reminding Karl August of his duties as his behaviour was providing the many enemies of the Anglo-Bavarian langue with new ammunition. He asked Karl August to invest all his energy in his duties as grand prior and to give a good example to the public. Still Karl August continued in his old habits. In 1792 the grand prior moved to Munich but, when his father Karl Theodor died in 1799, he lost his great protector and he was cold-shouldered by the court of new duke elector, Max IV Joseph. Soon the post of grand prior was taken away from him and he moved to Vienna. After he lost most of his lands in the treaty of Lunéville, he was compensated in the general act of the German states (*Reichsdeputationshauptschluß*) in 1803 with the possession of Lindau on Lake Constance. Following Austrian pressure, he exchanged Lindau with the possessions of Regécz and Sárospatak in Hungary. In 1806 he designated himself Prince Bretzenheim von Régecz and became a member of the Hungarian diet.

An asset for the Anglo-Bavarian langue was surely the much improved relations between Munich and the Roman curia. The ties between Karl Theodor and Pope Pius VI were improved even more when the duke elector visited Rome in June 1783. Things became even more simple for Bavaria when, in 1785, the curia agreed to establish permanent papal nuncios in Munich.

That the Bavarian lands were not an enclave of quietness and unbroken political continuation but were very much involved in the web of international politics in central Europe became apparent when the great storm of the revolution broke out in France in July 1789. Although the events in France were geographically distant, they soon began to affect the Anglo-Bavarian langue and its members. That the aristocratic sovereign Order of St John was threatened in its very foundation by the French Revolution was clear for everyone. Even after the first wave of terror had passed, the French institutions took harsh actions against the very existence of the Order in France. The national assembly considered the Order as a foreign sovereign possessing property in French territory and imposed taxes on its property. On 19 September 1792, the assembly decreed the Order extinct within the French territories and its possessions were annexed to the domains of France. This was a disastrous financial blow for the knights. The loss of the possessions of the three French langues deprived the Order's treasury of 392,974 *livres* annually. Compared to the situation before 1792, the total receipts were reduced by over 60 per cent. The French national assembly also withdrew the citizenship of all those Frenchmen who were members of any foreign-based Order of chivalry which threatened the very existence of the three French langues: Provence, France, and Auvergne. Subsequently Grand Master Rohan declined to acknowledge the new French Republic. The disastrous financial effects were much worse than the political repercussions. The commanderies in the countries of the Allied Powers where the Order still kept its possessions could not be made to increase their responsions or make other contributions to the Order's treasury. In 1796 much of the plate of the Order had to be melted down to make coins, as the large loans from neutral and friendly sources had been exhausted.

When sketching Rechberg's role in the Bavarian grand priory and its context, one also has to mention the mysterious institution of the so-called Bavarian 'Illuminates'. During his sojourns in Malta between 1783 and 1788 and again in 1798, Rechberg had sometimes to face rumours that he and his Bavarian brethren in the Order were members – or at least – had been 'infected by this sect'. There is no documentation whatsoever that Rechberg was ever a member of the 'Illuminates' but he did know very well that some important members of the Bavarian grand priory were active as Illuminates. One of them was *Balí*

Johann Baptist von Flachslanden. In fact, how far fantasy and false exaggerations can lead one astray is shown by Elizabeth Schermerhorn in her oft-quoted book *Malta of the Knights* – which follows Broadley's totally unreliable book on Freemasonry in Malta – who maintains that, after the Anglo-Bavarian langue had been installed, 'the new cult (of Freemasonry) penetrated to the most sacred precincts, and the Bavarian prior of St John's (sic) dabbled in Masonry, and Bishop Estling (sic), with the secret name of Philon de Biblos, acted as intermediary with the head lodge in Bavaria'. Various publications have stated that Masonic ideas and the subversive concepts of the Illuminates had infiltrated the Order and Malta with the Bavarians which in the long run contributed to the fall of the Order. As is often the case, this is a mixture of truth and fiction: the key figure was *Abbé* Casimir Haeffelin.

The 'Order' or better 'secret society' of the *Illuminées* or Illuminates had been founded in 1776 in the Bavarian town of Ingolstadt by the professor of law Adam Weishaupt. It was based on the philosophy of radical enlightenment and anti-clericalism and developed on a programme of education, society, and science. It preached the removal of the obligations and borders of confessions, classes, and nations. There were three grades in the 'Order'. The novices had to learn humanity by reading the works of Schiller (*Fiesco*), Lessing (*Nathan, Emilia Galotti*), Goethe (*Egmont*), and Wieland (*Agathon*) and the new social revolutionary pamphlets of Mably and Morelly. The second grade (the *Minervales*) had to study the stoic philosophy of Seneca, Epictes, Plutarch, and Sallust. The third grade (*Illuminates*) were to concentrate on the atheistic-materialistic works of Holbach and Helvétius. With this training, the Illuminates aimed to ethico-moral perfection and to prepare for social and political change in Europe. This programme opposed nationalism, patriotism, egoism, individualism, and religious borders and 'chains'. Following persecution between 1784 and 1790, the number

79

of the active Illuminates was drastically reduced. It has, however, to be made clear that there was always a strict separation between Illuminates and Freemasons. In general, it was impossible for Illuminates to become Freemasons later. But even most contemporary Freemasons were anything but radically anticlerical or antifeudal. As modern historians rightly observe, the eighteenth-century Freemasons were certainly not mixed up with revolutionaries or rebels. The Masonic lodges were a heterogeneous coterie of conservatives, absolutists, physiocrats, liberals, Catholics, Protestants, deists, and atheists. The Freemasons and the Bavarian Illuminates therefore should not be mixed up with the Jacobites or French Democrats who, after 1789, rose to power and took drastic measures against their political enemies.

The programme of the Illuminates aimed at a soft 'evolutionary' revolution which was to be achieved by a secret infiltration of the important posts in the state. Of such undercover activities, the Bavarian court was especially afraid. After 1781 some Masonic lodges joined the Illuminates. In 1784 the Illuminates in Bavaria experienced internal conflicts when some of them favoured Karl Theodor's proposal of exchanging Bavaria for Belgium while others strictly opposed the idea of Bavaria falling into the hands of the Austrians. That the Illuminates were themselves never really united is also shown by the opposition of some of them to the plan of handing over the properties of the Jesuits to the Order of Malta. On 23 November 1784 an anonymous Illuminate in Vienna drew up a *Formalia* which regretted that the establishment of the Anglo-Bavarian langue had wasted a chance to infiltrate this institution immediately.

That some leading members of the langue led secret lives was strongly rumoured but could not be proven. The Order's *ricevitore* and one of the masterminds of the Anglo-Bavarian-Langue, Casimir Haeffelin, and his circle were active Illuminates. Haeffelin's declared enemies, the conservative party of the former Jesuits at court, especially Ignaz Frank

– very much afraid of Haeffelin's next moves and projects – had always tried their best to put his name in a bad light. This did not have much effect until the head of the commission of the investigation and punishment of the Illuminates, Kaspar von Lippert, a friend of Frank's, discovered that Haeffelin was also a member of the secret society with the name of *Philobiblios*. Not long afterwards even the papal nuncio Zoglio was informed who duly reported the affair to the Curia. In a list of 15 November 1790 which included 91 names of notorious Illuminates, Haeffelin is listed as 'bishop, main protector according to a letter from the priest Beermiller and other sure indications'.

However, the prosecutors admitted that Haeffelin was too clever and hard for them to get a real grip on him and it was feared that he could resume his career one day. Many maintain that Haeffelin kept contact with the Illuminates even after 1790 despite these accusations. In 1795 customs officers in Düsseldorf discovered a secret archive of the Illuminates where Haeffelin was mentioned as a leading member. On 28 December 1800 Papal Nuncio della Genga (later Leo XII) wrote that he knew for sure that Haeffelin had resumed his activities as an important member of the Illuminates, while in 1803 the Austrian court and the papal nuncio in Vienna suspected that Haeffelin was still in contact with the society. Haeffelin's former membership was recalled in 1817 when the pope refused to appoint him cardinal in spite of the Bavarian King Max I Joseph's strong recommendations. That same year Haeffelin officially regretted his connections with the Illuminates and played down his importance in the secret society.

Owing to his influential friends and through his friendship with the duke elector, in 1789/90 Haeffelin avoided a complete and open degradation. When, following the French Revolution, political fear of subversive infiltration set in motion a new wave of investigation against the Illuminates in Bavaria, Karl Theodor could not protect his friend

Haeffelin any more. The *abbé* and bishop lost his power in the ecclesiastical council and at court and he was replaced as vice-president of the council. Karl Theodor chose an elegant way out by promoting him to imperial baron in 1790 and with this farewell gift Haeffelin retired from the court and the active ecclesiastical politics – at least for a while. In February 1792 he was even released from his post as director of the administration of the schools in Bavaria. This, however, did not touch his position and activities within the Order of St John. He was sure that, when the days of Frank and Lippert were over, he would return to the limelight of the court and resume his career.

So, as from 1789 onwards, Haeffelin concentrated his activities more on his functions and role within the Order. In 1790 he represented the Anglo-Bavarian langue in Frankfurt a. M. at the election of the new German Emperor Franz II. During his forced political inactivity, in 1793 he found time to write a treatise on the statutes of the Order of St John especially intended for the brethren of the Anglo-Bavarian langue and suggesting some modifications to the old statutes. Possibly to stress his loyalty and to promote his conformist behaviour, in 1799 he published a treatise on the importance of the 'enlightenment of the nation' ('*Worin besteht die wahre Volksaufklärung?*'). After the death of Frank and Karl Theodor and under Max IV Joseph and minister Montgelas, he resumed his ecclesiastical and political careers.

Haeffelin was not the only important brother of the Anglo-Bavarian langue who was an active member of the Illuminates. In 1795, when the above-mentioned new list of members of Weishaupt's secret society was discovered in Düsseldorf, Commander Count Topor von Morawitzky, then a minister in the Bavarian cabinet, was again accused of being a tool of the Illuminates. From time to time, even Commander Count Törring-Seefeld, president of the chamber of the court, was accused of being a member of the society. The count was indeed an Illuminate, as were the commanders Baron von Seefeld, Baron Gumppenberg, Count Preysing, Count Taufkirchen, and Priest Commander Braun. One of the few knights who were both an Illuminate and a leading Freemason was Count Kollowrat, the grand prior of Bohemia (pseudonym *Numenus*). Another Illuminate in the service of the Order of Malta was Joseph Socher, the rector of the conventual church of the Anglo-Bavarian langue, who had already fallen victim to the first wave of sequestration of the Illuminates in 1784/85; he had to resign from his post and had been 'exiled' as parish priest to Oberhaching. The Bavarian knights' motives to join Weishaupt's secret society are not always easy to discern. In the case of Haeffelin it was clear: in addition to the intellectual challenge, he had become a member to extend his web of secret contacts.

Weishaupt found adherents even in the highest government circles. The most prominent Illuminates were the vice-president of the Bavarian administration Count Maximilian von Seinsheim and the future Bavarian minister of foreign affairs and architect of the 'modern' Bavaria Count Montgelas. When their membership in the secret society was discovered, they found temporary exile at the court of Duke Elector Karl Theodor's 'enemy' Karl August von Zweibrücken whose court in general was very open to new ideas. Karl Theodor's successor on the throne of Bavaria, Max IV Joseph, was himself once an active Freemason in Zweibrücken.

It is certain that Rechberg tried to remain aloof from this network of intrigues to concentrate on furthering his military career in the Bavarian army. As mentioned previously, between 1792 and 1797 there raged the so-called War of the First Coalition between France and Austria which was joined by several German states. The French revolutionary troops defeated the German troops in Western France and Alsace and the war soon reached the Rhine and had an impact on the duchies of Baden and the principality of Württemberg. The Order of St John lamented the loss of various commanderies in this south-western part of Germany. For a young, ambitious, and talented officer, it was the time and occasion to distinguish himself. During parts of these war campaigns Rechberg was joined again by his old acquaintance from the times of the Algiers Campaign, Friedrich von Vieregg, who was also serving in Isenburg's regiment. In 1797 Vieregg was promoted to major and, a few years later, Rechberg and Vieregg were again united in the Bavarian army. We will come back to this later on.

CHAPTER 5
A DANGEROUS MISSION AND THE LAST DAYS OF HOSPITALLER MALTA

In the meantime Rechberg's contacts with Malta had intensified again. Following the loss of the French territories in 1792, the balance of power in the Order of St John developed a new profile. The influence of the French langues declined while the German and Anglo-Bavarian langues gained more importance. In the autumn of 1795, the question of who should be nominated to the post of castellan of the Anglo-Bavarian langue was discussed in Malta. This post was held in rotation for a period of two years among members of this langue. Lieutenant to the Turcopilier Emanuel von Törring, Commander Streicher, and Turcopilier Flachslanden all suggested Rechberg as the most suitable candidate. We know about the ongoing negotiations through the letters of his father. Maximilian Emanuel informed his son Aloys that this position would earn Joseph Maria 300 *Louis d'or* in two years. After the term was over, there was a good chance that he would be honoured by the grand master with a commandery of grace. In fact, the distribution of commanderies – and in the period of absolutism this happened quite often – could be done directly by the grand master (*'ex gratia magistrale'*).

A few weeks later the council of the Order and Grand Master Rohan confirmed Joseph Maria's nomination to castellan and asked him to travel to Malta as quickly as possible to take up his post on 1 March 1796. To obey this order, arrangements had to be made with the Bavarian army and permission for a longer absence from Munich had to be given by the council of war. But while the young Rechberg was preparing for his tour to Malta, war against the French broke out again. To leave the Bavarian army at this time was clearly impossible and the Malta plans had to be aborted. This did not mean that contacts ceased; on the contrary, Joseph Maria was still aiming for lucrative positions within the Order. In the autumn of 1797, he discussed intensively with his family the possibility of taking over the commandery of Mindelheim St Johannes, until then reserved for his younger brother Johann Nepomuk. Joseph Maria calculated that the procedures to achieve that goal would take another year or so.

Things took a more dramatic turn early in 1798 when Joseph Maria received a call from the provincial chapter of the Bavarian grand priory. Flachslanden and Haeffelin's network of spies and agents in Germany, France, and Italy had sent thrilling news. In Munich Rechberg had a secret meeting with Haeffelin's close friend and collaborator, the priest-commander of Aham, Philipp Vacquier de la Barthe, who had obtained a packet of alarming letters and notes, some secretly copied from the French, Russian, and Prussian representatives at the congress of Rastatt. The dispatches by François Gabriel de Bray, the Order's representative at Rastatt, and the letters of the Knights Lomellin, Ferreti, and Schönau expressly informed the grand master that the French were planning to take Malta soon. From de la Barthe, Rechberg got to know that these papers contained information about Napoleon's plans for a forthcoming expedition to Egypt, in the course of which Malta would be seized. Other documents contained Russian plans to save Hospitaller Malta from the French. The choice fell upon the experienced soldier Rechberg to carry these documents to Malta, a mission that had to be kept under utmost secrecy. Time was pressing. To take leave from the Bavarian army was easier now as the French Wars had officially ended with the peace treaties of Campo-Formio in October 1797. On 17 March Rechberg was given a passport personally signed by Austrian Archduke Joseph Johann von Habsburg. Passing the French lines in Northern Italy with these documents increased the risk of this mission to Malta.

The new French actions against the Austrians in Northern Italy and the campaigns of the new star on the military firmament, Napoleon Bonaparte, made the subsequent journey south to an unpredictable adventure. The previous year Napoleon had successfully invaded Northern Italy and defeated the Austrians at the Battle of Lodi, driving them out of Lombardy. The victory of the crucial Battle of the Bridge of Arcole had opened for Napoleon the way to central Italy and allowed him to take over the Papal States. The Treaty of Leoben he signed with the Austrians gave him control of most of Northern Italy. A few months later he marched on Venice and forced it to surrender.

By late March Rechberg, accompanied by Baron Pocci, had left Munich. Crossing the Austrian territory was no problem but the difficulties started after passing Verona when they started encountering French military contingents and guards. Rechberg and Pocci continued to travel south, disguised with the Cisalpinian cockade. Every passport check and investigation by French or Italian officials turned into an adventure and lottery. In the case of any acute threat of being stopped and physically checked by the French, Rechberg had decided to burn the papers he was carrying. The two travellers had to turn to Italian guides since, because of the wars and destruction of roads and post-stations, there was no regular post-coach service any more, which slowed them down considerably. At first they had intended to take a passage from Genoa to Malta but the French were then blocking the port for foreign ships. Boarding a French ship to Malta appeared too risky. There remained the option to find a Maltese *speronara* or brigantine in Leghorn which they reached via Mantua and Florence. There Rechberg and Pocci embarked on a merchant vessel bound for Malta.

They must have thought that the toughest part of the journey now lay behind them but, just one day after the vessel had left Leghorn, it was attacked by a French corsair. Putting up a fight against the strongly armed French ship appeared useless and the crew and the passengers soon surrendered. Fortunately the corsairs were mostly interested in material things and showed no interest in the papers Rechberg was carrying. After the corsairs had seized the freight, there were some wild discussions amongst the French about what to do with the passengers. Since these were seen to be just a burden for the French vessel to continue its cruise, they were moved to another French ship. But even here they did not stay for long. After an odyssey from port to port on the north-west coast of Italy, the crew and passengers were set ashore at Civitavecchia.

Rechberg continued his voyage with some help from other members of the Order and some bills of exchange sent from Bavaria. On 4 June, he finally reached Malta and was welcomed by his comrades from the Anglo-Bavarian langue, namely Count and Commander Joseph von Lodron, the lieutenant of the turcopilier, Count Emanuel von Törring; the Conventual Conservator Commander Friedrich von

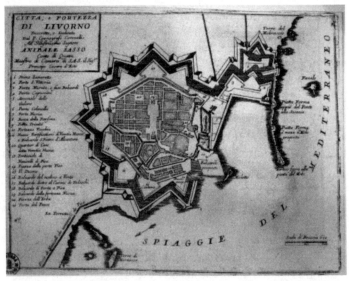

Plan of the port and fortifications of Leghorn (*c.* 1700)

Preysing; and the commander of Stöckelsberg Count Ludwig von Seeau, as well as the chaplains and conventual priests Joseph Betzl, commander of Munich; Ferdinand Haintlet, commander of Altötting; Deacon Alois von Schiltenberg; and the custodian of the *Auberge de Baviere*, Joseph Splinder. Rechberg had met Betzl, who had obtained a doctorate in philosophy and theology in 1783 at the University of Ingolstadt, a few times in Munich. According to the records of Grand Master Hompesch's secretary Charles Joseph Meyer de Knonau, there were five Anglo-Bavarian knights (including Rechberg) amongst the 332 knights then present in Malta. We do not know if Rechberg immediately informed the Bavarians about the approaching danger or if he waited until his meeting with Grand Master Hompesch.

Many things had changed since Rechberg had left Malta in 1788, not the least because of the election of a new grand master the previous year. Mainly thanks to Haeffelin's secretive and influential work – and also the events in France – Ferdinand von Hompesch had been elected as the first-ever German grand master. Haeffelin had come to Malta in the autumn of 1796 when it was being whispered that Grand Master Rohan was dying and started networking on behalf of Hompesch. The Bavarian bishop pointed out to many that, in such stormy times, the election of a representative of the German empire – a symbol of political stability and a bulwark against the French liberals – would bring the Order back on the right track. In a letter to Duke Elector Karl Theodor, Hompesch himself stressed how much the Bavarian influence and the contacts of his brother, the Bavarian Minister Karl von Hompesch, had helped him to be elected in July 1797.

After an audience with Grand Master Hompesch to whom Rechberg handed over the documents about the coming French attack, he was taken back to his rooms in the Anglo-Bavarian auberge. Trying to calculate the forces the Order could throw against the attackers, Rechberg soon noticed that the Order's biggest sailing ships were not in the *Porto Grande*.

He was informed that they had left for a caravan. Indeed on 29 April 1798 the *San Zaccaria* and the frigate *Sant'Elisabetta* had left port to look for North African corsairs under the command of Lieutenant-General *Balí* Paul Julian Suffren de St Tropez whom Rechberg knew from the Algiers campaign. When the vessels glided out of the impressive *Porto Grande*, no one knew then that it would be the Order's very last caravan. The ships first headed north towards Sicily. Near Pozzallo, the crews of some trading vessels informed them that they had seen a Tunisian corsair pink. For several days the search for this vessel did not bear results but on 21 May – not very far north of Gozo – they encountered the Tunisian corsair which tried to escape but the *San Zaccaria* and *Sant'Elisabetta*, utilizing a favourable wind, proved too fast. When the first demands to surrender were ignored, the *San Zaccaria* opened fire with her 26 12-pounder guns on the upper deck and the 12 8-pounder guns on the quarter deck. Since they had no intention of destroying the corsair, the heavy 24 18-pounder guns on the lower deck were not brought into action. After a relatively short fight, the corsair pink surrendered.

On boarding the vessel, the knights discovered that the Tunisian reis or captain and 29 men of the crew had been killed and 18 had been wounded. The remaining 77 Muslims were taken slaves. The ships of the Order suffered no casualties. St Tropez sent the Tunisian chebec to be repaired in Girgenti since, because of lack of wood in Malta, the Order preferred to repair its ships in Sicily. The captured ship was manned with a 27-man-strong prize crew and sailed north, while the *San Zaccaria* and *Sant'Elisabetta* took the captured corsairs on board and sailed back to Malta where the ship arrived on 26 May to await further instructions. Because of their contact with the corsairs, the crew and officers of the ships of the Order were not allowed to go ashore. The Order had very strict quarantine regulations and contacts with ships or passengers from North Africa or the Levant were regarded as especially dangerous in transmitting diseases. The captured corsairs were detained in a special quarter on Manoel Island, the quarantine island.

Two days were spent waiting in the port until a caique brought over a messenger who delivered further instructions to St Tropez. The *San Zaccaria* and *Sant'Elisabetta* were ordered to depart again to look for corsairs and to sail to Girgenti to escort the captured chebec and two grain ships for the *Massa Frumentaria* back to Malta. If there no diseases broke out on board during this tour, the crews would be allowed to go ashore after their return. The cruise through the Malta channel and along the coast of southern Sicily was rather uneventful with no news of corsairs or pirates. After taking on some water and provisions, the convoy composed of the *San Zaccaria* and *Sant'Elisabetta*, the two grain ships, and the Tunisian chebec, left Girgenti on 6 June. On its way to Malta, a strange thing happened when the convoy encountered a Maltese *speronara* whose crew told them of a huge French fleet approaching Malta and that there was some uncertainty regarding its intention. Although he had instructions not to proceed to Malta but to seek refuge with his ships at Messina in case of any threat to Malta from superior foreign fleets, *Balí* Paul Julian Suffren de St Tropez kept course for Malta. One might question the reasons for that decision. The fact is that even later St Tropez did not fervently defend his Order against his French comrades. A letter by an anonymous German knight to the representative of the Order at the Congress at Rastatt a few weeks later labelled St Tropez as one of the main traitors.

With a good wind, the ships sailed in south-easterly direction and when in the morning of Saturday 9 June they passed Gozo and approached Malta's northern coast – and following the warning by the crew of the *speronara* not very much to their surprise – they saw a huge fleet of ships-of-the-line, frigates, and transport vessels. The eyewitness Ovide Doublet, Hompesch's French secretary, wrote: '*Never had Malta seen such a numberless fleet in her water. The sea was covered*

91

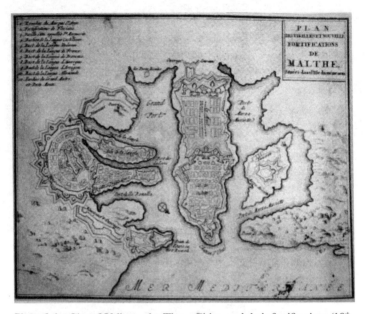

Plan of the City of Valletta, the Three Cities, and their fortifications (18th-century French engraving)

for miles with ships of all sizes whose masts resembled a huge forest.'
After some time it turned out that they were French vessels:
it was Napoleon and his expedition forces for the campaign
of Egypt. The harbour entrance was blocked by this huge
number of vessels. Although the Order's officers and the
crews were very suspicious and on the alert, the French did
not show any sign of hostility. When St Tropez signalled that
his ships were on their way to Malta's main port, the French
responded immediately and created a corridor for them to
pass through. In the afternoon of 9 June, the *San Zaccaria* and
Sant'Elisabetta entered the *Porto Grande*. Little did the knights,
officers, and crews know that they had participated in the last
caravan of the Order of St John ever and that in a very few
days the rule of the Order over Malta would come to an end.

Grand Master Hompesch's passivity during the subsequent
events is still a mystery. Even Rechberg's diary does not offer

any clues about it. Although the Order's plenipotentaries at the congresses of Rastatt and Campo Formio had indicated that there might be something going on in the French military headquarters against Hospitaller Malta, and the papers which Rechberg had delivered to Hompesch presented detailed information about what was expected and even indicated how to solve the situation, the grand master seems to have refused to believe about the approaching danger. Hompesch was not even suspicious when the French spy Henry Poussielgue, the first clerk in the French legation at Genoa, visited Malta in December 1797 to carry out his investigations. In March 1798 a French vessel was sent to Malta by French Admiral Breuys, ostensibly to carry out some repair work but in reality to check once more the situation there. Surely Hompesch must have counted on Austria's and Russia's protection in case of need. At least some French knights were informed that, already in the summer of 1797, the French Minister of Foreign Affairs Delacroix and Napoleon had developed plans to organize a *coup d'état* in Malta and to nominate the powerful Spanish minister Manuel Godoy as grand master. These plans were at first halted by the Royalists and Conservatives in the French *Directoire*, but in September 1797 Barras, with the support of Napoleon and the army, did away with the legal opposition and removed the Royalist parliamentary deputies and the situation changed completely and the plans were resuscitated. *Balí* de la Tour du Pin then requested Hompesch to order a general check-up of the state of the defences and to bring the bastions, gun batteries, and munitions up to date. Hompesch, however, did nothing.

This spirit of apathy and isolation had prevailed in Malta since before Hompesch's time and explains some of the events of June 1798. Way back in April 1796 Ovide Doublet, Grand Master Rohan's French secretary, had written to Rechberg's acquaintance Commander Joseph de Maisonneuve who then had toured Bavaria and was staying in Switzerland: '*Nothing succeeds with us here. This security, or rather this state of apathy, to my*

Joseph Vernet, The Port of Toulon (c. 1760)

mind inconceivable, disheartens and disgusts me .... A continual change of front, a complete indecision, chimerical fears, and hopes equally chimerical – such is our pitiable and unhappy policy.' The huge French fleet composed of 500 vessels which had left Toulon on 19 May and approached Malta on its way to Egypt was definitely not a chimera ....

Although the bulk of the French fleet had gathered at Toulon, other contingents had joined from Genoa and Civitavecchia. In fact the 70 ships carrying the Civitavecchia contingent, commanded by General Louis Desaix, and their escorting frigates had arrived off Malta already by Wednesday 6 June. Not to provoke suspicions Desaix had immediately written to Caruson, the French consul on the island, to inform Grand Master Hompesch that the Order had nothing to fear from the French ships which were on their way to Egypt. Desaix also requested permission for some of his ships to enter the *Porto Grande* to take on water and supplies. The officers of the few French ships which entered the harbour paid immediately for the provisions and goods they took and behaved impeccably. They kept insisting that they were on their way to Egypt. That same day two Greek merchant vessels sailed into the *Porto Grande*. Because of the presence of the French fleet, not much attention was paid to them. The captains informed the authorities that they were carrying grain and their crews were checked by the sanitary officers and nothing suspicious was found. It only turned out later that these vessels were carrying weapons and that their crews were well-trained soldiers to support the coming French landing operations. According to Rechberg's diary, some specially trained soldiers and spies disembarked from this ship who mixed with the local population and spread the rumour that all French knights were traitors and ready to hand over the island to Napoleon. This must have caused considerable confusion; when the French attack really came, the Maltese militia seized several French knights, some of whom were injured and even killed.

No incidents were reported on 7 and 8 June and life in Malta continued more or less its normal ways. According to Hompesch's Swiss secretary Charles Joseph Meyer de

Napoleon Bonaparte
at the time of the
Egyptian campaign

95

Dominique Vivant
Denon (c. 1810)

Knonau – who fervently tried to defend his master in his book *Revolution de Malte* (1799) – Hompesch had already gathered the Maltese militia and the troops of the Order on 6 June but this is not confirmed by other sources. At 5.30 a.m. on Saturday 9 June, the crews of the watch-towers at Gozo signalled that they were seeing an armada of men-of-war on the horizon. It soon turned out that this was the bulk of the French fleet which Hompesch still seemed to believe was on its way to Egypt. As the French fleet sailed along the coasts of Gozo and Comino, some incidents took place that should have warned the knights. The French eyewitness Dominique Vivant Denon – a scholar and artist who had visited Malta already in 1778 – describes how a French bark tried to land some soldiers at Comino but was refused by the signals of the watch-tower there. When the French ships approached Valletta, two Maltese caiques sailed out of the *Porto Grande* to sell them some tobacco.

This was exactly the time when Lieutenant-General *Bali* Paul Julian Suffren de St Tropez and the ships of the

Order had returned to Malta. Early in the afternoon, the *San Zaccaria* and *Sant'Elisabetta*, escorting two transport vessels and the captured corsair vessel, wove their passage through the French ships to Malta's main port. Later in the afternoon, the vessels moored in the inlet between Vittoriosa and Senglea. The fact that the vessels passed unmolested gave the impression that there was no danger for the Order.

As the ships cast anchor, Rechberg could observe a hectic scene, with small boats and caiques moving from one side of the port to the other. After most of the soldiers and crews had alighted from the *San Zaccaria* and *Sant'Elisabetta* – it was around 4 p.m. – a launch from Napoleon's flagship *L'Orient* entered the *Porto Grande* with a message. The French messenger Marmont proceeded to the residence of the French consul Caruson who was told to submit to the grand master a request to allow the French fleet into the harbour to take on water and that the French crews and soldiers should be exempted from undergoing quarantine.

There were then already rife rumours about the hidden intentions of the French to take Malta and Hompesch convened the council for six o'clock, whose members included Rechberg's friend, *Bali* Törring. With one dissident voice, that of the Spaniard de Vargas who remarked that since France was an ally of Spain the fleet should be admitted, the members of the council urged Hompesch to enforce the regulations of 1756 that only four ships could enter at any one time. Later that evening Caruson boarded a small caique and took the message back to Napoleon. In the meantime the Order's treasurer, Commander Bosredon de Ransijat – one of the leading traitors –played a trick on Hompesch by reading to him a letter he claimed he had just received from the former knight Deodat de Dolomieu who was on board of one of Napoleon's ships. This letter said that there was no reason for any preoccupation. The French fleet was only carrying Napoleon's troops to Egypt and the French only requested to take on water and provisions in Malta.

97

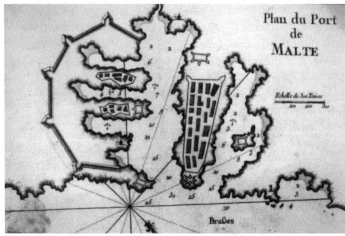

Plan of the ports of Malta (French engraving, *c*.1770)

Bonaparte, of course, knew that the Order would allow only four French ships at once to berth in the harbour but feigned to be personally offended and ordered Caruson to write a harsh letter on his behalf. In the early hours of 10 June, Bonaparte dictated his reply:

> The Commander-in-Chief is indignant to learn that you will not grant permission [to water] except to four vessels at a time – what length of time would be required therefore to water and victual 500–600 sails? This refusal has surprised us and we intend to obtain by force what ought to have been accorded by virtue of that hospitality which is the fundamental rule of your Order.

The long-prepared plans for the attack on Malta were then set in motion. Not to give early warning to the Order and thus give it time to prepare, Bonaparte did not sent the French consul with the message back to Valletta but kept him on his flagship until the following morning. By that time the French troops had already started landing on some of the Maltese shores. In fact the so-called 'declaration of war' which Bonaparte had ordered Caruson to write on his behalf only reached the grand master about two hours after the French already had set foot ashore at St Julian's. An anonymous German knight later claimed to have seen signals to the French ships in the night between the 9th and the 10th coming from the residence of the Knight Tousard.

When Caruson did not return to Valletta in the late evening of 9 June, the rumours of an impending French attack had grown stronger and the council of war was again convened. It was composed of *Balis* Neveu, Sousa, Frisari, Tousaint de la Tour de Pin, Thiusi, Renate de Bardonnenche, Filippe Jean Charles de Fay, and Antoine Etienne Tousard. Of these, at least Bardonnenche, de Fay, and Tousard secretly sided with the French. The loyalty of the Turinese Knight Frisari and the Portuguese Knight Sousa was – to say the least – suspect. A survey of the available forces was not very promising. There were 200 French, 90 Italian, 25 Spanish, 8 Portuguese, 5 Bavarian, and 4 German knights, 50 of whom were either too old or too ill to fight. The most important tasks were divided thus: Marshal Abel de Loras assumed

Fort Manoel (French engraving, *c*.1780)

command in Valletta; *Balí* Vittorio Nicolas Vachon de Belmont, grand prior of Toulouse, was placed in charge of the Floriana landward defences; Fort Ricasoli was under the command of *Balí* de Tillet; while Fort Manoel was under the command of the Portuguese *Balí* Gurgao and the French *Balí* La Tour St Quentin. The shore defences were commanded by Lieutenant-General *Balí* Suffren de St Tropez and Captain General Knight Commander Pierre Anibale de Subiras. The strategically important bays of St Julian's and St George's stood under the command of the Knight De Preville. The Regiment of Malta was stationed in Valletta under Knight-Commander Johann Baptist Heinrich Pfiffer von Wyher. The countryside cavalry and the militias were led by the Order's seneschal, Prince Camille de Rohan, aided by his lieutenants, *Balís* Tommasi and Thenissey. This division of responsibility meant that, of the six top commanders responsible for the defence of Malta, four were French.

CHAPTER 6
FIGHTING UNTIL THE END

Although he had just returned to Malta, Joseph Maria von Rechberg was entrusted with the command of Fort Tigné on Dragut Point at the entrance of Marsamscetto harbour; despite his young age he was already reputed a veteran of the French wars. The fort had been commanded by the engineer and knight Antoine Etienne Tousard, but since there seemed to have been rumours about his loyalty, he was replaced by Rechberg. The Spanish artillery officer Caamaño was detailed to assist Rechberg.

Fort Tigné was the last major fortified work built by the knights. Designed by the Order's chief resident engineer, Stephane de Tousard, in 1792, its construction had been entrusted to the Maltese engineer Antonio Cachia. It was named after *Balí* Renate Jacques de Tigné who donated over 1,000 *scudí* towards its construction. The foundation stone was laid on 7 May 1793. Later Grand Master Rohan donated another 6,000 *scudí* and *Balí* de Tillet a further 500 *scudí* for its erection. The fort was officially inaugurated on 9 July 1795. After blessing the new fort, the prior of St John's conventual church, Raymond Albino Menville, celebrated Mass in its chapel and blessed the titular painting of St Stephen hanging over the main altar. The diamond-shaped casemated construction and the use of the polygonal fortification system showed some influence of the latest techniques of fortress-building but its small size was not suited for a long siege. The wide ditch was provided with three musketry galleries located in its three corners. The glacis on its land-front was heavily mined.

Although Rechberg noted that some of the outwork and ditches were still not completed, he was experienced enough

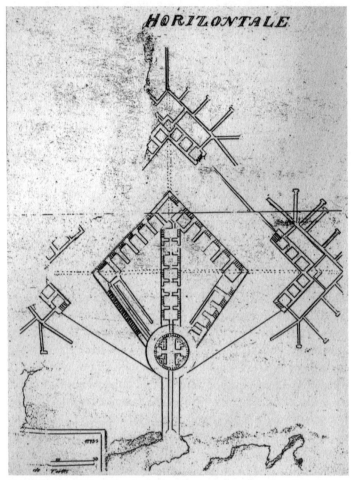

Cross-section of Fort Tigné, showing the casemated interior of the fort and the mine tunnels

to realize that it could be defended very effectively with a relatively few men. The fort's guns (12 24-pounders, six 18-pounders, six 12-pounders, and four 4-pounders) could do great harm to any ship entering Marsamxett Harbour and to troops attempting to land on St Elmo Bay at Valletta.

The fort was also armed with 12 mortars (six shell-firing and six *petreros*) of different calibres. There were, however, obstacles. Of the 28 guns of the fort, only 15 were in a state to be used. Rechberg also soon found out that the Maltese *cacciatori* troops he was commanding were only provided with a limited quantity of powder and cartridges. The *Reggimento dei Cacciatori*, a volunteer light infantry regiment of chasseurs, had been raised by Grand Master Rohan in 1777 and recruited from Valletta, the *Porto Grande* conurbation, and the country villages. In 1798 it numbered about 500 men. Detachments from the *Cacciatori Maltesi* under *Balí* Neveu were also stationed at Forts Ricasoli and Manoel.

The other armed forces of Malta then consisted of the *Reggimento di Malta*, the only regular infantry regiment with approximately 1,000 infantrymen. To these must be added 500

'Governor' (commander) of Fort Tigné, with the fort in the background

Colonel of the Regiment of Malta   Officer in the Regiment of Malta)

soldiers from the galleys and sailings ships, 400 artillerymen, and the grand master's personal guard, numbering 200 men. There were also the urban militia made up of the regiments of Valletta, the three cities of Bormla, Senglea, and Birgu, and the old capital of Mdina; the six country regiments of militia; and the so-called *Bolla* battalion, formed of all those persons generally excused from frequent military training because of their important social functions, such as lawyers, teachers, notaries, etc. All these forces numbered on paper up to 7,000 men. Their value in actual fighting was, however, very limited and only some of them were actually called up.

Already, following the sequestration of the Order's French possessions in 1792, there were rumours about French plans to conquer Malta. Joseph Maria's brother Johann Nepomuk was then in Malta and he observed how Grand Master Rohan had ordered an intensified training of the militia and a re-organization of the defensive forces. Johann Nepomuk's report on the matter to his brother Aloys in 1792 has an element of disillusion. Three-quarters of the convened militia-men did not know how to handle arms at all. All knights had been overnight promoted to captains of local districts of militia, therewith becoming responsible for the training of these troops, although many lacked experience. According to Johann Nepomuk, it was ridiculous to see the knights trying to train these troops every Sunday without being able to communicate with them as they did not know Maltese. The men, on the other hand, very often did not know Italian or French. Rechberg attributed many of the military problems of the Order to these difficulties in communication.

Colonel of the Regiment of Malta

Napoleon's forces then consisted of 36,826 well-trained and experienced troops, while the ships' crews numbered another 12,781 men. These troops stood under the command of some of the most illustrious generals in French history: Berthier, Junot, Desaix, and Hilliers. Napoleon himself was in overall command of the military and naval operations. The four admirals, Brueyes, Blanquet-Duchayla, Villeneuve, and Decrès, had to execute his orders even against their own judgement. An experienced soldier like Rechberg must have analysed and calculated sharply the little possibility they had to resist a massive French attack.

REGOLAMENTO Toccante al Battaglione delle MILIZIE DELLA CITTA' VALLETTA.

In MALTA nel Palazzo, e Stamperia di S. A. S. MDCCLX.
Per D. Niccolò Capaci suo Stampatore .)(Con Licenza de' Superiori .

Regulations & Standing Order Procedures of the Valletta Battalion of 1760

He could not have known the exact figures of Napoleon's forces, but he knew exactly the small number of troops the Order could gather and – what was more important – the very limited fighting spirit amongst many knights and troops. It was obvious that many of the French knights were not willing to raise their arms against their French compatriots. Rechberg's own notes more or less confirm what other eyewitnesses have said about the numbers: there were then around 330 knights, a regiment of roughly 1,000 soldiers, the grand master's guard of approximately 200 men, two regiments of marine soldiers with 600 men, the *Reggimento dei Cacciatori*, and – in theory – a thousand or so men from the local militia.

Late in the evening of 9 June, Rechberg, his assistant Caamaño, and a contingent of hastily gathered Maltese *cacciatori* moved to Fort Tigné and prepared themselves to resist the attacks. There were also some of the gunners from the *San Zaccaria* posted at the fort. Because of the general confusion, only a limited quantity of provisions, powder, bullets, and cartridges could be transported to the fort. There were strange reasons given for this lack of provisions: the caretakers of the keys of some of the powder magazines could not be found or had deliberately disappeared. Rechberg's old acquaintance, Chevalier de Bray, who was not present in Malta in 1798, claims that it was treason which prevented the fort from being properly supplied with gunpowder and munitions. Rechberg does not say so in his own notes but he blames the general confusion and the lack of preparation for the situation. Shortly after Rechberg and the majority of his *cacciatori* had arrived at Fort Tigné and prepared the guns and inspected the ditches and walls, *Balí* Camille de Rohan called and asked Rechberg to send one of his men to Birkirkara to hand a message to Chevalier St Felix who was in command of the Birkirkara battalion. A few minutes later Rohan left and Rechberg and his men continued to prepare the fort for an assault.

In the early morning of Sunday 10 June, the French started their actions with three simultaneous landings: General d'Hilliers at Mellieha Bay in the north of Malta; General Desaix on the opposite side of the island at Marsaxlokk; and General Vaubois on the east coast at St Julian's Bay. The attackers surely expected a harder resistance. There was some fighting at Marsaxlokk Bay and at Delimara Point. Fort St Lucian, overlooking Marsaxlokk Bay, under Chevalier Du Pin de la Gueriviere, held out until the morning of 11 June when all the ammunition for the 18 cannon was exhausted. There was hardly any resistance at St Paul's Bay and Mellieha. At St Julian's, Commander De Preville surrendered immediately without firing one shot. At 6 a.m. the grand master was told that the French had landed on St Julian's Bay and that the enemy soldiers were already pillaging Birkirkara and the nearby villages. The Maltese troops wanted to march to St Julian's but were stopped by the colonel who was then killed by the Maltese. It was said that no fewer than 7,000 men landed at St Julian's without any opposition, about 3,000 in Marsaxlokk Bay, and the same number at St Paul's Bay. By 8 a.m. on 10 June, most of the coast of Malta was already in French hands.

By then Rechberg in Fort Tigné had already successfully defended his posts against the first French attacks. Well trained by his experience in the French wars in the Palatinate, he knew about the enemy's tricks of approach. In fact in the early morning of the 10th, the men at Fort Tigné observed some groups of people dressed in civilian clothes approaching the outworks of the fort. Their clothes were, however, not in the local fashion and Rechberg took them as disguised French soldiers. In fact these people were carrying arms and the alerted *Cacciatori* at the outworks opened fire and made them retreat.

Rechberg was then in Fort Tigné waiting for more munitions. He did not know yet about the great harm which had been caused by the traitor Bardonnenche who was in

107

Commander of the artillery

charge of munitions and ordnance. At 3 a.m. on the 10th, *Bali* de la Tour de Pin, Knight Commander Thiusi, and 16 other knights had started to carry the gunpowder from the magazines at Cottonera which held 11,000 barrels to the Cospicua wharf to be carried by boat to Valletta and the outlying works and fortifications and to Fort Tigné. On Bardonnenche's order, some traitors had, however, hidden many of the horse-drawn carts needed for the operation. In fact it appeared that many members of the Maltese militia were only supplied with five cartridges of gunpowder mixed with coal dust and bullets made of leather pellets. Bardonnenche himself, when approached by knights and officers who were running out of munitions, answered that the magazines were empty. Many weeks later the former representative of the Order at the Congress of Rastatt, François Gabriel de Bray, received a letter – dated Malta, 20 June – from an anonymous German knight who blamed the shameful surrender of Malta mainly on Commander Bardonnenche and other French knights who did not provide appropriate and functioning cartridges, powder, and munitions. It was these persons who had also purposely misinformed and tricked the Maltese militia.

After the successful defence against the disguised French soldiers in the early hours of 10 June, there were only a few hours of rest. After 8 a.m. the fighting reached Fort Tigné again. As long there were enough munitions, Rechberg could offer a stiff resistance to the French assaults. The guns of Fort Tigné gave valuable support when, at around 11 a.m., a galley, two galeottes, and a chaloup, all under Captain General Soubiras, left the *Porto Grande* to attack the landing of more French troops at St George's and St Julian's bays. The wind had dropped and, while the oar-driven vessels of the Order could manoeuvre easily, the French men-of-war could not approach the coast to defend their transport boats. Although equipped with only limited munitions, Soubiras sunk a French chaloup and a transport vessel and damaged several others; at midday, however, a breeze sprung up and, since some French frigates were drawing nearer, Soubiras made a quick retreat. The success of this retreat was greatly helped by the guns of Fort Tigné which held the French

The battery at Ghorhar, with Fort Tigné, Fort St Elmo, and Fort Manoel in the background (on the right)

frigates at bay. A few weeks later, a copy of an interesting letter reached the Bavarian court via secret channels provided some more background to this episode. In the letter addressed to Count Litta in St Petersburg, *Balí* Loras said that he himself had requested the grand master very early in the morning of the 10th to send all the Order's galleys out to sea to block the landings at St Julian's and St George's bays. At this time there was a very calm sea with no wind which were the ideal conditions for the galleys. Some of the French ships were too far away to open fire and would have refrained from firing out of fear of hitting their own troops and, because of the lack of wind, they could not have moved closer. Hompesch, however, hesitated and some other officers complained that Loras's proposal could not be put into practice as some of the crews and gunners had been taken to man the fortresses and the bastions. So it was only late in the morning that Soubiras was ordered to sail out with some of the ships.

On the 10th in the evening, some French vessels tried to enter Marsamscetto harbour and to land troops there but the guns of Fort Tigné prevented them from doing so. The French commander in charge of the landing in the districts west of Fort Tigné and the port of Marsamscetto was the general of the infantry Claude-Henri Belgrand de Vaubois – the future commanding officer of Malta. Vaubois's brother, Richard Fulgentio Belgrand, was then serving as a conventual chaplain in Malta and he later left the Order to serve as an officer in his brother's troops.

Vaubois soon realized that it was impossible to land troops within Marsamscetto without taking Fort Tigné. In the night between the 10th and the 11th, the French therefore posted heavy artillery to fire on the fort. This bombardment from land was co-ordinated with another from some ships-of-the-line and frigates. The whole day of 11 June a rain of shells, bombs, and bullets hailed down on Rechberg's fort. Still, when some French ships approached the coast later that day, they came under strong fire from Fort Tigné and had to turn back. The fort then surely demonstrated its solid and technically advanced construction. At midday of the 11th, a special danger emerged when the French tried to install a battery behind the walls of a church on a hill called 'M'havrab' (sic) to direct it against Fort Tigné. It is likely that Rechberg confuses the names and the church referred to was the Sliema chapel of Our Lady of Nativity, also called Porto Salvo, tas-Sliema or *del buon viaggio*. To prevent that Rechberg and artillery captain Caamaño trained some of the 24-pounders and 18-pounders of the fort in the direction of the church and opened fire. After more than two hours of bombardment, the church and all of the 18 private villas which once stood on the hill were knocked down. Of course, even the French had retreated from there. Rechberg got to know from some messengers that the French were now trying to install another battery consisting of four high-calibre cannon and two howitzers behind the hill in the dead angle of the Fort Tigné guns.

The stiff resistance of Fort Tigné was an exception. In other locations the knights showed anything but bravery and the traitors achieved their aims almost everywhere. By the afternoon of 10 June, the French were already in possession of most of the Maltese countryside. Prince Camille de Rohan and the Maltese cavalry under his command had retired to the shelter of the Floriana fortifications. There was no resistance at Rabat and Mdina which the French troops entered at 2.30 p.m. Chaos and uncertainty prevailed nearly everywhere. Fifteen hundred militia troops mutinied at Zebbug and tried to kill the knight who tried to bring them to order. By the late afternoon of 10 June, all the island, except for the *Porto Grande* conurbation and the villages of Zebbug, Dingli, Zurrieq, Siggiewi, and Qrendi, was occupied by the French. Although Napoleon had strictly forbidden plundering and looting, several incidents were reported. According to Rechberg, the French by then had landed a total of 15,000 troops.

111

Meanwhile even the island of Gozo, which was held by just 300 regular troops and 2,000 militia, had fallen to the attackers. Napoleon had sent General Reynier with 4,000 troops to land at Ramla Bay. Although the attack had been fixed for the early morning, strong winds had delayed the landing until the early afternoon. There was some resistance and gun fire from the Ramla battery and Chevalier de Megrigny with a small garrison held Fort Chambray at least a few hours. However, by the evening Reynier had seized both the fort and the Rabat citadel. To put some more pressure on the Maltese and the Order, Napoleon played a psychological trick. Reynier had sent some French prisoners of war he had made in Gozo to Napoleon on board of *L'Orient*. According to the eyewitness Vivant Denon, Napoleon interrogated them and then released them with the words: '*I don't want to make prisoners of war. As you have raised your arms against your French comrades, you will also know how to die. So go back to Malta as long it is not in my possession.*'

Because of the bad organization and apparent indecision of the leading knights, there was panic in Valletta all day long on 10 June. The capital and Floriana were encircled by the French under General Desaix who, after nightfall of the 10th, had moved his troops from Marsaxlokk to occupy the Cottonera lines and Fort Ricasoli. Lieutenant-General *Bali* Paul Julian Suffren de St Tropez, who was in command of parts of the Cottonera Lines and Fort St Michael, showed surprising cowardice and fled to Valletta without offering real resistance.

The confusion in the city, amongst the Maltese as well as amongst the knights, had not ceased. The hectic and chaotic movements could even be observed from the French fleet, as the eyewitness Dominique Vivant Denon reports. Hompesch had the Order's treasurer Bosredon Ransijat, who had openly refused to fight against his French compatriots, imprisoned at Fort St Angelo but he did not do much else. He just sat in his palace, attended by his aide-de-camp, Chevalier Saint-Priest, and made no attempt to coordinate resistance. This had disastrous consequences as there was no general who could carry out this co-ordinating. Everything was in the hands of the – rather inactive – grand master. Some eye-witnesses blamed Hompesch's *aide-de-camp*, Chevalier Saint-Priest, for having blocked and wrongly communicated the grand master's orders. The individual commanders of the various forts and strong points were left to themselves and many were indecisive as to what to do. The spreading of false rumours and commands by the traitors worked well. In one instance this led to disaster when it was rumoured that someone had opened a secret door in one of the Floriana bastions. When, in the evening twilight, a company came marching from this side it came under fire from a company of Maltese infantry stationed near St John bastions. It later emerged, however, that this was a company under Commander Neveu which suffered various casualties from this friendly fire. Neveu himself was also wounded.

Meanwhile, a group of influential Valletta residents had gathered at the *Banca Giuratale* in Merchants Street to discuss what could be done in these circumstances. Later in the evening they decided to send a delegation to Hompesch to suggest an armistice. After some hesitation this delegation was met by the grand master in the magisterial palace who received their plea but did not respond.

Early the following morning, when the French started their assault on the walls of Floriana and Porte des Bombes, the extent of the treachery of many of the French knights became very evident. Porte des Bombes and this part of the Floriana walls were commanded by Chevalier François d'Andelart who gave the order to light up the bastions to get a better view on the advancing French but this was soon exposed as a trick to offer the French musket and light artillery a better sight of the defenders. D'Andelart was subsequently killed by the Maltese infantry posted on the bastions. Sheltered by their huge bastions, the Maltese had no problem to fire at the

113

Piazza San Giorgio with the Magisterial Palace in Valletta

French who retreated after two hours. Also in the early hours of 11 June some other French knights, including Chevaliers Du Roux, Mondion, and de Quenoy, were accused of treason and lynched by their Maltese soldiers. Chaos and uncertainty prevailed that morning and the locals were very much afraid that the French would immediately start to bombard Valletta from the landward side, especially when the French special troops were observed moving and mounting heavy artillery and mortars near Msida. These guns were, however, directed against Forts Tigné and Manoel and not against Valletta and its civil population. The eyewitness Meyer de Knonau observed how the guns of Forts Tigné and Manoel killed many French pikemen who had approached the walls of Floriana from the Marsamxetto side. By then there was no direct communication any more possible between Forts Manoel and Fort Tigné and Valletta. This is confirmed by the eyewitness Dominique Vivant Denon.

In all that chaos Rechberg, his assistant Caamaño, and their soldiers performed a miracle to organize and bring some coaches full of gunpowder and provisions from Floriana to

Fort Tigné. At certain moments, these transports had to be forcefully defended against some rebellious Maltese, whose opposition was so strong that a coach carrying barrels of water was lost.

In the evening of 11 June, the French played some other tricks to try to demoralize and to irritate the resisting crews of Forts Tigné and Manoel. They set some houses and wood at Gzira and Sliema on fire. Well-versed with the French tricks, Rechberg prevented his men from contacting the local population and some Maltese priests who offered their spiritual support and might have been instructed by the French to spread false rumours and demotivating news. But still, in the evening of 11 June, news somehow filtered through that in Valletta the rebels against Hompesch and the loyal knights had seized the magisterial palace and that the

Plan view of Marsamxett Harbour, showing Valletta with Fort St Elmo and Fort Manoel and Fort Tigné protecting the northern approaches to Valletta

knights who had put up some resistance had all been killed. Rechberg and his men did not believe that this was the full truth, although they could see with their telescopes that there was some confusion and chaos in the capital. A huge fire must have been started in the middle of the city since heavy smoke could be observed. The contact between the capital and Forts Manoel and Tigné with messengers had broken down since the early hours of the 11th.

Meanwhile events in Valletta had taken a rather sad turn. A few hours after daybreak, Hompesch – beleaguered by the locals and by the members of the Order asking for orders and advice – finally gave in and decided to ask for an armistice. At 9 a.m. a messenger of the Order arrived on Napoleon's flagship and handed this request to General Berthier. It was agreed that a French delegation would visit the grand master in the afternoon to negotiate the matter further. At 3 p.m. this delegation, headed by General Junot, Napoleon's senior *aide-de-camp*, followed by Henri Poussielgue and the ex-knight, the scientist Deodat de Dolomieu, proceeded to the grand master's palace where they met Hompesch together with his French secretary Doublet and four high-ranking members of the Order, including *Balí* Tommasi. The rest is history and does not need to be repeated over here in great detail. The armistice was provisionally fixed for one day and the Act of Capitulation was signed in the early hours of Tuesday, 12 June. On the same day a decree to execute the Convention was signed, relative to the surrender of the city and forts to the French. The document was signed by the Knights Frisari, Ransijat, and Amat; the Maltese Baron Mario Testaferrata; and the advocates Gio Nicolò Muscat and Benedetto Schembri who was then the president of the *Tribunale della Rota*.

All this was not known to the soldiers in Fort Tigné and Rechberg had no intention of surrendering, maybe in the hope of relief forces which, of course, never arrived. Perhaps he was hoping that the British squadron which was then sailing off Italy would come and engage the French but Nelson then had no idea that the French fleet was at Malta. This he only got to know some days later, when most of the knights had already left the island. From Rechberg's own notes and correspondence, one might presume that he – like *Balí* Loras – was hoping that Hompesch would order all reliable troops to gather in Valletta and try to hold out until the British navy arrived to relieve them. Contemporary experts calculated that Valletta could have resisted for at least two months. This plan was all the more promising as Napoleon and the French admirals knew well that they could not risk a long siege as their large fleet of transport vessels and carriers was very vulnerable to British attacks.

To prevent the crew in Fort Tigné from sleeping and resting, the French kept a constant fire with muskets and also lit up fires all through the night. But even Rechberg had used the night for some special actions. In the very early hours of the 12th, when it was still dark, he had sent his assistant Caamaño and the French Knight Tignay in disguise to Valletta. The two knights managed to enter Floriana but on the way to Valletta they were attacked by Maltese rebels. Tignay escaped but the Spanish knight was killed. Through some by-ways, Tignay proceeded to the grand master's palace but found the entrance occupied by many Maltese rebels and French troops. Seeing that, Tignay believed the case of the Order was lost and he did not return to Fort Tigné.

When the two knights failed to return to the fort, Rechberg decided to check the situation himself. He provisionally handed over the command of the fort to the most experienced soldier, a certain Folim, who was instructed to keep the fort by all means. Dressed as a civilian, Rechberg managed to pass the French lines and to enter Floriana and proceed to the corner of the magisterial palace. This was the moment when the Act of Capitulation was being signed inside but this was not known to Rechberg who did not dare to proceed further or risk to communicate with other knights. If he had

117

done that, he would obviously have been recognized. For Rechberg, it must have appeared that Hompesch and most of the leading members of the Order had fallen into the hands of Napoleon's troops.

In the meantime, the bombardment and assault on Fort Tigné had started again early in the morning of 12 June. That made the return of Rechberg to the fort a most risky and life-threatening undertaking. After he had managed to reach the casemates again, decisions had to be taken about what was to be done. Rechberg was too loyal and proud to hand over the fort when there was still the possibility of holding out longer. In his account *Revolution auf Malta* of 1840, the Swiss historian Friedrich Hurter summarized what his compatriot, the knight and eyewitness Joseph Meyer de Knonau had observed in 1798: '*On 12 June, the French moved into Valletta and took possession of all the important military posts and bastions. By then only the Forts of St Thomas, Manoel, Tigné, and Bormla kept on resisting.*' On the 10th and 11th, Fort Tigné and Fort Manoel and the troops of *Balí* Gurgao and La Tour St Quentin could still communicate by means of signals but this was interrupted on the 12th owing to the French advance and the heavy gun smoke.

By midday of 12 June, the garrisons of Fort St Thomas, Fort Manoel, and the troops at Bormla, learning what had happened in Valletta, surrendered but Rechberg and his *cacciatori Maltesi* at Fort Tigné kept on fighting. As the three musketry galleries could be supplied through underground tunnels, the French infantry found it hard to approach the fort. Through the treachery by Tousard and Bardonnenche, the French knew that the glacis around the ditch was defended by 36 mine galleries reaching out like tentacles which would blow up an enemy daring to cross the glacis. The French infantry therefore hesitated risking a frontal attack.

There was some tension when, by midday of the 12th, the soldiers and *cacciatori* in Fort Tigné, after the wind had blown away the heavy gun smoke, discovered that the French

flag had been raised in Valletta, Floriana, and over Fort
Manoel. Many of the Maltese militiamen now showed signs
of mutiny. Rechberg immediately ordered them to lay down
their arms and to leave the fort. That meant that the soldiers
in the fort were reduced to 80 men, although these trained
and loyal men were enough to keep the French at bay. Later
in the afternoon, however, most of the powder and munitions
started to run out. The worst problem was the lack of fresh
water. Aware that supplies would soon run out, Rechberg
ordered his men to fire only if they had a very good chance
of hitting their targets. The heavy bombardment soon started
to show effects, greatly damaging some of the outworks and
even endangering the roofs inside the bastions. Provisional
repairs enabled the structure to hold out until darkness set in
and the bombardment ceased.

In the evening there was hardly any gunpowder and
munitions left and, despite of the continuous ongoing repair
work, it was clear that the badly damaged roof of the fort
would soon collapse. Rechberg now decided to hold out a
few hours more until darkness came and then to try to escape
secretly. The men themselves planned to escape in small
groups through an underground tunnel leading to a small
boat basin on the beach below facing Valletta or through
the fort's portico which lead to a staircase leading down to
the shore. As everywhere around them had already been
occupied by the French, such an attempt of escape must
have been very risky, if not impossible. In fact hardly anyone
managed to escape. A popular tradition within the Rechberg
family and in the Rechberg estates in Swabia maintains that
it was Joseph Maria who had fired the last shot against the
French invaders.

Rechberg's own notes do not make clear what happened
to him immediately after he secretly left the fort in the evening
of 12 June. He comments that some of the soldiers of Fort
Tigné fell in the hands of the French, while some others were
captured by Maltese rebels. His notes report that the rebels

treated the men of Fort Tigné very badly. Considering his rank, we can presume that he was detained and interrogated by the French and then, like the few other knights from the Anglo-Bavarian langue, released and allowed to take up residence again provisionally in the *Auberge de Baviere*. There he caught up with what had happened in the previous days and hours in Valletta.

In the convention signed on board of the French flagship *L'Orient* on 12 June, the Order renounced all rights of sovereignty and ownership over the islands of Malta, Gozo, and Comino in favour of the French Republic. Another important article guaranteed the Maltese the right to continue to exercise the Catholic religion and to retain their property and privileges. No extraordinary taxes were to be levied.

With some bitterness and shame, the Bavarian knights observed that some of the traitors, like Ransijat and Doublet, were immediately taken into French service and saw to the destruction of the Order's government. Chevalier Lascaris became one of Napoleon's secretaries, while Chevalier de Greiche kept his position as senior chamberlain. Tousard was promoted chief officer of the engineers and went with Napoleon to Egypt. In all, between 30 and 50 French knights joined the French forces. Another shady figure was Commander Filipe de Amat, the former Spanish *chargé d'affaires*. On 17 June he gave a sumptuous dinner in honour of the new masters of Malta. Later Napoleon requested for Amat a good pension from the Spanish government for his services as 'mediator' between the Order and the French Republic. There were lists drawn of the quantity of armour and weapons which fell into the hands of the French: 1,500 guns of various calibres, over 20,000 muskets, 12,000 barrels of gunpowder, provisions for six months, and three million gold and silver guilders.

Many accounts and reports – at that time and later – have been written about the events of June 1798 in Malta. The letters and reports of the eyewitness Rechberg certainly rate amongst the most reliable and accurate. According to the experienced soldier, the fall of Malta only was made possible through the treachery. Without the traitors behind the walls of Floriana and Valletta, the French would have never managed to enter the capital so quickly. After the capital and nerve centre of command was ruled by chaos and treachery, it was impossible to keep an organized and well-planned defence of the other key positions of defence, namely the forts of Cospicua, St Angelo, St Michael, St Elmo, Manoel, and Tigné. Analysing the situation from the modern point of view, it was only because of the energetic and talented Rechberg that Fort Tigné held out for so long. In other words, besides the traitors the main culprit for the fall of Malta was the lethargic Grand Master Hompesch. His passiveness could be even less excused by the fact that he had been informed in great detail about what was going to happen through the papers and documents which Rechberg had handed over to him less than one week before the arrival of the French fleet.

The knights observed how, on 13 June, the French liberated all remaining slaves on the island. Unfortunately Rechberg gives no figures in his notes, but the numbers in the history books vary from about 600 up to 2,000, a number which seems exaggerated. Archival sources mention that, between 17 June and 27 September, 597 former slaves left for North African ports. The French did not lose time in abolishing the old system. On 14 June Napoleon ordered that all municipal officers, government employees, judges, commissioners of health, heads of the Religious Orders, and curates had to swear allegiance to the French Republic.

Rechberg was amongst the first knights to leave Malta. On 16 June, an order was circulated enjoining most of the French, Italian, Spanish, German, and Bavarian knights to leave the island in three or four days' time. The new government provided them with passports. The French historian Olivier de Lavigerie in his *L'Ordre de Malta depuis la Révolution Française* writes that Rechberg left Malta without an indication of his destination. It is documented that Hompesch left Malta in the early hours of 18 June on board an Austrian merchant vessel and was escorted as far as the island of Mljet in the Adriatic by the French frigate *L'Arthemise*. Archival sources say that Hompesch was accompanied by about 20 knights and some priests of the Order. From the Bavarians, there was for sure *Balí* Count Emanuel von Törring, the Conventual Conservator Commander Friedrich von Preysing, and Commander Ludwig von Seeau on board. Rechberg is not listed among the knights who accompanied Hompesch on his voyage to Trieste.

There is, in fact, a lack of archival documents which makes it difficult to establish what happened to Rechberg. According to a letter from his brother Franz Xaver to his sister-in-law Nanny, Joseph Maria had sailed from Malta together with some other knights on a ship from Ragusa. He would have arrived in the then Austrian port town of Trieste on 15 July 1798. We know for sure that he was in Trieste on 20 July as on this day he wrote a letter to his brother Aloys reporting what had happened in Malta the previous month. But, as Hompesch arrived in Trieste only five days later (other sources say on the 27 July), Rechberg could not have sailed with the grand master but he must have gone on a different vessel.

Rechberg had used his last days in Malta to observe the military and naval strength of the French. He could see the French refurbishing one of the galleys of the Order and manning it exclusively by a Maltese crew to join the French fleet on its way to Egypt. Rechberg later got to know that 'his' old *Santa Maria del Pilar*, on which he had undertaken the Algiers campaign, was renamed *Berouse* and taken into French service. The frigate *Sant'Elisabetta* was renamed *Carthagenoise*, while the *San Zaccaria* was called *Dego*. When the Order surrendered, the building of another third rate, the *San Giovanni*, was nearly completed. The ship was finished during the French occupation and named *L'Athenien*, the English later seized it, renamed it HMS *Athenien*, and incorporated it in the British navy.

Napoleon left a garrison of 3,000 men, 5 companies of artillery, and a medical unit on the island. The French troops were lead by General Vaubois and Brigadier General Chanez, who commanded the infantry in Valletta and the surrounding forts and Brigadier General D'Hannedel who commanded the artillery and engineers.

CHAPTER 7
IMMERSED IN THE ORDER'S STRUGGLE FOR SURVIVAL

The voyage of the Austrian vessel with Hompesch on board from Malta to Trieste was a long and complicated one. Stormy weather and some blockage by French ships had prevented quick progress. In early July, Hompesch and his friends had stopped for some days in Ragusa (modern Dubrovnik). On 25 July, together with the small group of other French, German, and Bavarian knights, Hompesch arrived in Trieste, then part of the Austrian Empire. Grand Master Hompesch took up residence in the palace of the Russian general Osaco. As mentioned previously, Rechberg had arrived in Trieste some days earlier and, despite his disagreement with the grand master's role in the handling of the French attack, he had waited for the arrival of the head of his Order. As in the meantime he got to know that the French gazettes were celebrating the fall of Malta as a big triumph of Napoleon's skills, Rechberg sat down and compiled a report to give the picture from his point of view. This he sent to his brother who would insist its publication in the magazine *Schwäbischer Merkur*.

Rechberg did not intend to return to Munich for the time being to resume his military service but to stay in Trieste to observe events as they unfolded. For the next months Trieste served as the new headquarters of the Order and the exiled Hompesch. On 25 July Bavarian Duke Elector Karl Theodor gave Rechberg a passport valid for 18 months granting him freedom of movement. Soon after his arrival, Hompesch organized a meeting of a provisional council which chose Rechberg as the emissary to negotiate with Emperor Franz II in Vienna about the provisional establishment of the

Order's headquarters in Trieste and – despite the loss of Malta – the guaranteeing of its privileges as an independent sovereign power. That Rechberg was chosen for such an important mission was no surprise. Considering his exploits in June 1798, it was obvious that there was hardly anyone else who could claim to be more loyal to the Order. On 29 July the governor of Trieste, Count Pompejus Brigido von Bresowitz, issued a passport for Rechberg describing him as a knight of Malta travelling on a mission on behalf of his grand master. Rechberg arrived in Vienna on 4 August. Franz II showed a positive attitude towards further support for the Order. Suggestions that the knights should establish their headquarters in Vienna were put aside because most of the knights in Trieste insisted to stay at a port town which would leave them all options open to continue their naval activities. Trieste, with its fortress and huge port, was an ideal choice. Rechberg and most of his brethren then still believed in a quick return to Malta. The emperor promised to support these plans.

By late August 1798 Rechberg was back in Trieste informing the grand master about what had been achieved in Vienna. In the next weeks there was hectic correspondence between the headquarters of the grand master and various agents at the European courts and knights in different countries. Plans were developed for a combined Austro-Russian army to oust the French from Malta. The troops were to be carried on English and Russian vessels. That there was a good portion of optimism and naïveté in these plans does not to be stressed. By November Rechberg was again in Vienna, most likely to sort out the possibilities of the re-conquest of Malta. From his letters it emerges that Rechberg himself was quite sceptical of these plans. According to him, Malta could only be re-taken in full concord with the English. Russian and Austrian efforts would not be enough by themselves.

At the same time Rechberg reported about the events in Malta and the situation in Trieste to Duke Elector Karl

Theodor, to Grand Prior Karl August von Bretzenheim, and to the powerful Johann Baptist von Flachslanden. In addition to all the bad news, there was some positive outcome for Rechberg personally. Bretzenheim and the provincial chapter of the Order suggested that his valiant fight against Napoleon should be judged as due fulfilment of his vows and caravans and that he should therefore be promoted to the rank of a knight of justice.

Because of the political upheavals and the diaspora of the knights to various countries, however, the general council of the Order which could approve this new status could not be convened and Rechberg was officially accepted as knight of justice only in the summer of 1799. There was also an echo of his competent and brave conduct in Malta in the Bavarian army. His patent as lieutenant-colonel in the fourth fusilier regiment commanded by Baron von Dallwigh was issued in Munich on 27 December 1798.

By means of various communications, Flachslanden kept Rechberg and the other members of the Bavarian grand priory informed as to how things in Bavaria should or could proceed further. He clearly pointed out that, according to him, Hompesch's time was over. That the grand master had played an unfortunate role – to say the least – in the affair of the surrender of Malta was obvious. But that was not the main cause to remove Hompesch. Flachslanden explained his larger and global vision of politics to the leading Bavarian knights. With France being lost for the Order; Protestant Prussia showing a rather secular attitude; and the German states being too weak, there was only Austria and Russia to rely on. Already Hompesch's secretary Meyer de Knonau had pointed to Russia as the new main point of reference for the Order in some of his letters. Flachslanden fully agreed with this position. Rechberg knew that the basis for that had already been laid in the previous years. In fact, because of his close relations with his elder brother Aloys – whose career at the Bavarian court then took off and who in the following years would become minister and privy councillor of the new Duke Elector Max IV – Joseph Maria was certainly amongst the best informed of men. Between 1797 and 1799 Aloys represented Bavaria at the Congress of Rastatt. In 1799 he was for a short period acting ambassador of Bavaria in St Petersburg. The news from the side of the Order he received from Flachslanden who held Aloys von Rechberg in high esteem because of the latter's discreet and loyal character.

The pace of the new development was set in the East. In the summer of 1797 the new czar, Paul I, had founded a Russian grand priory. The capture of the messenger with Paul's document offering protection of the Order on 9 February in Ancona had given Napoleon an excuse for further measures against Malta, allegedly in danger of falling into Russia's hands. The convention of 4 (Russian calendar) / 15 January 1797 which incorporated the Russian grand priory in the Anglo-Bavarian langue was ratified by Duke Elector Karl Theodor on 30 November 1797. On 28 February 1798 Paul I confirmed the duke elector's ratification and the new name of Anglo-Bavarian-Russian langue was created. From the point of view of Grand Prior Bretzenheim and his Lieutenant Flachslanden – meaning the Bavarian position – this creation was in those days the only logical step which could guarantee the survival of the Order's property in Bavaria if not in the German Lands in general. That Duke Elector Karl Theodor was soon to die and that this would change the whole situation in the spring of 1799, neither Rechberg nor Flachslanden could foresee in the summer of 1798.

The involvement of Russia and its czar in the affairs of the Order had gone even farther. On 29 November 1797 Paul accepted the title of protector of the Order. He and his wife, Czarina Maria-Feodorowna, were invested with the grand cross of the Order. So were their sons, Grand Duke Alexander, Constantine, and Nicholas, and the Prince of Condé, Louis Joseph de Bourbon, who was then an *emigré* in Russia and whom Paul appointed as the grand prior of Russia. The grand priory of Russia was then composed of eight *balì* grand crosses, 14 commanders, two commander chaplains, five knights of justice, and six knights of honour.

From this moment on the epicentre of action was transferred to St Petersburg. In the following months Flachslanden duly informed Rechberg about the ongoing events. For the moment, the Bavarian side could only observe what was happening. At the end of July 1798, the news about the fall of Malta reached St Petersburg. On 26 August / 6 September 1798 the grand priory of Russia officially protested against the surrender of Malta. Flachslanden had commented to Rechberg on this forthcoming protest already in early August. He had then written to Grand Master Hompesch on the matter. When the news of the fall of Malta reached St Petersburg *Balì* Giulio Litta, Paul's advisor on the Order, did not want to gather a convent of all the knights but hurried up to have a meeting of the members of the Russian grand priory and 'his creatures' only. The tribunal which would discuss the role of Hompesch and the possibility of his abdication was formed of Duke Besborodko, Duke Alexander Kourakin, Count Cobenzl as the representative of Austria, Commander Count Wielkorski, the Prussian Commander Count Buxhöwden, two French knights, two clerics from the Catholic Grand Priory of Russia, and the Kurlandian knight, von Heyking.

This protest was based on the accounts of *Balì* Charles Abel de Loras and the forged report of the aged *Balì* Tigné about the fall of Malta which had reached St Petersburg a couple of days before. The manifesto of the Russian grand priory accused Hompesch of weakness if not outright treachery. Because of his behaviour and the handing over of Malta to the French, the Russians – in flagrant disobedience of the Order's statutes – did not regard Hompesch as grand master and thus they did not feel obliged to obey Hompesch any more. That Paul was behind this manifesto is only too obvious.

Balì Giulio
Renato Litta

On 12 May 1798 the new Bavarian *chargé d'affaires* Baron von Reichlin had arrived in St Petersburg. He was present in late August when the knights gathered in the Order of Malta's palace in St Petersburg to formulate the protest. Chancellor Besborodko secretly informed Reichlin that Paul intended to form an alliance with England and Turkey which would include a clause that Malta had to be given back to the Order and that all possessions of the knights of St John in Germany would be preserved. On 10 September 1798 (Russian calendar) Paul published a manifesto declaring the deposition of Hompesch. The manifesto was subscribed by the knights of the Russian priory, Prince Condé, and the 41 French commanders and knights who had followed him to St

Petersburg, 13 knights from other European countries, and, finally on 23 October, by the chapter of the German priory.

On 27 October/7 November the Russian priory assumed the right to appoint a new grand master and they chose Czar Paul. On the same day *Balí* Giulio Litta was appointed as lieutenant of the grand master and ten more commanderies were added to the grand priory. On 13/24 November 1798 Paul accepted the dignity of grand master and soon afterwards he donated the Russian priory an additional annuity of 216,000 roubles to create new commanderies. St Petersburg became the capital of the Order. Hompesch's protests were rather weak and mostly remained unheard. Most of the Bavarian knights kept a rather neutral attitude. Meanwhile in St Petersburg, the actions went on. On 29 November / 10 December 1798 the new 'grand master' Paul I founded a second grand priory of Russia, the so called Russian Orthodox Priory. Contrary to its name, this priory also included Armenian Orthodox and Protestant members. Count Nicolas Soltykoff was appointed as its head, an idea which had already come up a couple of months before. The commission set up by the Order to report on Paul's idea of creating a Russian grand priory for non-Catholic subjects included the *Balí*'s Montaroux, Frisari, Ventura, and the Bavarian Count *Balí* Törring. The knights of this priory had either to serve four caravans in Malta or to serve in the national army of Russia. This new institution, which was granted an annual revenue of 216,000 roubles, included 98 commanderies. As its founder, Paul reserved for himself the right of the first appointment of the commanders. The foundation of this new priory was announced by the czar to the European sovereigns on 21 December 1798 (Russian calendar). While the Catholic priory of Russia became the destination of many French and some Italian refugees, the Orthodox priory 'became the prey of the reigning favourites', as the historian Walishewsky rightly observed.

131

Paul I as
Emperor of
Russia and
Grand Master of
Malta

Paul's shadow, *Balí* Giulio Litta, took things in hand and, without any warrant, appointed Chevalier la Houssaye as head of the chancery; his brother Mgr Lorenzo Litta as almoner; and Chevalier de Vetry as head of the treasury of the Order. Things for the Order in Russia became easier when Mgr Litta, archbishop of Thebes, was appointed papal nuncio at St Petersburg. As lieutenant of the grand master, Litta received an annual income of 10,000 roubles. His brother, the papal nuncio, received the same sum of money as almoner of the Order. Houssaye – the chancellor – and de Vetry – the treasurer – were obviously Giulio Litta's creatures. After Houssaye's death, from November 1800 onwards Joseph de Maisonneuve exercised the functions of vice chancellor.

132

Paul clearly instrumentalized the Order as a vehicle and a symbol in a fight against European liberalism, democratism, and anarchy. Consequently some of the old statutes were condemned to lose their significance. The abolition of the vow of chastity was discussed intensively. Giulio Litta himself received a dispensation from Paul to marry a rich Russian noble widow. Only the highest offices of the Order were to remain celibate for the time being. Members were to be of honest descent, with a pure moral and impeccable education, and profess loyalty to monarchical ideas. Obviously the Order of Malta became a Russian court order.

On 8 September 1798 the Bavarian ambassador Baron Reichlin – himself a knight of the Bavarian grand priory – had sent from St Petersburg an interesting memoir with a resumé of the situation of the Anglo-Bavarian langue. It came to the hands of Bavarian councillor Aloys von Rechberg who immediately informed his brother Joseph Maria. According to Reichlin, the only real option for the Anglo-Bavarian langue was to follow Russia. Any attempt to insist on a separate Bavarian policy or even to keep the ties with the langues of Castille and Aragon – where even the king of Spain had styled himself as acting grand master – would lead to a conflict with Russia. Reichlin knew about the plans to sequester the lands and possessions of the Bavarian grand priory in case of the death of Duke Elector Karl Theodor and warned against any attempt in this direction. A sequestration would greatly damage Bavaro-Russian relations in general. On 12 October 1798 Baron Reichlin – now with a clearly Pro-Russian attitude – sent another communication from St Petersburg. Some 'favourable' members of the Russian court had recommended that Duke Elector Karl Theodor should intermediate between the Russian Court and Grand Master Hompesch. The Bavarian sovereign should convince Hompesch to abdicate and this would help avoid a threatening division within the Order of Malta. Rechberg's letter show that there were the plans to compensate Hompesch with the Grand Priory of Bohemia if he resigned as grand master.

Despite these comments, the position of the Bavarian grand priory and the Bavarian government in general concerning the rapid developments in Russia in the autumn and winter of 1798 were not clear. This had very much to do with the sickness and death of Duke Elector Karl Theodor and the hostile position of his successor Max Joseph and his secular-minded circle of diplomats and ministers. In late autumn the grand priories of Bavaria, Bohemia, and Germany still hesitated to recognize Paul's 'election'. That it was the Bavarians especially who were making obstacles in this direction made Paul furious. The background of the matter deserves to be laid out here in more detail as the protagonist of this book became involved in it and it also effected and was affected by the global political framework of the time.

That the Bavarians had sent a delegation to Hompesch to Trieste in the late summer of 1798 was interpreted by the Russians as an affront against the decrees of the chapter of the Russian priory and Czar Paul's position in general. In fact the Bavarian grand priory had sent a delegation to Hompesch, officially to congratulate him for his escape from the French; in reality it meant to find out what Hompesch intended to do. On 24 August 1798 this delegation headed by Count Maximilian von Arco arrived at Trieste and delivered the letters from Duke Elector Karl Theodor and Grand Prior Karl August von Bretzenheim. Their fellow-brother Rechberg was then absent from Trieste and carried out his diplomatic mission in Vienna. According to the papers of Hompesch's secretary Charles Joseph Meyer de Knonau, *Balí* Törring and the Bavarian priest Heintlet in 1798 stayed all the time with Hompesch in Trieste.

On 12 October 1798 Hompesch addressed a letter to all sovereigns in Europe protesting against the illegality of the 'Russian' convention. Even in the last years of Karl Theodor's reign there was a strong party at court which favoured a rather neutral role for Bavaria in the conflict between France, Austria and Russia. Bishop Haeffelin, the receiver of the Bavarian grand priory, was not re-installed at court yet and there was a wait-and-see policy and playing for time. During Hompesch's exile in Trieste, *Balí* Flachslanden was acting procurator of the German langue.

Bavaria's hesitant attitude – advocated by the minister of foreign affairs Vieregg, a relative of Rechberg's old friend Friedrich von Vieregg – kept on irritating Paul I. To send a signal when, on 13/24 November 1798 he accepted the dignity of grand master, the Bavarian ambassador Baron Reichlin – although a knight of the Order himself – was not invited to the ceremony. That Reichlin was excluded from this ceremony was also 'thanks' to a memoir of Bishop and Grand Cross Casimir Haeffelin concerning the line of policy of the Bavarian grand priory and the Bavarian government which recommended not depending too much on Russia. *Balí* Litta came to know Haeffelin's document and so the Bavarians became once more suspect at the Russian Court. It was also known that Haeffelin and some Bavarian knights were still keeping close contacts with Hompesch. On 2 November 1798 the Bavarian *chargé d'affaires* in St Petersburg Reichlin warned again the court at Munich that every decision in favour of Hompesch would provoke Paul. But from Munich there did not come the slightest sign of agreement to Paul's proclamation as grand master. This silence was the result of internal disorientations as to where to direct the policy of the Bavarian grand priory and that of Bavaria in general in the turbulent period of 1798 / 99. It appears that Flachslanden and Haeffelin could not harmonize their ideas about how to direct the Bavarian priory. Flachslanden – more the opportunist character who saw quick riches and promises in Russia – clearly favoured Paul as the new grand master and 'light to follow'. Haeffelin – maybe more far-sighted and a supporter of a finely tuned balance of power – did not want to abandon the ties with Austria and the Curia and was well aware of Bavaria's position in the centre of Europe. He never wanted to go in confrontation with Popes Pius VI and Pius VII who did not acknowledge Paul as the new grand master. Flachslanden, on the contrary, in 1798 did not care about the old and feeble Pius VI who was living in exile, at the head of a seemingly defunct church. Throughout the autumn and winter 1798/99 the Alsatian nobleman worked for the acknowledgement of Paul as grand master by the German knights.

Haeffelin – on the contrary – seemed to have worked on a scheme to re-unite the knights in Vienna. On Haeffelin's side there were *Balís* Taufkirchen and Vieregg. Rechberg knew that Taufkirchen had secretly visited Hompesch in Trieste again on 11 December 1798. Rechberg himself seemed to have kept neutral towards these two poles of Bavarian policy. His main aim was to resume his career in the Bavarian army and to stay loyal to the Bavarian court. Still he could not avoid getting involved in the intrigues and secret moves of his Bavarian compatriots and fellow brethren in the Order.

For Bishop Casimir Haeffelin it was still the imperial court in Vienna and the Curia in Rome which promised to be in the long run the points of reference and orientation. Pope Pius VI already had expressed his disapproval when he heard about the so called disposition of Hompesch by a decree of the Russian priory. When Pius got to know that on 27 October / 7 November 1798 Czar Paul was acclaimed grand master by the Knights of the Russian grand priory and some knights of other langues which had fled to St Petersburg after the fall of Malta he strongly protested. The strong disagreement between Paul and the Curia finally led to the expulsion of the papal nuncios from Russia. This so called acclamation of Paul was clearly contrary to the instructions of Pope Pius VI – still the nominal head of the Order – that representatives of all the langues of the Order should participate at the election. Even Pius VI's successor Pius VII continued to withhold from

Paul the title he coveted until his death in March 1801. Also the Austrian emperor Franz II was everything but pleased with this development but he kept silent because he needed Russia in alliance against France.

In late October 1798 Rechberg was secretly contacted by Count Preysing to support him in a most risky action. Preysing had been instructed by Flachslanden to go on a secret mission to Malta to check out the situation on the island and the chances of success of a Russian military intervention to seize Malta. Rechberg himself – who did not want to be drawn on the Russian side – refused to join Preysing but he gave him some of his plans and other material that could prove useful for the expedition. Instead of Rechberg, it was Baron Donnersberg who joined Preysing on this expedition in the winter 1798/99. The situation in Malta then was most delicate and dangerous and it was difficult to reach the island. After the Maltese had risen against the French on 2 September, General Vaubois had retreated with his troops to Valletta, Floriana, and the Three Cities. By 18 September a Portuguese squadron had began a naval blockade of Malta. This blockade was continued later by the British. Preysing and Donnersberg knew that *Bali* de Barres was still in Malta keeping secret contacts with Hompesch in Trieste. De Barres was later exposed and subsequently expelled from the island by British General Sir Alexander Ball in October 1800. Another source for the Bavarians were the observations and letters of the former captain general of the Order Pierre Annibale de Soubiras who had been imprisoned by the French and was only released in September 1798. When Soubiras sailed on board of a merchant vessel to Naples he encountered the above-mentioned Portuguese squadron and was interrogated about what had been happening in the meantime in Malta.

The outcome of this mission was rather disappointing for Flachslanden and the 'Russian party'. The Bavarians found out that Napoleon had left 3,000 infantrymen and three companies of artillery under General Vaubois to garrison the island. The once so glorious ships of the Order had suffered a rather sad destiny. The sailing ships had been broken down or converted into French warships. One galley had joined the French fleet on its way to Egypt. The other three galleys, *La Vittoria*, *San Luigi*, and *San Pietro*, were sold to the bey of Tripoli. The Bavarians were told that at first Napoleon's troops had been widely welcomed by the Maltese but soon dissatisfaction with the anti-clerical French regime had become widespread. Things escalated when the French started to sequestrate Church belongings and precious liturgical instruments. On 2 September 1798 a large section of the Maltese population had risen against the French. Two French attacks against the Maltese ended in complete failure. Then General Vaubois tried to use naval power. A frigate and 12 chaloups sailed to St Paul's Bay and tried to land infantry to attack the Maltese from the rear. This, however, had already known by the locals and Maltese contingents were already expecting the French at St Paul's Bay and prevented them from landing.

With the help of the British, the French were then besieged in Valletta and the fortified area around the Grand Harbour. Thanks to the wise and diplomatic actions of the British commander-in-chief Alexander Ball, the Maltese population was then very much pro-British and there was a strong antipathy against the return of the Order. There would also have been a great resistance against a Russian take-over.

In Bavaria and amongst the Bavarian grand priory, however, Russian influence was growing stronger and stronger. The effects of this development are shown when Czar Paul replaced Haeffelin as the receiver of the Anglo-Bavarian langue by Count von Arco in November 1799. That the mysterious and inscrutable Haeffelin, following his continuous contacts with Hompesch, had become much disliked and suspect by Paul I is documented by the new grand master's decision to suspend the pensions of Haeffelin and of the Bavarian minister in Rome, Antici da Pescia. Joseph Maria and Johann Nepomuk von Rechberg's positions in the Order – thanks to their rather

Aloys of Rechberg

neutral position – were more or less untouched by these new developments. Joseph Maria for the moment concentrated once again on his Bavarian army service. Little did they know that Johann Nepomuk would soon lose his candidacy for the commandery of Mindelheim St Johannes.

The situation for the Bavarians became worse when on 24 November 1798 – after the convening of a provincial chapter – the representatives of the Bavarian grand priory declared that the Order could not ignore the statutes by condemning Hompesch and the 'traitors' of June 1798 without hearing their version of events. It was furthermore stated that a decision over the magistry would be only taken by a chapter formed

139

by representatives of all the langues of the Order. In the eyes of Paul, with this statement the Bavarians had excluded themselves from the rank of '*confrères bien intentionnés*'. Other rumours did not help to calm Paul. Already in December 1798 the Austrian diplomat Thugut in St Petersburg had indicated that if Max Joseph von Zweibrücken took over the Bavarian lands, this would spell the end of the Order of St John's possessions in Bavaria.

Needless to say Thugut tried his best to poison the atmosphere against Max Joseph von Zweibrücken who – as a former French army officer – was accused of being pro-French and who obviously stood in the way of Austria's secret wish to annex Bavaria. As the new *chargé d'affaires* of the Order at the imperial court at Vienna, Paul appointed *Bali* de Ferrette. Some Bavarian knights still did not seem to have understood the global importance of Paul's 'Maltese' policy and his choleric character. Karl Theodor – the great protector of the Anglo-Bavarian langue – was still alive, when in early January 1799, some Bavarian knights protested again against Hompesch's forced deposition and the 'usurpation' of the magistry by Czar Paul in October/November 1798. Paul became furious and the Bavarian *chargé d'affaires* in St Petersburg was told to leave the country. But this was just a small indication of what was to come. However, some soft correspondence helped to placate the czar and the situation had returned to normal again by late January 1799.

Still this incident must have made clear how fragile the Bavaro-Russian relations were and how 'delicately' the czar would react against any action against his role as the protector and grand master of 'his' beloved Order of St John. It was especially surprising that the party in Bavaria which worked on the dispossession of the Order in Bavaria had gained ground more and more. The main opponents were still Duke Karl August von Zweibrücken and, after his death, his brother and successor on the throne Max Joseph. Already by 1783 Karl August had drawn a secret instruction and memoir stipulating the dispossession of the Bavarian priory and commanderies. The main argument was that in these 'modern' times no anachronistic institution should form a state in a state and 'waste' the national income and resources. Of course, another reason was that the Zweibrücken family of the House of Wittelsbach strongly opposed Karl Theodor's wish to create a lucrative post and income for his illegitimate son Karl August, count of Bretzenheim, at the expense of the Bavarians and the House of Wittelsbach. At least by November 1792, these secret plans by the court of Zweibrücken were known to Rechberg who had discussed them in his letters to his brother Franz Xaver. Aloys von Rechberg had been trained as a diplomat in Zweibrücken.

This oncoming danger was also known to the Bavarian diplomats abroad. Reichlin, the Bavarian *chargé d'affaires* in St Petersburg, took the situation so seriously that, on 20 December 1798, he sent his secretary Baron Sulzer to Munich to explain personally the tense situation in St Petersburg concerning the question of the Order of Malta. After a fast journey Sulzer reached Munich on 6 January 1799 and handed over the letters from St Petersburg. He was immediately ordered to meet the minister of foreign affairs, Vieregg. Sulzer reported what Chancellor Besborodko had communicated to him before he had left Russia. Among England, Austria, and Russia there was to be a complete harmony of views concerning the question of the Order. England had even indicated that the institution of a new English langue would be possible. It had also been universally agreed that Hompesch had to abdicate. That the Bavarians still supported Hompesch was a scandal and a most dangerous position to assume while surrounded by such super powers as Austria and Russia. It was only thanks to the influence of Besborodko and Litta that the furious czar had not expelled the Bavarian *chargé d'affaires*. Continuing the previous policy would be regarded as injurious to Russian interests. The Russians demanded the convocation of a chapter of the Bavarian grand priory which

141

should be concluded with a declaration expressing complete agreement with the measures of Czar and 'Grand Master' Paul. This declaration was to be confirmed by Duke Elector Karl Theodor and then sent to St Petersburg. All this did not just smell like blackmail; in fact it was just that.

It was difficult for the Bavarian court and the members of the Bavarian grand priory to answer this demand since Vienna's position towards Paul's 'election' seemed to be quite different to what was heard from Russia. So it was decided first to consult Vienna again. By December 1798 news had reached Munich that a separation of the Anglo-Bavarian langue from the Russian grand priory which had been officially incorporated in the langue just a year before had been discussed in St Petersburg. The man chosen to travel to Vienna was Grand Cross and Major General Count Friedrich von Vieregg a son of the Bavarian minister of foreign affairs. Vieregg was to take a letter from Duke Elector Karl Theodor asking Emperor Franz II to help restore relations between Russia and Bavaria. How this could be done with the additional request of the Bavarian ruler that the emperor, as the highest protector of the Order, should guarantee that the old statutes of the Order were obeyed is not quite clear. Vieregg had intended to go on to St Petersburg but Franz II insisted that he should remain in Vienna for the moment. That the Bavarian grand priory in itself was divided was pretty obvious. Haeffelin, Count Topor von Morawitzky, and their party favoured a neutral line and a policy of balance between Rome, Austria and, if possible, France and Russia. They wanted – at least for a while – to retain Hompesch as the official grand master. Another group – mostly centred in the court of Munich – wanted to make the destiny of the Bavarian grand priory depend on general Bavarian policies and therefore very much watched out to Vienna and St Petersburg. A third group around Flachslanden – the opportunists, so to say – had decided that only Russia could guarantee them their old prestigious posts and income.

On 7 January 1799 the pros and cons of the pro-Russian policy were discussed in a cabinet meeting in Munich. Count Vieregg rather pragmatically accepted Paul's usurpation of the post of grand master. The best defender of Hompesch and the line of the pope was Count Goldstein who demanded a commission to investigate the behaviour of the knights in St Petersburg and how a married man and a non-Catholic sovereign could be acclaimed grand master. In short the meeting brought about no positive results for the Pro-Russian group. By 10 January 1799 Vieregg had sent three letters and two postscripts to Reichlin in St Petersburg but they contained no acceptance of the Russian demands. That this attitude was to be expected was already indicated in a letter Flachslanden had written to *Bali* Litta on 22 November 1798 which especially blamed the influence of Baron Franz Karl von Hompesch – the Bavarian minister of finance and brother of the grand master – for the neutral if not the anti-Russian policy of the Bavarians. A couple of days later the more pragmatic party around Vieregg more or less succeeded to take the upper hand and on 26 January 1799 a paper was drawn up in Munich whereby the duke elector expressed his regrets that the attitude of the Bavarian grand priory could have insulted Paul. Karl Theodor himself, it noted, had never interfered in the Order's affairs (sic) but now he was going to use his power to make the Bavarian grand priory follow the Russian line of policy. Karl Theodor further indicated that he himself intended to convince Hompesch to lay all his power and authority in Czar Paul's hands. With this more positive news, Sulzer prepared to return to St Petersburg. With his departure for Russia delayed by bad weather, Sulzer could witness the death of Duke Elector Karl Theodor and, to his horror, the quick sequestration of the possessions of the Order of Malta in Bavaria. He knew exactly what reaction this would cause in St Petersburg and a return there was now out of question so he stayed in Munich. The Rechberg brothers soon felt the consequences of this change of power. In late

February 1799 a state commission came to Mindelheim to check the lands, property, ledgers, and all belongings of the commanderies of St Johannes and St Martin. Commander-candidate Johann Nepomuk von Rechberg was not present but he was informed about the proceedings in his residence in Munich. We do not know about his immediate reactions. It might have been that he – after some consultation with *Balí* Flachslanden – did not consider this sequestration as the last word. Flachslanden immediately set down to work to get this sequestration withdrawn. It is ironic that Mindelheim and the other commanderies in Bavaria were dispossessed under the supervision of the prince of Isenburg, Joseph Maria von Rechberg's commander in the war against the French in the 1790s.

The background of these events of February and March 1799 in Bavaria needs some more explanation. With Karl Theodor's death on 12 February 1799, a new era of Bavarian policy began. This era was marked by the rule of Baron Maximilian Joseph von Montgelas who under new duke elector (king as from 1806) Max IV acted as minister of state and was the real 'secret' ruler of Bavaria. In a few years after 1799 Montgelas gave Bavaria Europe's most modern constitution. His private memoirs are a good source to understand the reasons for the following actions. That in Montgelas' concept of a modern national state administered by a centralized secularized government there was hardly any space for an Anglo-Bavarian langue was obvious. During his visit to Munich in 1795, Max Joseph had already secretly renewed his old project to dispossess the Order in case of his succession as duke elector of Palatinate-Bavaria.

Max Joseph's approach to politics and government was very different from Karl Theodor's and certainly less aimed at pleasing the Bavarian nobility. This was especially felt in his ideas concerning the possessions of the Anglo-Bavarian langue whose confiscation would surely fit in the concept of contemporary nationalism and secularism. With the new government came an upheaval in the restructuring of the cabinet and exchange of posts. Many of the Knights of the Bavarian grand priory who held high government posts, like the Viereggs father and son, Baron Reichlin, and others had to go. The shrewd Flachslanden survived and Haeffelin's career even got a new boost. Baron Franz Karl von Hompesch, minister of finance even stayed in power but he died in 1800. In the meantime Max IV Joseph replaced Count Vieregg by the young Montgelas. In general Duke Elector Max IV Joseph and his minister tried to avoid a coalition with Austria and to keep at least a friendly neutrality with France. This policy was even supported by some knights of St John in Bavaria, one of them being Rechberg's old acquaintance François Gabriel de Bray who had then entered Bavarian service.

How far the knights had drifted politically is shown again in a secret memoir of 15 May 1800 sent by de Bray to Montgelas recommending that Bavaria should orientate itself towards France rather than towards Austria and Russia. The new French government under Napoleon would more and more turn to conservative and stable policies, de Bray noted. When Max Joseph finally assumed power, he set up a commission with some slight changes and augmentations to affect the old sequestration plan. According to this commission, a sequestration of the 28 commanderies which existed in 1799 in the Bavaria would bring the sum of 8 million German guilders. The commission was headed by the duke of Birkenfeld, a relative of Max Joseph's. On 16 February the duke elector's instructions were put into practice and the lands of the Order of Malta were seized. Therefore the constant warnings from the secretary of the Bavarian embassy in St Petersburg Sulzer not to touch the Order of Malta in Bavaria were left unheard. The duke of Birkenfeld informed Grand Prior Karl August von Bretzenheim that the actions against his institution had already started. The main reason for the sequestration was allegedly the fact that from the beginning the Zweibrücken branch of the Wittelsbach family had never consented to the foundation of an Anglo-Bavarian langue. The administration of the possessions and funds of the Order came in the hands of the 'administration of ecclesiastical goods'. Most Bavarian citizens welcomed very much the dispossession of the Order of Malta.

That *Balí* Flachslanden and Bishop Haeffelin were stunned by the rapidity of these actions may be explained by their diplomatic view of things. For them it was inexplicable and hard to foresee that the new Bavarian government would risk such a harsh opposition to Russia. When the sequestration actually took place the Bavarian knights started on subversive agitations against the actions and rumours were even spread that Duke Elector Max Joseph was driven by private speculation and mean business reasons. That this was not true is even confirmed by Montgelas's private diary – and he certainly cannot be called a dear friend of Max IV Joseph's. The consequences of this action would show that Bavaria was too tied up in the balance of international power to act out these measurements without previous international negotiations. Obviously the Bavarians thought that, in these troubled and hectic times, Czar Paul I as the nominal head of the Order would have been too busy with more pressing things to bother much about the events in Bavaria. But Max Joseph and his commission did not take into consideration the czar's verve and stamina in anything that had to do with his 'beloved' Order of St John. Rechberg got to know the news about the sequestrations in March 1799 in Trieste. For him they were a serious blow against his plans to continue working for the Order, especially since he was going to lose the income from a commandery. It made him decide to seek his fortune again in the Bavarian army. He immediately set down to write letters home to his family and to his brother Aloys in Munich asking for support in his intention to find again a good and well-provided post in the military. Indeed Aloys contacted his uncle Joseph Theodor Topor von Morawitzky – still member of the council of war – on behalf of his younger brother.

By the end of February 1799 when Baron Reichlin, the Bavarian *chargé d'affaires* in St Petersburg, communicated to Munich that *Bali* Litta had been fallen into disgrace at the Russian court no information about the events in Bavaria had yet arrived at St Petersburg. The news of the sequestration reached St Petersburg rather unexpected. Reichlin was not even informed by his new government. For his disappointment he got to know about it at an audience with Prince Besborodko who had learned about it from the Russian minister at the imperial diet at Ratisbon, Baron Bühler. By means of various unofficial other channels the news – not without exaggeration regarding the harshness and ruthlessness of the Bavarian government against the Order – reached the knights at St Petersburg. Paul's furious reaction was easy to imagine. Military actions against Bavaria were not impossible. On 20 March 1799 Baron Reichlin was officially instructed by the Russian government to leave St Petersburg within a day.

The Austrian minister Thugut's words were recalled, namely that the new Bavarian duke elector was a 'slave' of France. Soon the affair reached a most serious international level. To Thugut's delight, Paul regarded Max Joseph as a serious threat to the conservative order in Europe. So the hot-blooded czar discussed plans with the Austrians to end the role of this *Chevalier des regicides français*, as Max Joseph was called. Bavaria would be conquered and placed under an Austrian commission. The Russian generals Korsakoff and Sowaroff were already informed about the matter. If these plans had been carried out, Thugut's daring plans to bring Bavaria under direct Austrian power would have been completely realized. That the 'imperial spleen' for the Order of Malta was an ideal tool to instrumentalize Paul politically had long been realized by the Austrians. Already on 15 February 1799 Thugut had written to Vienna that interest in the Order of Malta was the only solid subject in St Petersburg.

That Paul ordered immediately 50,000 men under General Korsakov to attack Bavaria unless the priory was restored – as some modern historians maintain – is, however, not true. All that Paul did was to order the Russian corps which was marching to the Rhine against the French to begin the 'second war of the coalition' to regard Bavaria as an enemy country. That the Russians would really dare to attack Bavaria did not seem all too likely but the duke elector was suspicious of the role of his neighbour Austria. The Bavarian requests to Prussia that its envoy in St Petersburg, General Tauenzien, should act as an intermediary to soften Paul's anger and to make him start official negotiations with Bavaria again were all in vain. Tauenzien knew Paul only too well to expect the czar to be willing to discuss any action against 'his' Order. The man who spoke to Paul about the matter was the Russian envoy in Bavaria, Baron von Bühler. Most likely it was Flachslanden who had contacted Bühler to solve the situation. Paul was only willing to normalize relations with Bavaria once the possessions of the Order were restored completely and Bavaria joined the alliance against France. Paul also demanded that a delegation of the Bavarian knights should be sent to St Petersburg to pay homage to him as grand master of the Order.

In his memoirs Montgelas blamed Duke Wilhelm von Birkenfeld, a relative of the new Duke Elector Max IV Joseph, for the precipitous sequestration of the Order's belongings. But he surely had to assume a large portion of the blame himself as well. According to Montgelas, the sequestrated goods and assets of the Order were to be used again for the schools. All in all, 8 million guilders were expected to flow into the Bavarian treasury. Bühler, the Russian envoy at the diet at Ratisbon, immediately protested against the measure while Flachslanden also sent two memoirs against the Bavarian government to St Petersburg. Through the Prussian envoy at the congress of Rastatt, Count Goertz, – the former mentor of Aloys von Rechberg and a close acquaintance of Montgelas – by 22 February 1799 the Bavarian cabinet got to know that memoirs had been sent from Bavaria to St Petersburg which put the Bavarian government in a bad light. In these memoirs it was even maintained that the dispossession of the Order of Malta in Bavaria was a direct attack on the honour of the czar. Most presumably Goertz had got to know about Flachslanden's writings. In March 1799 the 'Russia-expert' Sulzer was ordered to write a detailed rescript about how to solve the momentary difficulties. It was even mooted to send him again to St Petersburg to calm down the furious czar.

In Bavaria the situation was indeed precarious. When Max Joseph turned again to Prussia for help to calm the czar, the Prussian court expressed their friendship with the Bavarians, but showed no willingness to get involved in the difficult matter. The only solution left was to abandon the old policy of neutrality and to follow the Austrians in their war against the French. Only with the support of Austria could relations with Russia be normalized again – or so it was hoped. By April 1799 the Bavarians were still playing for time and hoping that Austrian diplomatic skill would prevent them from having to return the sequestrated lands to the Order. The 8 million German guilders gained – so Max Joseph argued – were essential for the Bavarian budget. The congress of Rastatt was still on and Bavaria kept hoping that Malta might be returned to the Order and so Paul would be satisfied for the moment. But the situation was not solved by this approach and, in May 1799, Montgelas took things in hand. The all-powerful Bavarian minister and former illuminate and admirer of Napoleon's France was himself a strong opponent of the Order which he regarded as a useless institution and would – if one did not stop it – infiltrate the Bavarian government and court as the Jesuits used to do. But, for the moment, reasons of state forced Bavaria – so Montgelas clearly saw – to take a step back. Even during the negotiations in Rastatt, things did not turn out in Bavaria's favour. Very negative for its position were the comments by the Prussian delegate Jacobi that Bavaria had sequestrated the property of the Order as a favour for the French *Directoire*.

On 2 May 1799 Montgelas sent the archives of the Bavarian grand priory to Duke Wilhelm von Birkenfeld who was requested to study the documents and decrees to find the best way to re-install the Order in Bavaria but with the least cost for the government. As a special Bavarian envoy to St Petersburg was chosen another knight of Malta, Rechberg's old acquaintance François Gabriel de Bray, who had become a good friend of the new strong man in Bavarian policy, Baron Montgelas. Before de Bray accepted this delicate post, he insisted to be given the grand cross of the Order of Malta and Bavarian citizenship. Because of his new friendship with Montgelas and Flachslanden, this was soon granted. It is interesting to note that even a clever and experienced man like de Bray thought in 1799 that it would be possible to make Paul resign the magistry. In St Petersburg de Bray also acted as a minister of the Bavarian grand priory.

Now Max Joseph depended on the help of a man he otherwise very much hated: *Balí* Flachslanden. The duke elector knew that Flachslanden – way back since his time in Zweibrücken – had for years intrigued against him. But now the shrewd *Balí* was the best person to submit Bavaria's position to Czar Paul. In fact in the spring and summer of 1799 Flachslanden's position as the head of the pro-Russian party in Munich became so powerful that some believed that he was a possible candidate to replace Montgelas as minister of state. Without doubt Czar Paul would have very much liked this development and even the princess of Baden, who had visited Munich, openly showed her full sympathy for Flachslanden. But it was obvious that Flachslanden's position greatly depended on the mercy of the czar and it was well known that Max IV Joseph believed that a one-sided turn to the Eastern power would not benefit Bavaria in the long run. So Flachslanden did not reach his ambitions.

On 21 May 1799 Max IV Joseph and his councillor Aloys von Rechberg, Joseph Maria's elder brother, discussed the situation: it was obvious that it would be impossible to insist on the sequestration of the Order's possessions. But for further actions it was decided to try to keep the Maltese question always separate from the general political negotiations. Montgelas could convince Max Joseph to write to Paul to politely justify his previous actions. In fact, on 22 May the duke elector wrote to Paul explaining that the sequestration was just putting into practice an old plan of 1788/95 when the situation was completely different. The actual sequestration of February 1799 was only carried out to check the income and procedures of an institution about which he (Max IV Joseph) never had been fully informed about by his uncle Karl Theodor and which he had therefore never confirmed. Max Joseph reminded Paul that the Zweibrücken branch of the Wittelsbach family had never agreed upon the installation of a new institution of the knights of Malta in Bavaria. Therefore his sequestration of 16 February 1799 was only a temporary action. This last sentence was the crucial point which left many options open for the future. The funds of the priory were not touched at all and everything was to be re-installed. The basic concept of this letter followed Bühler's suggestions to satisfy the wishes of the czar best. To keep the façade and the sovereign reputation of the duke elector, the forced re-installation of the Bavarian grand priory was styled as a new foundation. In late June, the Rechberg brothers and their fellow brethren were convened to a provincial chapter of the Bavarian grand priory in Munich where the new developments were discussed and Flachslanden was officially authorized to negotiate with the Bavarian court.

When, on 5 July 1799, the Russian envoy Baron Bühler – who had been present at the negotiations at the end of April in St Petersburg – returned to Munich, he was immediately received by Max IV Joseph to discuss the re-installation of the Order in Bavaria. The duke elector officially lifted the

151

sequestration and, by 11 July, the flag of the Order was flying again on the conventual church of St Michael in Munich.

At the same time negotiations continued regarding the old and new holders of the Bavarian commanderies and there was vivid exchange of letters between Joseph Maria, Johann Nepomuk, and Turcopilier Flachslanden about the re-installation of Johann Nepomuk or maybe Joseph Maria as commander of Mindelheim St Johannes. Already before it had been discussed among the Rechberg family that Joseph Maria – who by then had fulfilled his obligatory four caravans in the Order – should take over the commandery of Mindelheim St Johannes and therewith enjoy its full income. Indeed in the official list of the members and commanders of the re-installed Bavarian grand priory of 7 August 1799 Joseph Maria appears as holder of the commandery. He also was listed among the beneficiaries of the income of a commandery of grace which would bring an income of over 1,000 guilders. This would have compensated him for his expenses which he had incurred during his voyage to and sojourn on Malta the previous year. Because of several administrative problems he, however, had to wait some more years to enjoy this income. In the list of August 1799 his brother Johann Nepomuk features as beneficiary of a sum of 150 guilders per year from the commandery of Schierling. The holder of this rich commandery was Joseph Maria's old friend and comrade, the veteran of the campaign of Algiers Count Friedrich von Vieregg.

In June 1799 a letter from Czar Paul had arrived in Munich installing Flachslanden as the official Russian representative in the negotiations on behalf of the Order of St John. On 12 July 1799 *Bali* Flachslanden, acting as the plenipotentiary of the new 'Grand Master' Paul I, and Montgelas, plenipotentary of Duke Elector Max IV Joseph, signed a treaty re-installing the Bavarian grand priory and the bailiwick of Neuburg according to the old organization and structures. The former commanders and members of the

Anglo-Bavarian langue were to be officially re-instated. An important detail was that the duke elector had to acknowledge Paul as the new grand master. It was further decreed that the Bavarians had to abandon all contacts with Hompesch. On the other hand, Paul confirmed Max IV Joseph as founder of the institution which meant that he had the right to appoint 18 new commanders since the sequestration of the possessions of the Anglo-Bavarian langue in Bavaria had made such offices extinct.

The negotiations between Flachslanden and Montgelas were finalized with the 'preliminary convention' of 17 July 1799 ('*Präliminarkonvention*') which officially stipulated that Max Joseph had declared for himself and his successors to re-establish the possessions and rights of the Order in the duchies of Bavaria, Sulzbach, and Neuburg, and in the Upper Palatinate. The foundation charter of 6 August 1781 as well as the charter of re-union and incorporation ('*Reunions- und Inkorporationsakte*') of 22 April 1782 were to form the basis of a new convention which would feature some slight modifications and additions. A new inclusion was – obviously – the incorporation of the Russian priory; it was also stipulated that if the Anglo-Bavarian knights were to serve in the Bavarian administration or perform military duties, their salaries were to be paid by the government. This applied in the case of Joseph Maria von Rechberg who was then a major in the Bavarian army. The duke elector was made responsible to re-establish the commanderies while the czar had to be fully acknowledged as grand master. As a result the Anglo-Bavarian langue had to obey to the grand master as long as his orders did not clash with the rights of the pope as the spiritual head of the Order. The duke elector was to be acknowledged as the founder of the Anglo-Bavarian langue and the acts of the re-unification were issued in his name. Paul guaranteed all open and secret articles and promised to protect them against any foreign intrusion.

The separate articles mainly concerned the inheritance of the grand priorship in the dynasty of the duke elector. Article

20 decreed that the post should always be an appanage of a prince of the family of the elector of Bavaria who was, of course, dispensed from the vow of chastity. Therefore the four-year-old Karl Theodor, duke of Bavaria, was now officially grand prior. The post carried with it an appanage of four commanderies and 50,000 guilders which was a considerable relief for the Bavarian budget. *Bali* Flachslanden was appointed as the grand prior's plenipotentiary. This article meant that Karl August, count of Bretzenheim – the illegitimate son of the late Karl Theodor – was removed from his post of grand prior, although he did not intend to give up his old prestigious post and incomes so easily. He soon came to heavy conflict with Max IV Joseph and the other members of the house of Wittelsbach.

Since St Michael church and the annexed monastery was already being used for another purpose, Max Joseph suggested that the church of the Theatines with its annexed monastery should be handed over to the Order instead. But the eviction took a very long time and the Bavarian grand priory never really made use of the Theatine church as its conventual church. The foundation – or better re-foundation – bull was ratified by Paul on 13 November 1799. Already in June 1799, during the proceedings of the re-installation of the grand priory of Bavaria and the bailliwick of Neuburg, Montgelas had secretly discussed how to dispossess the Order again when time and circumstances would allow it. 'Who can found institutions, can also dissolve them,' – said Montgelas. What he also had in mind was that even the Austrians were far from ready to acknowledge Paul officially as the new grand master. Although Montgelas intended to delay the complete restoration of the Order's lands and possessions, Flachslanden – even when he was then in St Petersburg – had kept a very careful eye on the developments through his agents. The secretary of the Bavarian *chargé d'affaires* Sulzer, who learned to know and to dislike Flachslanden in St Petersburg in 1800, sent constant warnings of the shrewdness and the growing influence of the *bali* to Munich. Flachslanden had to be kept away by all means from infiltrating his power in Bavarian politics. These warnings by Sulzer found ready ears in Montgelas and Aloys von Rechberg who had been a member of the Bavarian delegation to St Petersburg in 1799. Rechberg – a highly acknowledged expert in analysing political situations – had made the acquaintance of the czar and was able to interpret his character. Montgelas and Aloys von Rechberg did their best to isolate Flachslanden from the court of Munich but they could not do this very openly as the *bali* had a most powerful protector in Czar Paul. Despite this re-establishment of the Bavarian grand priory, it clearly emerges from his letters to his brother Johann Nepomuk of the summer of 1799 that Joseph Maria was quite sceptical about the survival of the Order's possessions in Bavaria. With some surprising farsightedness, he commented:

.... the madness of Czar Paul about the Order might be over in a few years, the [Russian] interest is anyhow more set on the island of Malta than on the institution itself. What will happen in Bavaria when the Russian interest slows down? One has to consider that the re-establishment of the Order in Bavaria was a forced affair. So one should hurry to get a commandery and therewith gain at least a few years of pension ....

In the meantime, on 30 March/10 April 1799, Paul had set up the sacred council of the Order which consisted of the Acting Lieutenant of the Grand Master *Bali* Count Nicholas Soltykoff; Grand Marshal *Bali* Hereditary Grand Duke Alexander of Russia; Grand Commander *Bali* Prince Peter Lapoukin; Grand Hospitaller *Bali* Count James Sievers; Grand Admiral *Bali* Johann Lamb; Grand Turcopilier *Bali* Johann Baptist von Flachslanden; Grand Chancellor *Bali* Theodor Rostoptchin; and Grand *Bali* Johann Baptist von Pfürdt-Blumberg. Only two, Flachslanden and Pfürdt-Blumberg were Catholic and professed in the Order.

155

Rechberg was kept fully informed about the directions in Bavarian politics through his elder brother. The duke elector then was hardly the master of the situation but he was driven by the global upheavals. On the global political level, Bavaria was once more requested to side clearly with Russia and Austria against the French in the raging war of the second coalition. On 29 May/9 June 1799 in St Petersburg, Paul laid down that the Bavarian troops were to join the Russian contingents in central Europe. When the Bavarian court agreed, the Russian General Korsakoff, the commander of the Russian troops at the Rhine, would join the Bavarian forces. Baron von Bühler was now officially accredited again as Russian envoy in Munich where he rented a flat in the house of Rechberg's father. Max Joseph also felt obliged to promise the Russians a contingent of 20,000 men in the campaign against France. Like his comrades, even Joseph Maria von Rechberg prepared his company of cavalry to fight the French.

In the meantime, in early summer, preparations had started for the journey, as demanded, of a delegation of Bavarian knights to pay homage to Paul. Rechberg's older brother and councillor of the duke elector thought it would be wise to combine it with an extraordinary delegation led by the Bavarian Duke Wilhelm – the brother-in-law of Max Joseph – and he himself as Bavarian councillor to negotiate a possible wedding of the Churprinz and the Russian Great Duchess Catherine. We will come back to this later on. Montgelas – who in the end still believed that Bavarian neutrality was the best solution to survive in a Europe deeply shaken by the French Revolution and the Napoleonic re-shaping of whole countries and nations – did not like the thoughts of the czar at all. As he knew that the coalition of the leading conservative powers in Europe – Prussia, Austria, and Russia – were far from united in their plans to fight France and the new democratic ideas, he still played for time. But it was clear that Bavaria had to do some 'sacrifice'.

In the end, the situation which Montgelas had tried so vehemently to oppose could not be avoided: Bavaria joined the coalition with Russia and Austria against France. At the same time there was a hectic diplomatic correspondence between St Petersburg and Vienna because former Grand Master Hompesch – then still residing in Trieste – kept on protesting all the time against his dispossession and that the Russian Orthodox and married Paul had usurped the post of grand master. As Trieste was then Austrian territory, Paul – *de facto* but not *de jure* grand master of the Order – demanded Vienna to silence Hompesch. Still in the spring of 1799 the problem that there were two claimants for the office of grand master remained unsolved. In June 1799 there came rumours from Vienna that the Austrians intended to force Hompesch to abdicate and to make Paul resign from the magistry to make Archduke Johann – Leopold II's son – grand master. Many Bavarians now clearly preferred Paul – if they ever had to choose – to the disliked Austrian.

But these were just rumours and Paul even put so much pressure on Austria that the emperor forced Hompesch to resign the magistry in early July 1799. However – at least by canonical law – without the approval of the Holy See, neither Franz II nor Paul could force Hompesch to abdicate. In fact it was only in 1802 that the curia ratified this abdication. Despite of the Holy See's hesitation, quite soon the grand priories of Germany, Bohemia, Venice, Capua, Barletta, Messina, and Portugal and, following their liberation from the French, those of Lombardy and Pisa, acknowledged Paul as grand master. Now the Bavarians also recognized Paul as the new grand master. On the other hand, because of pressure exerted by their king, the Spanish priories of Catalonia, Navarra, Aragon, and Castille refused to acknowledge the czar. Even the grand priory of Rome followed the attitude of the Holy See and refused acknowledgement. Still, at this time, Hompesch was not downgraded by the Holy See. In fact the invalidity of Paul's magistry was pointed out by many. As a schismatic,

Paul could never head a Catholic Order. Paul was married and only a honorary grand cross and therefore not even a full member of the Order. After Paul's death the procedure to elect a new grand master returned to normal and was conducted in conformity with the statutes. Even the Bavarian court which had to accept Paul's magistry agreed that every election of a grand master had to be approved by the pope.

Just to silence any '*malcontents*' on 9/21 August 1799 the chapter of the Order in St Petersburg communicated to the Bavarians that Hompesch had abdicated. Still late in 1799 Paul, as grand master of the Order, communicated the new regulations to the remaining priories and bailiwicks of the Order. Article 10 of these regulations is most interesting and clearly shows the instrumentalization of the Order for the new political programme: '*The present war against the French must be considered as a war against the Infidels; therefore every campaign of six months should be acknowledged as a regular caravan.*'

Now when with the convention of 17 July 1799 (*Präliminarkonvention*) the Anglo-Bavarian langue – or better *Langue Anglo-Bavaro-Russe* – was again put on solid jurisdictional ground, a delegation of obedience (*Obidienzabordnung*) was sent to St Petersburg. This delegation was headed by Duke Wilhelm von Birkenfeld and included Baron Aloys von Rechberg and the secretary Sulzer. It left Munich on 19 August 1799 and arrived in St Petersburg on 26 October 1799. A deeper reason for the sending of this high-ranking delegation was to agree to a treaty of protection by Russia. That this move was not made out of the free will of the Bavarians but was imposed by the Russians was obvious. It clearly went against Bavarian neutrality but, for the moment, Montgelas and Max Joseph thought they could not do otherwise.

Another delegation which was to concentrate solely on the affairs of the Order, and composed of Flachslanden, Count Preysing, Count Arco, and Chevalier de Bray, had already departed to St Petersburg on 23 July 1799. It carried the homage of the Bavarian grand priory and the ratified document of the re-installation of the priory. De Bray's choice had been approved by his friend Montgelas. His travel diary gives a good account of the events. On 5 August the delegation reached Berlin where negotiations and discussions with members of the Prussian government were carried out. In Mitau (today Jelgava) (29 August) they had an audience with Louis XVIII of France who was living there in exile. When they finally reached St Petersburg, the delegation took up lodgings in the *Hôtel de Malta*, but soon they moved to the *Hôtel Apraxin* which was found more comfortable. During his stay in the Russian metropolis, de Bray was a most watchful observer and he composed a 'Mémoire sur la Russie' which was such a sharp, critical and clinical analysis of Paul's court that when it was read in Munich it suddenly caused such international interest that the Russian authorities took strong offence. On 19 February 1800 de Bray returned to Bavaria. Only Paul's death in March 1801 saved de Bray from further serious Russian actions. After his recall de Bray was temporarily posted on 15 October 1800 in London as *envoye extraordinaire* of Bavaria. De Bray's *Memoire* clearly shows how much the Bavarians knew about Paul's unbalanced and moody character and his arrogant and undiplomatic attitude towards the other European conservative powers never made it possible for the anti-French coalition to really work.

That Paul had had himself be acclaimed as grand master of the Order was still a hotly discussed '*politicum*'. To Austria, Prussia, France, Spain, and England, it did not much matter that Paul was married, and Russian Orthodox, and therefore in flagrant breach of the old regulations of the Order. It was the Russian ambitions in the Mediterranean which were causing headaches in Vienna, Berlin, Madrid, Paris, and London. From this point of view alone, it was unthinkable that Malta would be returned to an Order headed by the czar. Especially for Austria, Paul's acclamation to the grand magistracy had been a shock – so de Bray wrote – as there were still many of the Order's commanderies in Hapsburg lands. De Bray simply called Paul's direct and prominent involvement in the Order's activities a *'fantaisie'*. But the Bavarian delegation could do nothing else for the moment other than to come to some arrangement with Paul as well as possible. The delegation was again showered with medals and decorations in St Petersburg. In his 'memoire' de Bray indicates that, in Malta and the old institution of the knights of St John, Paul saw the integral symbol of an united conservative Europe against its (= his) enemies, the French republic, and the Turkish empire. Very much vainglorious and overambitious, Paul saw himself in the historical role to fulfill this mission.

The negotiations in St Petersburg in late summer 1799 also had some effect on the inner organization of the Anglo-Bavarian langue – or *Lingua Anglo-Bavaro-Russe* as it was now called in some documents. It was clear that the Russian accent was growing stronger. The czar's son Grand Duke Constantin was made the new turcopilier while *Balí* Nikolaus Soltykoff became the grand master's plenipotentiary. 'Grand Master' Paul appointed Count Arco as the *charge d'affaires* of the Order in Munich and also receiver of the Bavarian grand priory. Flachslanden's deference to the Russian Court also had its effects. Paul bestowed on him two rich commanderies in the Russian priory and the Alexander Nevki Order. For renouncing the right of succession to the grand priorship in favour of the offspring of the house of Wittelsbach, Flachslanden received an additional pension of 2 400 guilders. The other members of the delegation were also showered with gifts.

Flachslanden's stay in St Petersburg was, however, not only marked by success. Something must have happened before the Order's council meeting of 9 /21 January 1800, as *Balí* Grand Duke Constantine of Russia replaced Flachslanden as turcopolier. In fact Flachslanden's star in St Petersburg was waning. His old service in the Russo-Turkish war was not forgotten and his prominent and helpful role in the Anglo-Bavarian langue made him invited by Paul to dinner every evening. But, all of a sudden, this conciliatory atmosphere came to an end as a result of internal intrigues and conflicts. When Flachslanden participated at a meeting of the sacred council of the Order presided over by Paul, the turcopilier made some suggestions against Vice-Chancellor de la Houssaye's programme to change the old statutes. The suggestions made de la Houssay very much afraid – perhaps rightly so – that Flachslanden was aiming at the post of lieutenant of the grand master and he believed that the turcopilier aimed to oust him. De la Houssaye won the support of Marshal Soltykoff and Chancellor Rostoptchin for his intrigues against Flachslanden and indeed these three succeeded to make the court believe that Flachslanden was a dangerous intruder in Russian politics. As a result Paul started to ignore Flachslanden and the entire Bavarian delegation, which soon left St Petersburg and returned to Munich.

By then Rechberg had long since returned from Trieste to Munich. By the early summer of 1799 he had left Trieste and travelled via Linz and Passau to the Bavarian capital. His correspondence shows that he was entrusted with the delicate mission to co-ordinate the contacts between Hompesch, who soon was officially to resign the magistry, the imperial court in Vienna, and the Russian court. There was still the plan to compensate Hompesch for his abdication with of the grand priory of Bohemia, an idea possibly developed by Flachslanden to silence the former grand master. That the Austrian knights strongly opposed such plans was only logical. Finally Hompesch was forced to resign without receiving any valid compensation.

Back in Munich, new tasks and missions awaited Joseph Maria. In these turbulent and hectic times, the new Bavarian court under Duke Elector Max IV Joseph certainly needed men like Rechberg for various missions and projects. In the summer of 1799 he was sent to Prague to negotiate with the Russian representative the route of the Russian army in their future campaign against the French and to try to prevent it from marching across Bavarian territory.

In late 1799 Rechberg is back in South Germany, apparently negotiating with some high-ranking members of the Order regarding his provision as a knight of Malta. But these negotiations seemed to have failed. Although listed as commander of Mindelheim St Johannes, he still does not seem to have benefitted from the full income of this commandery. In a letter of March 1800 to his elder brother Aloys, he refused to take his oath as a professed knight before these financial affairs were solved. Considering the newly established good contacts of Aloys and the Russian court, he wrote to his brother after his return from St Petersburg inquiring if he could help him acquire a new commandery. It was known that Paul, after his acclamation as new grand master, had drastically financially refounded and expanded the Russian grand priory – then still part of the Anglo-Bavarian langue.

At the same time Rechberg also kept his options open regarding the continuation of his Bavarian army career. This was the time when the Bavarian military system was again deeply reshuffled and changed. In the spring of 1800 there were negotiations between Rechberg and the military administration about a new engagement but things led nowhere. The key issue was the little money the Bavarians offered for such positions. Hoping for a good position, Rechberg already had spent 2,000 guilders to provide himself with suitable equipment for a high-ranking officer.

In the meantime the situation in central Europe had escalated. As stipulated in the coalition's treaty, Austrian, Russian, and Bavarian troops had started attacking the French. Rechberg joined the Bavarian troops in April 1800. In early summer, he was entrusted with co-ordinating the contact between the Bavarian court and the imperial army headquarters. According to him, there were relatively good chances for a success against the French. The united troops were well provided and their numbers were superior to the French northern army. Napoleon himself was in command of the French southern army which achieved an important victory against the Austrians near Marengo on 14 June 1800. North of the Alps, the allies tried to block General Jean Moreau's troops at the Danube near Ulm. It was mainly the lack of organization in the allied troops which caused their heavy defeat near Ulm on 27 June 1800. Rechberg's contingent escaped imprisonment and retreated to Ingolstadt.

On 2 July Rechberg fought in the battle near Ampfing where the allied troops triumphed. In subsequent weeks and months, he was again involved in diplomatic missions and acted as Bavarian military delegate in the imperial troops' headquarters of Austrian Archduke Johann Baptist Joseph von Habsburg. It was mainly due to General Moreau that the French won a decisive victory at Hohenlinden, near Ebersberg – the seat of the Bavarian grand priory – in Upper Bavaria, on 3 December 1800. The battle ended with over 4,000 Austrian and Bavarian casualties. Rechberg then continued his service as emissary and courier between the Austrian and Bavarian courts and headquarters and was also involved in the negotiations with the British delegate Lord Wickham who was then touring Bavaria. The consequences of this war were dramatic, especially for Bavaria. While the French troops marching towards the Bavarian capital, Max Joseph fled to Amberg in Northern Bavaria. The possessions of the Order were, however, not touched – at least for the moment. The war of the Second Coalition ended with the treaty of Campo Formio. Rechberg then served at the headquarters of the exiled Bavarian court at Amberg in the Upper Palatinate.

It was only then when peace was restored that the duke elector returned to his capital. From now on Max IV Joseph and his cabinet started clearly siding with the French. This went so far that the duke elector very much pushed forward for his eldest daughter to marry Eugène de Beauharnais, the

Eugène de
Beauharnais

first child and only son of Napoleon's first wife Joséphine. In the newly organized ministry, Montgelas could act out – with French backing – his commercial and agricultural reforms, ameliorate the laws, draw up a new criminal code, and equalize imposts without regard to traditional privileges. The secularization of the religious orders could be quietly prepared for. Still the lobby for the Order had been too strong to risk touching its possessions again – at least for the time being.

The end of the war also brought new tasks and challenges for Joseph Maria von Rechberg. His eventual appointment and mission to the Order's provisional headquarters at Catania had much to do with his previous impeccable and loyal conduct. Having kept his distance from the various parties within the Order – the one siding with the Austrians and the pope, the other with the Russians – made him the ideal choice to be appointed Bavarian representative at new Grand Master Tommasi's residence in Catania, especially since he was very much trusted by the Italian grand master under whom he had served in the Order's navy.

But let us return to the events which made the Mediterranean so interesting again for the Order. After Napoleon had been acclaimed first consul on 9 November 1799, slowly but steadily the relations between France and Russia improved. After the successful battle of Marengo against the Austrians on 14 June 1800, Napoleon even went so far – whether it was a mere pretence or a genuine offer is difficult to say – to offer Malta to Paul. The island was then still besieged by the British and the first consul knew very well that the French defenders in Valletta were in a desperate state and that General Vaubois could hardly hold out much longer. Much more than any other European king – so Napoleon communicated – Paul as grand master was the most legitimate ruler of Malta. It was obvious that Napoleon knew that Malta would sooner rather than later fall to the English. To have it in the hands of the Order – that is Russia – would be less problematic than if the island fell to the British who would foster their dominance in the Mediterranean. The Russians, of course, knew about these occult thoughts of Napoleon and for the moment tried to avoid an open clash with Britain. Therefore negotiations were drawn out on until the French surrendered in September and Malta came under the British. Still, in September 1800 it was discussed that Russia should recognize the Rhine as the frontier of France if Napoleon retreated from Italy, restored Egypt to the Sublime Porte, and guaranteed the possession of Malta to Paul as grand master.

In the winter of 1799/1800 Paul and the King of Naples had already developed plans to conquer Malta. Shortly before then, a Bavarian delegation and the Neapolitan Minister Duke Serra Capriola had gone to St Petersburg. Serra Capriolas's mission was to make Russia help to keep

Italy free from the much-disliked Austrians. But the question of Malta was another important item of discussion. The competent and versatile Russian *chargé d'affaires* in Naples, Alexeij Italinski, was instrumental in these developments. In the winter of 1798/99, Paul had already raised a contingent of troops under Prince Wolgonsky which were to be stationed in Malta after the defeat of the French. The chancellor of the German langue of the Order, Joseph Albert von Ittner, maintains that in 1800 preparations were already afoot in the port of Kronstadt to establish a small fleet stand under the command of the Order.

According to Serra Capriola, the Italian states and the Kingdom of Naples would have nothing against Malta being taken over by a joint Russian-English army. Paul, as the grand master, would be the nominal head over Malta in the same manner as the Order once ruled the country as a fief of the kings of Spain. Obviously the British and the Spanish would have never consented to this and so further international negotiations on the matter never materialized. But the Neapolitan continued to show Paul the kingdom of the Two Sicilies was very much in favour of the idea. During Serra Capriola's first audience in St Petersburg, the duke paid homage to Paul in the name of the Order's priories of Capua, Barletta, and Messina. Apparently a good job had been done by Baron Italinski, Russian *chargé d'affaires* in Naples. But Paul's days were counted.

Not only in Munich but also in other European countries it was believed that Paul's assassination was not just an internal Russian conspiracy but that English interests were somehow involved. In fact Paul was assassinated when France and Russia were drawing closer and closer. Indeed Paul had expressed to Napoleon the intention of transferring Russian trade more to the south. Besides the Black Sea, the Mediterranean therefore became a main sphere of interest for Russia with Malta remaining in the centre of Russian interest – not only because of the ties with the Order – but also from a global point of view. The above-mentioned Bavarian 'Russian-expert' Sulzer reported how, after the news of the fall of Malta to the British, the question of Malta became again a primary subject of discussion in St Petersburg. Most Mediterranean seafaring nations were not happy with the thought of Malta in British hands. Paul's position regarding Malta was very clear. On 24 October 1800 Baron Sulzer has written from St Petersburg to Munich: '*One has to know that the solution of the Malta question will determine the entire quality of the Russian-English relations.*' Paul was so sure about the return of Malta to the Order – that is to *him* as grand master – that he ordered the Russian academy of science to feature Valletta as a city under Russian dominion in the annually published *Almanach*! The British, of course, had other thoughts.

When Paul realised that England did not intend to return Malta to the Order, his anger led him to undertake various offensive measures. He ordered all English ships anchored in Russian harbours to be seized: in Kronstadt alone there were 100 English vessels. England then relied very much on tar, wood, and flax imports from Russia. All English goods in Russia were sequestrated and all pro-English members at the Russian court and cabinet were made to leave St Petersburg. The old Russian plan to conquer India was developed further and it was even rumoured that there was a joint French-Russian plan to attack India. Things were turning out extremely dangerously for England. A couple of weeks later, Paul was dead.

CHAPTER 8
BACK IN THE MEDITERRANEAN –
BAVARIAN ENVOY AND SPY IN CATANIA

P aul's unexpected death on 23rd March 1801 brought about a complete new re-assessment of the situation and subsequently new orientations in both the Order of St John and Bavaria. First Flachslanden's 'pro-Russian' party hoped that Paul's son Alexander I would continue his father's policies. The new czar declared that he was taking the Order under his imperial protection and he promised to try to reinstate it in all its rights, honours, immunities, and privileges. However, he refused to become grand master and appointed *Balí* Field Marshal Count Nicholas Soltykov as provisional lieutenant. Later – if Austria and the empire agreed – a chapter general would be convoked and a new grand master elected. Was Alexander perhaps hoping to gain a certain Russian influence in the destiny of Malta and the Mediterranean by such a moderate and neutral attitude? To make things clear: although Alexander refused the title of grand master, he kept the obligations stemming from being the protector of the Order. For a while, he was very interested that Malta would not be occupied by either England or France and he supported the island's return to the Order. This policy was shared by Count Worontzoff who became the new chancellor of the Russian empire in 1802. In the meantime *Balí* Soltykoff was told to stay on as lieutenant of the grand master with St Petersburg the seat of the Order. On a more global level, Alexander's decision to refuse the title of the grand master and his later decision to maintain a distance from the Order's affairs can be seen as an act of political pragmatism as well as 'spiritual' modernity. A newly-shaped Europe forged by the concept of national states would have prevented the Order from regaining its European possessions anyway.

Less than these more global considerations, what mattered to the knights for the moment were the pure facts. As long Paul had been alive, the German langue's possessions - the ones which had not been sequestrated when the French moved up to the western bank of the Rhine - could feel relatively safe but, after his sudden death, things took a dramatic turn. Paul's death did not lead to the unification of the different factions and parties within the Order. This divide was clearly visible when Hompesch again tried to revive his claims to the magistry but had lost the support of most of the remaining knights in the meantime. When Hompesch heard of Paul's assassination, in May 1801 he wrote to the Austrian minister Thugut to try to promote his rehabilitation as grand master. He – Hompesch wrote – had only temporarily (sic) resigned in 1799 not to endanger the Russo-Austrian coalition. This situation was now superseded and now Napoleon would not mind supporting his re-installation. The new czar, Alexander, would keep also a friendly neutrality. That this was anything but the full truth was most obvious.

At first Hompesch's claim was supported by the new French government which hoped that the British would leave Malta. After a few months, however, it was obvious that Hompesch was fighting a hopeless fight and soon even the French stopped supporting his case. The papacy remained possibly the Order's most influential supporter and the outcome of the Treaty of Amiens, concluded on 27 March 1802 and ratified on 18 April, definitely favoured the knights. Article 10 stipulated that Malta was to revert to the Order in full former sovereignty and that the new grand master should be elected by a general chapter to be held in Malta. The political environment imposed some changes in the centennial institution. The future Order would not contain any French or English langues but a Maltese one would be created. Malta's independence would be guaranteed by

France, Great Britain, Russia, Austria, Prussia, and Spain and the British were to hand the island back to the Order within three months of the treaty's ratification. But paper and written agreements did not matter anymore when the new emerging super-powers were heading to build their pre-imperialistic empires.

In general the Maltese opposed against the return of the Order and supported the British. The liberals and the merchant classes were especially quite opposed to the Treaty of Amiens and in June 1802 a high-ranking Maltese delegation petitioned King George III to ask for the protection by the British crown. The newly formed Maltese assembly formulated a new constitution which recognized the British king as sovereign lord on 15 June 1802. As was to be expected, the British kept Malta against the conclusions of Amiens. Its strategic importance was too obvious to give the island away. That the French then did not retreat from the Italian territory they had annexed, served as a welcome pretext for the British to keep Malta.

A pragmatic mind like Rechberg was, of course, a keen observer of the effects of the new arrangements on the Order's possessions in Bavaria and Southern Germany. The consequences of the Treaty of Lunéville (1801) between France and the German States were immediately felt. The German grand priory lost its possessions on the left bank of the Rhine which were annexed by France. But, for the moment, more disasters in Germany could be avoided. One cannot say that the members of the German langue remained inactive and did not try their best to prevent the oncoming disaster. When the German grand priory lost its possessions in Alsace and Lorraine with the treaty of Lunéville in 1801, Grand Prior Rink von Baldenstein demanded compensation from the emperor which was granted in the general concluding act of the deputies of the German empire (*Reichsdeputationshauptschluß*) and ratified on 27 April 1803 by Emperor Franz II and the German princes.

The German grand priory was to receive the abbeys of St Blasien, St Trudpert, St Peter, Schutten, and Thennenbach in the Black Forest as well as the county of Bonndorf and some more monasteries with their estates. But there were many obstacles in store. Immediately following this agreement, Archduke Ferdinand von Este-Modena, who had been lord of the region of Breisgau and the southern part of the Black Forest since the Treaty of Lunéville, protested against this compensation. The Order still gained enough international support for the return to Malta according to Article 10 of the Treaty of Amiens (1802), but England hesitated to respect these claims and all the efforts of the Order's diplomats proved in vain. In the following years various proposals and plans were made for the Order to settle elsewhere and take up its old activities.

Without the support of the Holy See, Hompesch's star had sunk rapidly. On 16 September 1802 the pope nominated *Bali* Bartolomeo Ruspoli as grand master and Hompesch once more resigned his claims to the magistracy. The former grand master moved to Montpellier where he lived on an infrequently paid pension from the French and died on 12 May 1805.

Although much to the displeasure of Montgelas, the commanderies and possessions of the Anglo-Bavarian langue survived even after Paul's death in March 1801. As long as the policy of the new czar could not be clearly seen, no new Bavarian attempts were made to sequester the Order's possessions. However things changed. On 12 April 1802 it was again confirmed that the post of grand prior should be permanently granted as an appanage to a son of the House of Wittelsbach. In fact the then seven-years-old Prince Karl Theodor, who was given the post after Bretzenheim's forced abdication, kept the title until his death in 1875. Anton von Rechberg – a younger brother of Joseph Maria – had for a while tutored Prince Karl Theodor. The daily business was taken over by Count Topor von Morawitzky. Things were moving steadily. In the council meeting of 14 /26 April 1802, the idea was mooted to separate the Russian priories from the Order. But this suggestion found no wholehearted support.

How influential the Bavarian knights still were was shown in 1802 when the vicar or substitute in the office of the grand master, the Russian General Field Marshal *Balí* Count Nicholas Soltykoff, sent a resolution to the pope asking that all remaining priories in Europe were to submit a list of candidates from whom the pope would select the grand master. On 15 / 27 March 1802, the representatives of the grand priories of Russia met to elect their magisterial candidate. Of the 13 names submitted, three belonged to the Bavarian grand priory although two of them, Count Topor von Morawitzky (Russia) and Flachslanden (French), were listed as members of other langues. The official Bavarian candidate was Rechberg's old friend *Balí* Taufkirchen who had no chance of being elected. *Balí* Giovanni Battista Tommasi received 23 votes, *Balí* Flachslanden 5 votes, *Balí* Gorjao 3, and *Balí* Pignatelli 2. Pius VII, however, had other ideas and on 16 September 1802 he appointed *Balí* Bartolomeo Ruspoli, of the grand priory of Rome, as grand master. Ruspoli, however, did not have the backing of a majority of the knights. Tension and uncertainty among the knights could be felt everywhere. *Balí* Ruspoli – then living in London – was certainly gifted with far-sightedness and political insight. Through his contacts with British leaders, he knew that there was hardly any hope that England would obey the stipulations of the Treaty of Amiens. He was also sceptical as to whether the extensive property which several European states had seized from the Order would ever be returned. All these negative perspectives made him decide to decline the magistracy.

On 9 February 1803 the seasoned former captain general of the Order's navy *Balí* Giovanni Battista Tommasi – then 71 years old – was elected grand master and soon after confirmed by the pope. Tommasi accepted and moved the

Grand Master Giovanni Battista Tommasi

Order's headquarters to Sicily, and therewith back to the centre of the Mediterranean. When, in early March 1803, Max IV Joseph learned that the pope had nominated Tommasi as the new grand master he quickly sent a letter of official congratulations. The same post also carried the announcement that the Bavarians were soon to send a *chargé d'affaires* to the new headquarters of the Order.

174

At first Tommasi resided in Messina, pending the possibility of his going to Malta. But when it became clear that England had no intention of giving back Malta to the Knights of St John, as had been stipulated in the Treaty of Amiens, Tommasi decided to establish the provisional Seat of the Order at Messina where he convened a general assembly of the Order in June 1803. A short time later he moved the Order's headquarters to Catania, a move supported by Naples. Minister Acton even hired some ships to carry some knights and delegates from Naples to Catania, to where the Order's archive and chancery were also transferred and sited in the large Augustinian convent in the city. In June 1803 Tommasi appointed Joseph de Maisonneuve as *chargé d'affaires* of the Order and receiver at St Petersburg. Flachslanden and Rechberg knew that already on 30 April 1803 Maisonneuve had sent a *mémoire* to the newly elected Tommasi giving an account of the internal affairs in Bavaria and the situation of the Bavarian grand priory.

English map of the Port and Straits of Messina (c.1790)

175

On 17 November 1802 the last meeting of the venerable council was held in St Petersburg to where it had moved after the fall of Malta. The council was officially dissolved on 25 April 1803 passing its power to the new grand master and sending the *insignia* of the magistry to him in Catania. Article X of the proceedings declares: '*The Priories of Russia and Bavaria form one single langue. Until now it has been known as the Anglo-Bavaro-Russian langue. Since the treaty of Amiens established that there were no longer to be any langues either in France or in England, the sacred council orders that henceforth this shall be known as the Bavaro-Russian langue.*' So in November 1802 the former Anglo-Bavarian langue became officially the 'Bavaro-Russian langue'. As a matter of fact the two grand priories of Russia continued to form, with that of Bavaria, one single langue. The affairs of this 'Bavaro-Russian-langue' were dealt with by the grand magistry at Catania.

For the German and Bavarian knights all these new and sudden moves meant a new orientation. Quite some of them favoured a return to the Mediterranean scene – connected with the hope of regaining Malta and resuming the Order's old role as a maritime power and a sort of policeman of the Mediterranean. Flachslanden then clearly found favour again in the affairs of the Order. During this last meeting of the sacred council of 5/17 November 1802 in St Petersburg, the Turcopilier Grand Duke Constantine was asked again to resign from his dignity in favour of the capitular of the priory of Bavaria Flachslanden. For Flachslanden – still the mastermind behind the Bavarian grand priory – it was essential to have a trustworthy and experienced representative at the new headquarters: his choice was Joseph Maria von Rechberg. This choice was all the more suitable since Rechberg had served under Tommasi who still held him – the valiant defender of Fort Tigné – in very high esteem. The Swabian baron knew Italian and French and had many contacts among the Italian knights. Throughout the summer of 1803 there were negotiations between Flachslanden and all-powerful Montgelas about harmonizing their concepts of a representative of the Bavarian grand priory and the Bavarian court at the grand master's court. In September Rechberg's new post was confirmed by the provincial chapter. Simultaneously the Bavarian court also confirmed him as Bavaria's official representative at the Order's headquarters. Rechberg who had spent the years 1801 and 1802 in the garrison in Munich was promised 1,000 guilders for the voyage and a daily provision of 2 guilders and 30 *kreuzer*. He also was to receive four-fifths from the responsions of an unnamed commandery for the next three years, which amounted to over 1600 guilders a year.

At first it was planned that Rechberg should leave Munich in November 1803 but, because of a riding accident he had to delay his departure for some weeks. On 14 February he received the instructions for his mission and duties from Montgelas.

A few days later Rechberg left Bavaria in low profile and in April established himself at the Order's provisional headquarters in the large Augustinian convent at Catania. His official position at the grand master's court was that of both *chargé d'affaires* of Bavaria and representative of the Anglo-Bavarian langue.

For the following year, Rechberg carried out a very discreet spying for the Order – mainly on the French plans and projects in the Mediterranean. In fact his correspondence with Flachslanden and with his elder brother are a treasure of information on Napoleon's hegemonial ambitions in the Mediterranean, North Africa, and the Near East; and French commercial interests and the English efforts to counteract these ambitions. He was partly supported in this intelligence work by Ovide Doublet, the former secretary of the French affaires of Grand Master Rohan, who lived in Rome and Naples for some time.

In 1804 and 1805 Napoleon still considered Malta, Southern Italy, and Egypt as vital stepping stones and connecting stations for his plans to conquer India. Way back in 1798, Talleyrand already had discussed sending 15,000 men from Suez to India to help the forces of Tipu-Sahib drive out the British. Rechberg pointed out several times that the French had not abandoned their old plans to regain of Malta, Cyprus, the Near East, and Egypt and he gave a number of concrete examples of French influence. Without French money, which passed via southern Italian ports to Alexandria and Damietta, the Egyptian beys would not have defeated the Mamelukes in 1804. On his visits to Messina and Reggio, Rechberg himself observed that many French agents, engineers, and spies used to arrive from Toulon, Nice, and Marseilles and board ships bound for Tripoli, Jaffa, Alexandria, Damietta, and Algiers. For many of them India was the final destination. In all the Red Sea and the Persian Gulf ports there were French agents aiming to destabilize the British colonies in India and the Far East. Rechberg very often received news and messages from India via Persia, Arabia, and the Near East before London whose ships had to sail around the Cape of Good Hope.

There was a regular flow of cash and arms to motivate the maharajas and chieftains of India to rise against the English. There was such a widespread infiltration that, in early 1805, the bankers of Alexandria did not have enough cash to pay the French bills of exchange. Rechberg noted that French money was secretly transported on Danish vessels to Alexandria to help the banks out but a few weeks later the British sent ships from Malta to stop these vessels. At the time a French peace treaty with Ottoman Emperor Selim III was in the making, which later would become an alliance against Russia and England. Rechberg also heard rumours about secret efforts to create a Franco-Persian alliance and met French agents going to Ali Shah.

Rechberg also kept an eye open about developments in Malta, the old residence of his Order, working closely with his old acquaintance Commander Nicola Bussi who in the

1790s had been captain of the *San Zaccaria* and who had been installed as the Order's representative in Malta in 1804. Bussi, who had lived for some time in England, should have been preparing for the transfer of the knights to their old residence but, because of English and Maltese resistance, nothing much was happening. The aged Tommasi's inflexible and stubborn position certainly did not help in this difficult affair. Rechberg soon realized that Tommasi was part of the problem that the secret negotiations with the Maltese representatives were not moving ahead. Tommasi strictly opposed establishing a 'Maltese langue' if the Order ever returned. His stubborn persistence to retain the old statutes and regulations did not help the Order's case and its popularity in Malta. Rechberg's old acquaintance de Bray received a 30-pages memoir from Tommasi praising the old values of the Order and noting that the Maltese should be grateful that the Order had ruled them for such a long time, a period when the population of Malta had more than tripled – so Tommasi wrote.

One of Rechberg's sources in Malta was the former custodian of the Auberge de Baviere, Joseph Splinder, who had remained on the island. Although Splinder was a rather unbalanced character, Rechberg could still draw some profit from his information. Whenever he could, Rechberg spoke with passengers and captains coming from Malta. If he ever actually visited Malta personally at the time, we do not know. Through his friends and contacts, he was surely aware that in Malta the memories of the Order's rule were starting to fade and only a very few knights had remained on the island. What was also certain was that the unwise behaviour of the French had made them many enemies. Rechberg read with great interest some memoirs about the incident at the Carmelite church at Mdina and the subsequent rising against the French. Rechberg knew that it was mainly one article in Napoleon's decree dated 13 June 1798 which had created tension. Article IV had stipulated that a religious Order could only possess one convent in Malta. As in many parts of Europe, even in Malta there was a confusion between the *Directoire* (Republicans) and the *Terreur* (Jacobins) and the new French Republic was widely associated with virulent anticlericalism.

The coming of the British did not mean that the Maltese started to enjoy the 'full rights' of a nation and *patria* as many had hoped. Soon the realities of a colonial status became visible. The British administration in Malta remained autocratic in the nineteenth century and political agitation kept growing. The staunch Maltese patriots never stopped asserting their countrymen's right to re-establish the old *Consiglio Popolare*. The wise and diplomatic behaviour of British Civil Commissioner Sir Alexander Ball prevented clashes between population and occupiers. Rechberg remained interested in everything nautical and he was sad to hear that 'his' old *Santa Maria del Pilar* had been broken up by the French during the blockade for firewood. The *San Zacharia*, renamed *Dego* by the French, after suffering some damage during the blockade was rotting away at Senglea creek and its wood being used for other purposes. The frigate *Carthagenoise*, the former *Sant'Elisabetta*, was broken up immediately by the British after General Vaubois's surrender.

It was not only politics and diplomacy which interested Rechberg while at the Order's headquarters. He also seemed to have taken considerable interest in Sicily's rich history and culture. He supported foreign visitors to the island, especially the painter and poet Karl Gotthard Grass from Livonia. He encouraged the gifted Grass, who had arrived in Sicily in 1804 together with the author Philipp Joseph von Rehfues, the architect Karl Friedrich Schinkel, and Johann Gottfried Steininger, to tour Sicily and to paint as many of the famous and typical sites of the island as possible. Grass dedicated his *Sicilische Reise, oder Auszüge aus dem Tagebuche eines Landschaftsmalers* to Rechberg. In the manuscript, he wrote '*Zueignung an Herrn von Rechberg, Freiherrn und Comthur des Malteser-Ordens, Rom, April 1808*'. The ambitious work, however, was only published after Grass's premature death (Rome, 3 August 1814) in Stuttgart in 1815. A copy of the book must have been acquired by Rechberg as it forms part of his legacy.

Through the letters of his elder brother Aloys at the court at Munich, Rechberg was informed that various princes and leaders were discussing the unification of the Teutonic Order and the Order of St John all through 1803 and 1804. The German priory of the Order of St John was very much in favour for this, as it still seemed that the Order could have the chance to regain most of their commanderies in the German lands and Malta. The council of the Teutonic knights, however, hesitated, although their Order had lost substantial possessions in the recent re-shuffles in Europe. Even the representatives of the Anglo-Bavarian langue were hesitant in pushing the projects. The Bavarian court furthermore very much resented the proposal that the Teutonic knights should be refunded with monasteries in Bavaria. There were also thoughts of refunding the Order for the loss of Malta with lands in the duchies of Baden and Württemberg in south-west Germany. But this was very much disliked by the local authorities and Austria. With very mixed feelings, Rechberg read his brother's hints that the all-powerful Montgelas and Max IV Joseph were still secretly working on plans to dissolve the Bavarian grand priory.

Rechberg and Tommasi could also observe that all the efforts of the Order's diplomats to re-establish their institution in Malta were in vain. However, various other proposals and plans were made for the Order to settle elsewhere and resume its old activities. An interesting option was offered by Gustav IV of Sweden who, in 1806, offered the island of Gotland to the knights who, however, refused as they feared that their claims on Malta would be lost forever; some European powers were rather sceptical about this proposal from the start.

Until his death on 12th June 1805, Tommasi did not achieve any progress in the efforts for the Order to regain its

Innico Guevara-Suardo, lieutenant of the magistry

old principality. After his death, the tensions and confusion became even more visible when *Balí* Giuseppe Caracciolo's election as grand master was not accepted by Pius VII. On 15 June 1805 the Order's council had elected the Neapolitan *Balí* Innico-Maria Guevera-Suardo to succeed Tommasi, but Guevera-Suardo was just confirmed as lieutenant of the grand magistry by a brief of Pius VII of 21 October 1805.

182

The pope – and a group of malcontent knights – had refused to accept Caracciolo as he was seen to be too much pro-British. Pius instead declared as permanent the appointment of *Balí* Innico-Maria Guevara-Suardo as lieutenant of the magistry and also recognized the magistral powers attached to this office. That meant that for the following decades there was no grand master but a 'lieutenant' heading the institution. Because of internal intrigues and difficulties, it took up to 2 / 14 February 1809 when in their capitular meeting both Russian grand priories recognised Guevara-Suardo as lieutenant of the grand magistry and therefore as head of the Order. The Order remained in Catania until 1826, before it was moved to Ferrara and finally to Rome.

In such a confusing situation, the Bavarian court and some members of the Bavarian grand priory, found no use in leaving Rechberg in Catania. Rechberg at first thought otherwise and pointed out that he still considered it necessary to keep a permanent representative of the Order and Bavaria in Catania. The network of contacts and information he had established were to be too precious to be lost; they could be of very good use not only for the Bavarian grand priory but also for the Bavarian court and politics in general. Max IV Joseph and Montgelas thought otherwise. By 1805 Bavarian relations with France had become too close. There was no interest to invest more in good contacts in an apparently moribund and anachronistic institution like the Order. In the end Rechberg obeyed the orders from Munich and prepared to leave Catania in June 1805.

In September 1805 Rechberg was back in the headquarters of the Bavarian general staff at Amberg. He came just in time to witness the outcome of the Treaty of Pressburg (Bratislava) of 26 December 1805 and the reward of Bavaria's Francophile politics. Thanks to Napoleon, Max IV Joseph received a royal title and important territorial gains in Swabia and Franconia to round off his kingdom. As Max I Joseph, he assumed the title of king on 1 January 1806. There was always some sort of give and take and, on 15 March, Max I Joseph ceded the duchy of Berg to Napoleon's brother-in-law Joachim Murat.

CHAPTER 9

A HERO OF THE NAPOLEONIC WARS AND THE CLOSING OF A CIRCLE

I n September 1805 the War of the Third Coalition started. When it became obvious that Bavaria would side with France, it was attacked by the Austrians whose army crossed the river Inn and marched to Munich. Once more the Bavarian court fled north to Amberg in the Upper Palatinate.

The outcome of the subsequent campaigns is well-known. Napoleon completely outsmarted the Russian and Austrian armies in the battles of Ulm and Austerlitz and the campaign ended in disaster for the conservative allies. Rechberg then served in the general staff of the Bavarian army. The campaigns of 1806 of the united French and Bavarian forces against Prussia saw Rechberg in the frontline of events. The Bavarian contingents were commanded by the Generals Wrede and Deroy. As lieutenant-colonel, Rechberg participated in the sieges of Glogau, Glatz, Brieg, and Breslau in Silesia.

The alliance with the French brought – at least for the moment – a very fruitful and promising outcome for Bavaria but it did not bring anything good for the Order. On the contrary, the century-old religious and military orders footed the bill when Napoleon shaped Europe more and more according to his secular ideas. By means of the Treaty of Pressburg (Bratislava) of 26 December 1805, the king of Württemberg and margrave of Baden sequestrated the commanderies of the German grand priory on their territory. Even a last desperate move by the representatives of the Order failed. On behalf of German Grand Prior Ignaz Balthasar Baron Rink von Baldenstein, the *Balís* Pfürdt

Bavarian King
Max I Joseph
(1806)

and Flachslanden negotiated with Max I Joseph, the newly appointed king of Bavaria, for the latter to guarantee the survival of the German grand priory's possessions. Again Joseph Maria's elder brother Aloys, councillor and minister at the Bavarian court, was of great help. King Max I Joseph was then on good terms with Napoleon and for some time the negotiations looked promising.

In fact such a treaty was concluded with Max Joseph on 28 January 1806, with the Bavarian king agreeing to protect the Order's possessions in Germany and to support compensation for the losses of its territories west of the Rhine. Some of the Order's possessions in southern Germany were incorporated

Crown and coat of arms of the
Wittelsbach-Family

in the Bavaro-Russian langue and therewith saved from
secular sequestration. It was planned that the offices of the
grand priors of Germany and of Bavaria were to be unified
in the person of the young prince Karl Theodor of Bavaria.
A decree of the sacred council of the Order of 21 June 1806
confirmed the convention.

But even Max I Joseph could not stop the exodus. In June
1806 Bavaria was itself forced by Napoleon to join the Union
of the Rhine-States (*Rheinbund*) – an alliance of German
states friendly to France. Napoleon's wish that all the member
states of the *Rheinbund* should sequestrate the property of the
religious Orders in their territory was fixed in the concluding
act of the Union of the Rhine-States (*Rheinbundakte*) of 12 July
1806. At the time of its dissolution, the German grand priory
had 34 commanderies, besides its residence of Heitersheim
and four houses (*Kameralhäuser*). The last time that the German
priory's possessions were confirmed by the German emperor
had been under Joseph II in 1780. *De facto* the German grand
priory ceased to exist in the summer of 1806. The principality
of Heitersheim and its estates fell to the duke of Baden. The
protests of Prince Prior von Baldenstein remained unheard
for he died soon afterwards on 30 June 1807.

Max I Joseph – more or less king by the grace of Napoleon – could do nothing against it. Napoleon's note of 22 August 1806 had already indicated the bad auspices for a survival of the Order's remaining possessions and had hinted that there should be no space in a modern secular state for such an institution. Max Joseph understood Napoleon's hint very well and finally agreed with his minister Montgelas that for his country's sake, the Bavarian grand priory should be sacrificed, a decision Czar Alexander I would object to. Even Joseph Maria's influential brother, the minister and councillor of the king, Aloys, could not prevent the subsequent actions, especially since in December 1806 Aloys was entrusted with the delicate post of Bavarian ambassador at the imperial court at Vienna and therewith he was moved away from the Bavarian court and the centre of decisions. Now with Bavaria on the side of the French, Aloys had the most difficult task of keeping a constant policy of balance between the powers. He showed himself as a most talented diplomat and held this office until the Congress of Vienna ended Napoleon's re-shaping of Europe. This re-shaping also had its effects on the Rechberg family. Until 1803, the possessions of the Rechberg family had been independent. After some negotiations between the Rechbergs and the Bavarian court, two-thirds of their possessions passed to Bavaria, the other part fell under the rule of Württemberg. In 1810 the Bavarian parts were incorporated in the kingdom of Württemberg.

The end of the Order in Bavaria came quickly and mercilessly. With the decree of 8 September 1808 all its possessions in Bavaria were sequestrated. The funds and riches, however, did not go to the state treasury but were used to endow the Bavarian bishop's seats. By early October 1808 a state commission arrived in Mindelheim from Munich and officially took over the properties of Rechberg's commandery of St Johannes in the name of the government. Because of his military duties, Joseph Maria von Rechberg was not present on this sad occasion. A few days later the long inventory list of the commanderies of St Johannes and St Martin at Mindelheim was sent to Munich. The suppression of the Bavarian grand priory did not automatically entail the suppression of all the titles of commanders and of knights of justice, so long as those bearing them were still alive. All holders of commanderies and even those who were on the waiting list for commanderies were compensated with pensions. So was Joseph Maria von Rechberg. At around the same time – perhaps as a sort of further compensation – he was bestowed with the title of 'royal chamberlain' at the Bavarian court.

The knights of the Bavarian grand priory and the bailiwick of Neuburg who did not yet hold commanderies received a pension of 1,500 guilders each. The title of the grand prior of Bavaria, however, remained in the house of the rulers of Bavaria. Even after 1808 it became a fixed post in the regulations of the appanages of the royal princes and it was connected with a stately revenue from the government's treasury. But, even after the suppression of the Bavarian grand priory, the 'Bavaro-Russian' langue lingered on for another two years in the two Russian priories. Nominally the langue survived with the Catholic grand priory of Russia until 1810. The official end of the two Russian grand priories came with a personal decree addressed to Count Soltykoff by Czar Alexander I on 26 February / 10 March 1810, titled 'Concerning the Disposal of the Capitals of the Order of St John of Jerusalem'. The 'economic aspect' was cited as the reason for the winding-up.

So the institution of the Order in the lands of Bavaria was gone but its exponents remained. In fact various knights of the Bavarian grand priory continued to play important roles in Bavarian politics, army, and society in the first decades of the nineteenth century. Besides Rechberg's prominent role in the Bavarian army and in the country's diplomatic service, there was the former receiver of the Anglo-Bavarian langue Bishop Casimir Haeffelin who had served as Bavarian *chargé d'affaires* at the curia in Rome since 1803 and who, in 1810, was additionally nominated Bavarian *envoye extraordinaire* at the court of the king of the Two Sicilies in Naples; there was also the priest and commander Maillot de la Treille in the ecclesiastical service at court; Karl Philipp Count von Vieregg, chamberlain of duchess Maria Leopoldine d'Este, Duke Elector Karl Theodor's second wife; Max Count von Taufkirchen; and Count Maximilian von Arco, officers and chamberlains of the Bavarian king. All of these kept on networking and helping each other in various projects and activities.

But not all of the former knights enjoyed good relations with the authorities. Although it had been decided in 1808 that the pensions for the commanderies should be paid until the death of the holders, this was very often not the case. A prominent case is Rechberg's old friend General Count Friedrich Joseph von Vieregg, grand cross of the Order of St John. Vieregg had received 5,000 guilders from the commandery of Landsberg since 1783 and another 5,000 guilders from the commandery of Schierling since 1799. These payments stopped in 1815. When Vieregg protested, the district treasury of the *Isarkreis* told him that they had been instructed to pay only as long as they had enough cash. When Vieregg protested to the king and threatened to bring the case to the Congress at Vienna, he was made to appear in front of a commission and was forced to retract his protests as these were impertinent and went against the royal law.

As the Bavarian grand priory and the Anglo-Bavarian-Russian langue breathed their last, Joseph Maria von Rechberg continued his brilliant career in the Bavarian army. As this book lays its emphasis on Rechberg's connection with the Order and Malta, this career will not be described in much detail. Between late 1805 and Napoleon's end in 1815, he participated prominently in nearly all important military actions in which Bavarian troops were involved. That meant that he fought with the French troops in most of their European campaigns until 1813 when the Bavarian king changed his policy and, considering Napoleon's sinking star, shifted to the allied forces of Austria, Russia and Prussia. From 1813 onwards Rechberg now fought against the French until Napoleon was exiled after Waterloo.

Thanks to Napoleon's genius, these wars were lessons of strategic and tactical thinking and planning and Rechberg could well absorb and analyse how his master acted. In the War of the Fourth Coalition Napoleon and his allies won at Jena-Auerstedt (October 1806) against the Prussians and at Eylau (February 1807) and later at Friedland (June 1807) against the Prussians and Russians. The Treaty of Tilsit restored peace for just two years. In the summer of 1809 the Austrians rose again but Napoleon, together with the Bavarian troops, defeated them at Wagram. A new peace, the Treaty of Schönbrunn, was signed between France and Austria. Rechberg participated

Bavarian officer in the Infantry (1813)

in most of these campaigns. His comrade, Major Eduard von Völderndorff und Maradein describes his exploits in some detail in his *Kriegsgeschichte von Bayern unter König Maximilian Joseph I* (1826). A few prominent stages of his career might

191

be mentioned. Rechberg's correspondence with his family further helps to re-construct his career and exploits.

In 1808 he was promoted commander of the first brigade of the first division of the Bavarian Army. His superior was Lieutenant General Count Bernhard Erasmus von Deroy. By that Rechberg held the command over the first infantry regiment, the second infantry regiment 'Kronprinz', and the first light battalion 'Habermann' quartered at Munich. Rechberg's biggest challenge came in 1812 when Napoleon requested the Bavarian king to contribute contingents for the campaign against Russia. Already the previous year Rechberg had been involved in the extensive preparations for war and was sent by the Bavarian court to Paris in the summer of 1811. According to the stipulations in the concluding act of the Union of the Rhine-States (*Rheinbundakte*), Bavaria was to contribute 33,000 men to the French campaigns.

Rechberg and his troops formed part of the famous *Grande Armée* with its over 300,000 men. He served in the 19th division of the sixth army corps of the Bavarian troops. The commander of his division was his old acquaintance Count Deroy under whom he had already served in the early 1790s in the Palatinate. Deroy's troops had gathered near Bamberg in Northern Bavaria in May 1812, from where they marched through Bohemia to Glogau (today Poland), crossing the river Weichsel and approaching the Russian border. The unification of the Bavarian troops with the French contingents took place on 12 June. From then on, Rechberg's 19th division marched in the centre of the *Grande Armée*. The troops first moved north to the Prussian city of Königsberg (today Kaliningrad).

The invasion of Russia started on 23 June 1812. The majority of the French troops and their allies proceeded through the Baltic lands and stopped in Vilnius where they were inspected personally by Napoleon. In subsequent weeks there were skirmishes between the allied troops and the Russians near Witebsk and Smolensk. When the Russian general Wittgenstein tried to interrupt the French supply line,

Napoleon sent Deroy's and Rechberg's division to the region of Polozk to block him. In the battles of 18 and 22 August the Bavarians triumphed over the Russians. Deroy was fatally wounded and General Karl Philipp von Wrede took over the command of the Bavarian troops. Meanwhile the central corps of the French troops marched farther towards Moscow; Rechberg's division stayed in the northern region of Polozk, entrusted with securing the northern flanks and to erect walls and ditches for a defensive line. The Russians avoided Napoleon's objective of a decisive engagement and retreated deeper and deeper into Russia. The first important battle was fought at Borodino, near Moscow, in September and it left over 40,000 Russian and 30,000 French dead, wounded, or captured. It was possibly the bloodiest of the Napoleonic wars. Entering Moscow was no triumph as, rather than capitulate, the Russians had set Moscow on fire.

In the meantime the situation around Polozk had worsened more and more. The autumn rains had changed the region into a swamp. The permanent lack of supplies, and provisions, namely food and medicine, had caused hunger, disease, and low spirits and decimated the Bavarian troops. Besides the dead in battle, over 1,000 soldiers of the 18th and 19th Bavarian division died through fever and hunger. Other had mutinied and tried to fight their way home. Even Rechberg started to suffer from fever. To avoid the spread of fatalism and mutinous behaviour General Wrede forbade the officers and soldiers from writing letters home. This also applied to Rechberg. The fever passed in December when the weather turned very cold. These extreme temperatures also took their toll amongst the soldiers, many of who died because of the cold or suffered frostbite. Because of these drastic losses the Bavarian troops had to be reshuffled and Rechberg was charged with establishing a new division out of the dispersed and exhausted contingents, known as the 'Brigade Rechberg'.

For Rechberg and for his comrades, however, the most difficult thing was not the battles but the sheer endless retreat from Russia to Bavaria in the winter of 1812/13. By January 1813 they had reached the town of Plozk in north-western Poland.

From the over 300,000 troops who had started the campaign, fewer than 20 per cent reached home. The cold, hunger, and the partisans dwindled their numbers every day. Still in the spring of 1813 there were rumours that Napoleon intended to raise a new army and move against the Russians again. For the moment, however, most of the French and allied contingents were on the retreat. After hearing about the miserable conditions and the dwindled number of most of his soldiers, Max I Joseph wrote to Napoleon asking to take the 'Brigade Rechberg' out of the line of action. The king was well informed that, despite Napoleon's disaster, Rechberg and his soldiers had performed brilliant work as they had continuously protected the northern flank of the main column of the army during the retreat under most difficult conditions and with only a few fit men. Therefore, on 24 March 1813, Rechberg, who was then on the way home to Bavaria, was promoted lieutenant-general of the infantry in Munich *in absentia*. In the very last battle of the retreat Rechberg's contingent had lost all its guns. After the Bavarian soldiers reached Bamberg the division was officially disbanded.

Back in Bavaria Rechberg joined the newly formed corps of General Karl Philipp von Wrede and was posted immediately to the Bavaro-Austrian border, where he stayed at Braunau on the river Inn in the expectation of a new Austrian attack. In the meantime his brother Aloys formed part of a high-ranking Bavarian delegation headed by Max I Joseph himself which negotiated in Vienna plans to switch allies. Following the treaty of Ried, as from 13 October 1813 Bavaria officially joined Prussia, Austria, Russia, Great Britain, Spain, Portugal, and Sweden in a new coalition. Bavaria was to participate with 36,000 troops against their old allies, the French. A few days before Rechberg had received orders to proceed with his division to the region of Landshut where the Bavarian general of the cavalry Wrede aimed to establish the headquarters of the unified Bavaro-Austrian troops.

After the French had been defeated in the 'battle of the nations' (*Völkerschlacht*) near Leipzig between 16 and 19 October 1813, General Wrede received intelligence that Napoleon intended to move his army through Fulda, Hanau, and Frankfurt a. M. back to France. Aiming to block this retreat, he proceeded with three divisions to the river Main near Hanau. In the battle at Hanau and Frankfurt, Rechberg led a Bavarian division. By a twist of destiny, his former brother in the Bavarian grand priory, Friedrich von Vieregg, again served in his division. Napoleon drove back the Bavarians and led his army back to France. As General Wrede was seriously wounded near Frankfurt, Rechberg was temporarily made general commander of the Bavarian troops.

Subsequently Rechberg and the Bavarians marched west with the allies aiming to defeat the French troops totally. They were involved in the battles of Brienne-sur-Aube (1 Februrary 1814), Bar-sur-Aube (27 February 1814), and Arcis-sur-Aube (20 March 1814). Some days later the allied forces marched into Paris and Napoleon abdicated on 10 April. By the time the Treaty of Paris was signed on 30 May 1814, Rechberg already was on his way home to Bavaria.

Rechberg's return to Munich was short-lived. In March 1815 news arrived that Napoleon had returned from his exile at Elba. That spring the allies (Russia, Austria, Prussia, and Bavaria) gathered 150,000 men to invade France and end Napoleon's regime once and for all. Bavarian Field-Marshal Karl Philipp von Wrede ordered his generals to see that all their divisions and regiments were put in the best order again. The Bavarians stood under the general command of the Austrian Field-Marshal Prince Schwarzenberg. Rechberg was

Troops from Badensia and Bavaria engaged in the retreat battles of
Napoleon's Russia campaign, 1812/13

appointed general and served as the highest-ranking Bavarian
officer in the Austrian headquarters co-ordinating the joint
Bavaro-Austrian campaign. At the end of May Rechberg
followed the Bavarian troops to Mainz and Saarbrücken.
Together with the Prussians and Austrians, the majority of
the Bavarian contingents marched through Belgium to join
with the British. On 18 June 1815 Napoleon was defeated
decisively by the English and the Prussians at Waterloo.

In July negotiations took place in Paris about the temporary
stationing of allied troops on French territory. Together with
Wrede, Rechberg, who had received personal instructions
from Max I Joseph, participated in the negotiations. The
Bavarian delegates were then not in an easy position, as the
Bavarian king did not intend to join the other German princes
and allies in their plan to reduce French power and territory
drastically. His 'pro-German' son Ludwig, however, was
among the allies hardliners. In the autumn of 1815 Rechberg
was in charge of the transfer of one division of the Bavarian
contingents (composed of three divisions) from Belgium and
France to Munich. Even when serving in the Bavarian army,

the old Maltese-Bavarian connection was not cut but kept on flickering from time to time. With some interest, Rechberg had observed the rising military career of a comrade in the Bavarian army, the Maltese nobleman Michele Sceberras Testaferrata, who was later made knight of the Order of St George of Bavaria and a chamberlain of the king.

The military careers of Rechberg and Vieregg – who had become a major-general – had taken off and earned them universal merits while the affairs of their Order of St John were proceeding far less positive. Of course, the Bavarian knights kept taking a keen interest as to what happened to their 'old' institution. Lieutenant of the magistry Innico-Maria Guevara-Suardo died in April 1814, that is a short time before the signing of the peace treaty of Paris of 30 May 1814, article 7 of which officially incorporated Malta in the British Empire. In Spain the king had declared himself as grand master of the Spanish priories. All these bad news did not seem to be the last words as the planning for the Congress of Vienna was already in the pipeline to settle the upheavals caused by Napoleon and to return Europe to calm waters. The Order placed its hopes in the oncoming gathering of Europe's diplomats and representatives. Vienna seemed to be the last chance for the Order to regain lost ground. In the meantime the Sicilian *Balì* Andrea di Giovanni e Centelles had been elected lieutenant of the magistry and confirmed by the pope.

That the Bavarian court watched developments at the congress very keenly was only too natural. The official Bavarian representative at Vienna was none other than Joseph Maria's elder brother, Aloys. One aspect was surely the question of the Order of Malta. A good observer and commentator was Count Montgelas the all-powerful Bavarian minister who relates in his autobiography that the Order demanded the restitution of its old possessions in several memoirs and pamphlets. The Order's envoy at Vienna was the Italian knight Antonio Miari, whom Rechberg knew from his first sojourns in Malta in 1783 and 1784. In 1785 Miari was placed in command of the flagship of the Order's fleet and later held several important posts. In 1798 Rechberg met the Venetian Miari again who was then Hompesch's secretary for Italian affairs.

In the congress Miari painted a much more positive picture of his institution than the bitter facts of the reality really showed. Miari claimed that all its belongings in Sicily and Sardinia were still in the Order's possession, and that the duchy of Parma and the Papal State had just restored to the Order its old assets and lands. Even the Bohemian priory was still in existence, while the old possessions in Lombardy and Spain would also be returned. The hard facts were, however, very different. As a result of the French Revolution, the three French langues had disappeared. In Spain the king had made himself grand master of the Hospitallers in his country and had sequestrated all their possessions. With Napoleon's conquest of North Italy, all the Order's possessions there were sequestrated, while those in the south of Italy were sequestrated in 1811. One year before the two newly founded Russian grand priories had been dissolved by Alexander I. that meant that in 1811, only the grand priory of Bohemia-Austria remained fully functioning.

At the congress, Miari demanded that, instead of Malta, the Order should receive another land to rule and to cover its duties and obligations, with all European powers guaranteeing the Order's neutrality and independence. England was to compensate the Order for the property it had lost in Malta. The congress should insist that all European sovereigns were to return the Order's property and lands they had confiscated. The future role and obligations of the Order would be newly discussed and stipulated. England was amongst the leading opponents to these proposals and, to the Bavarian minister Montgelas' pleasure, most European states considered these negotiations as too complicated and time-consuming to get started. So, after a short while, there

Joseph Maria von Colloredo-Wallsee, Grand Prior of Bohemia (1791 – 1818)

was a common agreement that the Order's demands should be not refused but slowly ignored. 'Good for us, because of the once-rich possessions which the Order had in our country and which a couple of years ago had been taken into the hands of the state', so Montgelas commented.

A disadvantage for the Order's standing then was the fact that it did not even have a grand master. After Tommasi's death in 1805 in the temporary exile of the Order at Catania, the council of the Order had elected Innico-Maria Guevera-Suardo, but the pope as the supreme head of the Order had only allowed him to carry the title of a plenipotentary (lieutenant) of the grand master. It was not until 1889 that Pope Leo XIII again allowed the head of the Order, Cecchi di Santa Croce, to use the title of grand master.

Even when the congress of Vienna offered such a disappointing outcome, the remaining knights in Bohemia and Austria did not give up. Plans were drawn up for the Order to be given either Lissa or Elba as its new residence. Through the re-erection of a Polish grand priory, the Order was to be re-established in Russia. In 1817 Count Ens proposed that the Order should be turned into a confederation; the Catholics were to remain subject of the Holy See but the Order would unify the Protestants and Orthodox branches as a sort of naval policeman. This project to re-establish the Order in the Mediterranean had already been proposed in a book published in 1815 by the councillor of the duke of Schwarzenberg-Rudolstadt, Friedrich Herrmann. But already the roots were being laid for a resurrection of the honourable Order on another level. This, however, goes beyond the framework of the lifetime of the protagonist of this book and the scope of this book.

After Vienna and the settling down of the previous European upheavals, even the men of the Bavarian ministries and higher officials were changed. The Rechberg family played an important part in this development. Joseph Maria von Rechberg's brother Aloys was recalled from his post as Bavarian ambassador and later held the positions of Bavarian minister of foreign affairs and in 1817 succeeded Count Montgelas. Joseph Maria's younger brother, Johann Nepomuk Xaver von Rechberg zu Elkofen, was promoted royal chamberlain and held various positions in the country's higher administration. In the last years of his service, he held the post of commissioner of forestry. Also for Joseph Maria von Rechberg, the end of the Napoleonic era meant a change in career. In late December 1815 he left military service.

In the months before Rechberg had tried hard to join the pool of potential candidates for Bavarian ambassadors and *chargès d`affaires* at foreign courts and had written several times to Montgelas offering himself as a suitable ambassador at the courts of Turin, Milan, Naples, or Paris. For the moment Montgelas and Max I Joseph ignored these offers but it was obvious that, sooner or later, a suitable position for the cosmopolitan, loyal, and experienced general would arise. In early January 1816, he was informed that he was earmarked for the position of Bavarian *envoye extraordinaire* at the court of Prussia in Berlin. On 26 January he was officially appointed as envoy with the rank of a minister. Rechberg accepted and served in Berlin until his retirement in early September 1825, officially owing to health reasons. That Rechberg offered to retire might have been also caused by the fact that the Bavarian government had provided the embassy in Berlin with much less funds than the embassies in Paris or Vienna. This was met with some bitterness by Prussia and was interpreted that the Bavarians were to give Berlin a diminished importance. Rechberg's applications to be transferred to other embassies during his spell in Berlin were constantly ignored. His performance in Berlin, however, must have been impeccable and there were never any complaints about his work and conduct. In fact during his time in the embassy he was awarded with the highest Bavarian medals and orders. He officially retired from active service in Easter 1826, with a yearly pension of 4,000 guilders.

While serving in Berlin, he could see that the Hospitallers were not completely forgotten in Prussia – at least the Protestant bailiwick of Brandenburg. On 23 May 1812 King Friedrich Wilhelm III founded a 'Royal-Prussian Order of St John' (*Königlich-Preussischer Johanniterorden*) with a simple cross of the Order as a symbol in memory of the bailiwick. All former members of the bailiwick of Brandenburg were admitted in this royal Order which had, however, rather the character of a court Order. The news from other countries were, however, rather depressing.

The restoration of the Order after the end of the Napoleonic era was a slow and difficult process indeed. In 1825 the grand priory of Messina was suppressed, followed in 1834 by that of Portugal. Some positive feedback did come from the Austrian-Bohemian grand priory which was still functioning. This was partly due to the protection of the powerful Austrian chancellor Klemens von Metternich, who would himself become a *balí* of honour and devotion of the Order. In 1818 at the congress of Aachen (Aix en Chapelle), Metternich had re-proposed the Order's case on the international platform. Discussions were held to re-install the Order in the Mediterranean as a charitable institution as well as an international naval police force, but nothing was concluded.

Andrea di Giovanni e Centelles died in Catania in 1821 and was succeeded as lieutenant of the magistry by the Milanese titular *Balí* of Armenia Antonio Busca who had close ties with Metternich, an important issue then as Austria, through dynastic connections and pure political interests, was again looking to dominate Northern and Central Italy.

Throughout all the years of wanderings in Malta, Catania, the battlefields of Europe, and in Berlin, Rechberg never had cut his close ties to his Swabian homelands. 'His' commandery at Mindelheim must have meant a lot for him. In fact, in 1820, he had the occasion – and the financial means – to buy some more parts of his former commandery and the adjoining farm for his private use. When Max I Joseph died in 1825 a new era of Bavarian politics began. His successor, the young King Ludwig I, removed many of the old guard of officers and diplomats. Among those who were replaced or resigned out of their own free will were Joseph Maria and Aloys von Rechberg. After Joseph Maria's retirement from Bavarian service in 1825, for most of the year he resided in Mindelheim, keeping himself busy administering his farm and property. Already during his active service he had taken great interest in the well-being of the former commandery of Mindelheim St Johannes. When the possession was running into heavy debts in 1815, Rechberg sold most of his huge and precious collection of paintings to Prince Ludwig von Oettingen-Wallerstein for 12,000 guilders to invest in

Mindelheim and to acquire the local brewery. The other parts of the year he spent in Munich and in the family residence at Donzdorf near Göppingen.

Throughout his service in Malta, in the Bavarian army, and in diplomacy, Rechberg had always interested himself in the arts. In his Munich residence he gathered an impressive collection of paintings by Italian, German, and Dutch masters, some of which are exhibited in the Alte Pinakothek collection in Munich and in the British Museum in London. His legacy of collected books and maps echo some of his Maltese connections. It includes a very rare collection of maps of all commanderies of the Order of St John, Johann Michael von Borch's *Lettres sur la Sicile et Malthe* (2 vols., Turin, 1783), an Arabic grammar, and books and maps on the Barbary coast and Algiers. Joseph Maria von Rechberg died of cholera at the age of 64 on 27 March 1833. He left no children.

SOURCES AND FURTHER READING REFERRING TO THE RESPECTIVE CHAPTERS

Introduction – A Knight and his principles

Boisgelin de Kerdu, Louis de, *Ancient and Modern Malta*, 3 vols. (London, 1805).

Castillo, Dennis, *The Maltese Cross. A Strategic History of Malta* (Westport 2006).

Freller, Thomas, 'Korsarenjäger, General und Gesandter – Joseph Maria von Rechberg und Rothenlöwen (1769–1833)', *Militärgeschichtliche Zeitschrift*, lxv, 2 (2006), 485–504.

Galea, Michael, *German Knights of Malta. A Gallery of Portraits* (Malta, 1986).

Galea, Michael, *Grand Master Emanuel de Rohan. 1775–1797* (Malta, 1996).

Gemeinder, Emil (ed.), *Joseph Maria von Rechberg: Kriegszug gegen Algier* (Schwäbisch Gmünd, 1971).

Hoppen, Alison, *The Fortification of Malta by the Order of St John 1530–1798* (Malta, 1999).

Maisonneuve, Joseph de, *Annales Historiques de l'Ordre Souverain de St Jean de Jerusalem depuis l'année 1725 jusqu'au moment présent* (St Petersburg, 1799).

Meyer de Knonau, Charles Joseph, *Révolution de Malte en 1798; gouvernement, principes, lois, statuts de l'Ordre. Réponse au manifeste du Prieuré de Russie* (Trieste, 1799).

'*Note des Prieurs Commandeurs et Chevaliers designés par S.A.S.E. pour former la nouvelle Langue Anglo Bavaroise*' (1783), Bayerisches Hauptstaatsarchiv München, Kasten schwarz 10132, II, ff. 801r–2r.

Panzavecchia, Fortunato, *L'ultimo periodo della Storia di Malta* (Malta, 1835).

Spiteri, Stephen, *Fortresses of the Cross. Hospitaller Military Architecture (1136-1798)* (Malta, 1994).

Testa, Carmel, *The French in Malta. 1798-1800* (Malta, 1997).

'Verzeichnis der Commenthuren', 'Verzeichnis der Ritter', Bayerisches Hauptstaatsarchiv München, Kasten schwarz, 10132, II, ff. ibid. 870r–5r.

Wismayer, Joseph, *The Fleet of the Order of St John 1530–1798* (Malta, 1997).

Chapter 1 – A youth in the shadow of the Cross of Malta

Archive of the Rechberg Family, Donzdorf, RA A 433, 613, 619, 630 (correspondence of Maximilian Emanuel von Rechberg).

Archive of the Order of Malta, Valletta, MS. 162, f. 11v (regulations for acceptance into the Anglo-Bavarian langue); ff. 152r–4v (= reception of Baron Joseph Maria von Sandizell); f. 266r (reception of Joseph Maria von Rechberg); MS. 163, ff. 72r–3v (= confirmation of the holders of the commanderies in Bavaria from 22 October 1784), ff. 74r–v (= schedule of the commanderies of the Bavarian grand priory with their responsions (drawn on 22 October 1784); MS. 273, ff. 278r–83r (= establishment of the Bavarian grand priory); MS. 273, ff. 286v–7v (= on the regulations and positions of the Anglo-Bavarian langue); MS. 273, f. 291 (= structure of the Bavarian grand priory and of the 28 Bavarian commanderies); MS. 586, ff. 214r–16r (= establishment of the Bavarian grand priory).

Aretin, Hubert von, 'Die Bayerische Zunge des Souverainen Ordens vom H. Johannes zu Jerusalem (Malteser Orden) 1782-1808', *RSMOM*, ii, 16 (July 1938).

Ay, Karl Ludwig, *Land und Fürst im alten Bayern. 16–18. Jahrhundert* (Ratisbon, n.y.).

Cavaliero, Roderick, *The last of the Crusaders. The knights of St John and Malta in the eighteenth century* (London, 1960),

Die Stiftsmäßigkeit des gegenwärtig in Bayern immatrikulierten Adels in Bezug auf das Hochstift Würzburg. Reprint of the edition of 1871. (Wiesbaden, 1981) (= Genealogy of the Barons and Counts of Rechberg).

Engel, Leopold, *Geschichte des Illuminaten-Ordens. Ein Beitrag zur Geschichte Bayerns* (Berlin, 1906).

'Etablissement de la Langue de Bavière', National Library of Malta, MS. 421, ff. 49r–53v; 203r–9v.

Freller, Thomas, 'Die "Malteserkrise". Anmerkungen zum bayerisch-russischen Verhältnis am Beginn der Regierungszeit Max IV. Joseph', *Zeitschrift für bayerische Landesgeschichte*, lxix, 2 (2006), 595–643.

Freller, Thomas, *The Anglo-Bavarian Langue of the Order of Malta* (Malta, 2000).

Gemeinder, Emil (ed.), *Joseph Maria von Rechberg: Kriegszug gegen Algier* (Schwäbisch Gmünd, 1971).

Hausberger, Karl, Benno Hubensteiner, *Bayerische Kirchengeschichte* (n.pl., 1985).

Journal politique ou gazette des gazettes (Bouilon), 1783, Janvier 2me quinzaine.

Kurbaierisches Intelligenzblatt, Munich (1782), xxvi.

Kurbaierischen Intelligenzblatt, Munich (1783), lxii (= List of commanders of the Anglo-Bavarian langue).

Münchner Staats-, gelehrte und vermischte Nachrichten (1782), cxcvi.

'*Note des Commandeurs et Chevaliers aspirant dans l'Ordre de Malte*' (1781), Bayerisches Hauptstaatsarchiv München, Kasten schwarz, 10132, I, f. 244r–v.

'*Note des Prïeurs Commandurs et Chevaliers designés par S. A. S. E. pour former la nouvelle Langue Anglo Bavaroise*' (1783), Bayerisches Hauptstaatsarchiv München, Kasten schwarz, 10132, II, ff. 801r–2r.

Panzavecchia, Fortunato, *L'ultimo periodo della Storia di Malta* (Malta, 1835).

'Piano dell'erezzione della Lingua di Baviera nell'Ordine di Malta, 1782', Archives of the Grand Magistry, Palazzo di Malta, Rome, LABR, I.

Rall, Hans, *Kurfürst Karl Theodor, Regierender Herr in sieben Ländern* (Mannheim–Leipzig–Vienna–Zurich, 1993).

Sherbowitz-Wetzor, Olgerd de, Cyril Toumanoff, *The Order of Malta and the Russian Empire* (Rome, 1969).

Steinberger, Ludwig, *Die Gründung der baierischen Zunge des Malteserordens* (Berlin, 1911).

'Verzeichnis der Commenthuren', 'Verzeichnis der Ritter', Bayerisches Hauptstaatsarchiv München, Kasten schwarz, 10132, ii, ff. 870r–5r.

Chapter 2 – A page in Malta – and a tense atmosphere

Archive of the Family of Rechberg, Donzdorf, HA K 34, F 11 (letters from Joseph Maria von Rechberg to his family); RA A 422 (documents and receipts of Rechberg's expenditure in Malta between August 1783 and May 1787).

Archive of the Order of Malta, Valletta, MS. 162, f. 114r; MS. 163, f. 236; MS. 273, f. 283r, f. 287r–v; MS. 586, f. 214r–v. (= appointment of Flachslanden as lieutenant of the grand prior and co-adjutor with the right of succession; bestowal of the turcopiliership on Flachslanden and its lieutenancy on Baron Friedrich von Vieregg).

Barz, Wolf-Dieter 'Die letzte Karawane des Johanniterordens von 1784. Betrachtet im Zusammenhang mit seinem Niedergang auf Malta', *Militärgeschichtliche Mitteilungen*, 44 (1988), 41–9.

Benhadda, Abderrehim, *Le Maroc et la Sublime Porte (XVIe-XVIIIe siècles)* (Zaghouan, 1998).

Bono, Salvatore, *I corsari barbareschi* (Turin, 1964).

Cavaliero, Roderick, 'The Decline of the Maltese Corso in the XVIIIth Century. A Study in Maritime History', *Melita Historica*, ii, 4 (1959), 224–38.

Cook, Weston Fr. *The hundred years war for Morocco: gunpowder and the military revolution in the early modern Muslim world* (Boulder, 1994).

Darmanin Demajo, G., 'La lingue Angla Bavara e la sua albergia', *Archivio Storico di Malta* Anno VII, xiv, Fasc. II (28 January 1936), 224–236.

Earle, Peter, *Corsairs of Malta and Barbary* (London, 1970).

Fontenay, Michel, 'Corsaires de la foi ou rentiers du sol? Les chevaliers de Malte dans le corso méditerranéen au XVIIe siècle', *Revue d'Histoire Moderne et Contemporaine*, xxxv (July–September 1988), 361–84.

Fontenay, Michel, 'Les missions des galères de Malte, 1530–1798', in *Guerre et commerce en Méditerranée, IXe-XXe siècles*, ed. M. Verge Franceschi (Paris,

1991).

Fontenay, Michel, 'The Mediterranean World, 1500–1800: Social and Economic Perspectives.', in *Hospitaller Malta 1530–1798. Studies on Early Modern Malta and the Order of St John of Jerusalem*, ed. V. Mallia-Milanes (Malta, 1993), 43–110.

Fontenay, Michel, Tenenti, Alberto, 'Course et piraterie méditerranéennes de la fin du Moyen Age au début du XIXe siècle', in *Course et Piraterie. 18e Colloque International d'Histoire maritime* (San Francisco, 1975; (Paris, 1975), 78–131.

Freller, Thomas, '"The Shining of the Moon" – The Mediterranean Tour of Muhammad Ibn Uthm□n, envoy of Morocco, in 1782', *Journal of Mediterranean Studies* xii, 2 (2002), 307–26.

Gemeinder, Emil (ed.), *Joseph Maria von Rechberg: Kriegszug gegen Algier* (Schwäbisch Gmünd, 1971).

Haeffelin, Casimir, 'Memoir' (1782), Bayerisches Hauptstaatsarchiv München, Kasten schwarz, 10132, I (= on the resistance of the French against the establishment of the Anglo-Bavarian Langue).

Lourido-Díaz, Ramón, *Marruecos en la segunda mitad del siglo XVIII* (Madrid, 1978).

Rodriguez Casado, Vicente, *Política marroquí de Carlos III* (Madrid, 1946).

Rossi, Ettore, 'Corrispondenza fra i Pascia di Tripoli ed i Gran Maestri dell'Ordine a Malta dal 1711 al 1766', *Rivista degli Studi Orientali*, 10 (1923–25), 414–32.

Rossi, Ettore, 'Il dominio dei cavalieri di Malta a Tripoli 1530–1551, e i rapporti dell'Ordine con Tripoli nei secoli seguenti 1551–1798', *Archivum Melitense*, vi, 2 (1924), 43–85.

Rossi, Ettore, 'Manoscritti e documenti orientali nelle Biblioteche e negli Archivi di Malta', *Archivio Storico di Malta*, Anno 2, 2, fasc. I (October-December 1930), 1–10.

Ryan, Frederick R., *The House of the Temple: A Study of Malta and its Knights in the French Revolution* (London 1930).

Steinberger, Ludwig, *Die Gründung der baierischen Zunge des Malteserordens* (Berlin, 1911).

Valensi, L., 'Esclaves Chrétiens et Esclaves Noirs à Tunis au XVIIIe Siècle', *Annales É.S.C.* xxii, 6 (1967), 1267–88.

Wettinger, Godfrey, *Slavery in the Islands of Malta and Gozo (ca. 1000–1812)* (Malta, 2002).

Chapter 3 – In the limelight of history – The campaign of Algiers

Antier, Jean Jacques, *Marins de Provence et du Languedoc. Ving-cinq siecles d'histoire du littoral français mediteranéen* (Avignon, 1977).

Archive of the Family of Rechberg, Donzdorf, RA A 692 (diary of Joseph Maria von Rechberg during his caravans in 1784).

Archive of the Order of Malta, Valletta, MS. 2221, MS. 6430, MS. 6431 (= 'Cariche in Convento' on the promotion of commanders and officers and with lists of captains and officers of the navy of the Order active in the 1780s).

Barz, Wolf-Dieter 'Die letzte Karawane des Johanniterordens von 1784. Betrachtet im Zusammenhang mit seinem Niedergang auf Malta', *Militärgeschichtliche Mitteilungen*, 44 (1988), 41–9.

Boisgelin de Kerdu, Louis de, *Ancient and Modern Malta*, ii (London, 1805).

Bono, Salvatore, *I corsari barbareschi* (Turin, 1964).

Cavaliero, Roderick, *Admiral Satan. The Life and Campaigns of Suffren* (London–New York, 1994).

Cervera y Jácome, J., *El Panteón de Marinos Ilustres* (Madrid, 1926).

Dauber, Robert L., *Die Marine des Johanniter-Malteser Ritter Ordens* (Graz–Gnas, 1989).

De Bray, François Gabriel, *Aus dem Leben eines Diplomaten alter Schule. Aufzeichnngen und Denkwürdigkeiten des Grafen François Gabriel de Bray* (Leipzig, 1901).

De Bray, François Gabriel, 'Un témoin de la Révolution française à l'étranger, d'après la correspondance inédite du Chevalier de Bray', *Revue d'histoire diplomatique*, Year 23 (1909), 354–597; Year 25 (1911), 559–90.

Earle, Peter, *Corsairs of Malta and Barbary* (London, 1970).

Fernán-Núñez, Conde de, *Vida de Carlos III* (Madrid, 1898).

Fernández Duro, Cesáreo, *La Armada Española, desde la unión de los reinos de Castilla y Aragón*, viii (Madrid, 1973).

Fontenay, Michel, 'Corsaires de la foi ou rentiers du sol? Les chevaliers de Malte dans le corso méditerranéen au XVIIe siècle.', *Revue d'Histoire Moderne et Contemporaine*, xxxv (July–September 1988), 361–84.

Fontenay, Michel, 'Les missions des galères de Malte, 1530–1798', in *Guerre et commerce en Méditerranée, IXe-XXe siècles*, ed. M. Verge Franceschi, (Paris, 1991).

Fontenay, Michel, 'The Mediterranean World, 1500–1800: Social and Economic Perspectives.', in *Hospitaller Malta 1530–1798. Studies on Early Modern Malta and the Order of St John of Jerusalem*, ed. V. Mallia-Milanes (Malta, 1993), 43–110.

Fontenay, Michel, Tenenti, Alberto, 'Course et piraterie méditerranéennes de la fin du Moyen Age au début du XIXe siècle.', in *Course et Piraterie. 18e Colloque International d'Histoire maritime* (San Francisco, 1975) (Paris, 1975), 78–131.

Gemeinder, Emil (ed.), *Joseph Maria von Rechberg: Kriegszug gegen Algier* (Schwäbisch Gmünd, 1971).

Gomez Vizcaino, Juan Antonio, *Antonio Barceló y Pont de la Terra. De Patron de jabeque – correo a Tenente General de la Real Armada* (Madrid, 2007).

Herrmann, Friedrich, *Über die Seeräuber im Mittelmeer und ihre Vertilgung. Ein Völkerwunsch an den erlauchten Kongreß in Wien. Mit den nöthigen historischen und statistischen Erläuterungen* (Lübeck, 1815).

Lang, Karl Heinrich Ritter von, *Memoiren* (Braunschweig, 1842).

Loth, Jules, *Le Chevalier des soirées de St Petersbourg* (Rouen, 1885).

Lynch, John, *Bourbon Spain 1700–1808* (Oxford, 1993).

Moreno, José, *Viage á Constantinopla en el año de 1784* (Madrid, 1790).

Mori Ubaldini, Ubaldo, *La Marina del Sovrano Militare Ordine di San Giovanni* (Rome, 1971).

Muscat, Joseph, *Naval Activities of the Knights of St John 1530–1798* (Malta, 2002).

Muscat, Joseph, *The Maltese Vaxxell. The Third Rates of the Order of St John. 1700–1798* (Malta 1999).

Panzac, Daniel, *Les corsaires barbaresques. La fin d'une épopée (1800–1830)* (Paris, 1999).

Rossi, Ettore, *Storia della Marina dell'Ordine di S. Giovanni di Gerusalemme di Rodi e di Malta* (Rome, 1926).

Shaler, William, *Algiers, political, historical, and civil…* (Boston, 1826).

'Spoglio della Corrispondenza attiva e passiva S. A. Ema. Il Gran Maestro Hompesch e di altre scritture e documenti restituiti dalla famiglia del fu Gran Maestro', Classe XXII, 'Relazione del Bombardamento di Algere dalla flotta Spagnola, Napoletana, Portoghesa e Maltese in Luglio 1784', Archives of the Grand Magistry, Palazzo di Malta, Rome.

Chapter 4 – Bavarian officer and member of the Order of Malta

Archive of the Rechberg Family, Donzdorf, HA K 34, F 5 (correspondence between Joseph Maria and his brother Aloys during the former's sojourn in Malta in 1785), ibid., F 11 (letters from Joseph Maria to his brothers during his military service in Munich in the late 1780s and early 1790s, and during his campaigns against the French in the mid-1790s), ibid. F 15 (documents referring to the nomination of Johann Nepomuk von Rechberg as candidate of the commandery of Mindelheim St Johannes); RA A 623 (correspondence of Maximilian Emanuel von Rechberg with his sons, referring to the exploits of Joseph Maria in the campaigns against the French in the mid-1790s.); RA A 625 (correspondence between Maximilian Emanuel von Rechberg and Joseph Maria); RA A 630 (correspondence between Maximilian Emanuel von Rechberg with Priest-Commander Johann Felix Eisele in May 1786).

Archives of the Order of Malta, Valletta, Malta, MS. 163, ff. 72r–3v (= confirmation of the holders of the commanderies in Bavaria from 22 October 1784); f. 73 (= appointment of 'il Nobe. Gio. Nepomuceno

Barone de Rechberg' as candidate-commander of the commandery of Mindelheim St Johannes); ff. 74r–v (= schedule of the commanderies of the Bavarian grand priory with their responsions (drawn on 22 October 1784); MS 274, f. 121r (details of the responsions of the Anglo-Bavarian langue, filed 17 September 1787); f. 188v (= 'onoraggi, gaggie, e varie spese, relative alle ricette compresevi quelle degl'agenti' for the Anglo-Bavarian langue); MS. 861, ff. 401–12 (= list of expenses and use of money on behalf of the Anglo-Bavarian langue (1785–96), f. 413r (= responsions paid from Mindelheim in April 1798); MS 2195, ff. 1–189r (= list of the commanderies of the Anglo-Bavarian langue and the respective pensions for the holders and other dignities).

Barruel, A., *Nachrichten zur Erörterung der Geschichte der Entstehung, der Fortschritte und Folgen der Jakobiner in und außer Frankreich* (London, 1802).

Bayerisches Hauptstaatsarchiv, München, Gr Fasz. 742, No. 80/1 (= minutes of the provincial chapters of the Anglo-Bavarian langue and the Bavarian grand priory 1784–94); No. 82 (= minutes of the provincial chapters of the Anglo-Bavarian Langue and the Bavarian Grand Priory 1781–1802); No. 84 (= 'Responsioni Baviera pro anno 1796'); No. 87 (= minutes of the provincial chapters of the Anglo-Bavarian langue and the Bavarian grand priory 1783–87).

Bayerisches Hauptstaatsarchiv, München, Kasten blau 428/5 (former based in 'Königliches Kreisarchiv', Munich, Serie A, General Registratur, Fasc. 742, 44 ecclesiastical affairs, Nos. 73–87) (= documents on the administration of the inner affairs of the Anglo-Bavarian langue).

Broadley, A. M., *History of Freemasonry ... in Malta from 1800* (London, 1880).

De Bray, François Gabriel, 'Mémoire sur l'importance de conserver l'Isle de Malte dans les mains de ses Souverains actuels' (1794), National Library of Malta, Valletta, MS. 1259, ff. 1–27.

Développement de la motion de M. Camus relativement a l'Ordre de Malte (Paris, 1790).

Distler, Uwe, *Franz Albert Leopold von Oberndorff. Die Politik Pfalzbayerns (1778–1795)* (Kaiserslautern, 2000).

Du Moulin-Eckart, Richard, *Bayern unter dem Ministerium Montgelas 1799–1817*, i (Munich, 1895).

Fichtl, Wilhelm, 'Aufklärung und Zensur', in *Krone und Verfassung* (Munich, 1992), 174–85.

Flachslanden, Johann Baptist, 'Examen de la Motion relativement à l'Ordre de Malte et Réponse sommaire par un Citoyen de l'Ancien Ordre du Tiers Etat' (February 1790), Archive of the Order of Malta, Valletta, MS 6406.

Freller, Thomas, *The Anglo Bavarian Langue of the Order of Malta* (Malta, 2001).

Gemeinder, Emil (ed.), *Joseph Maria von Rechberg: Kriegszug gegen Algier* (Schwäbisch Gmünd, 1971).

Gumppenberg, Ludwig A., 'Das bayerische Gross-Priorat des Johanniter-Ordens', *Oberbayerisches Archiv für vaterländische Geschichte*, iv (1843).

Habel, Heinrich, *Landkreis Mindelheim* (Munich, 1971).

Haeffelin, Casimir, 'Aus den Statuten des Ordens St Johann von Jerusalem zu Malta. Denen Brüdern der Englisch-Baierischen Zunge zum besseren Verständniß der üblichen Wörter und richtigen Wissenschaft mitgeteilt. Anno 1793', Bayerisches Hauptstaatsarchiv, München, Cod. Germ. 4282.

Haeffelin, Casimir, 'Travel diary Malta 1796/97', Bayerisches Hauptstaatsarchiv, München, GR fasz. 742/79.

Hammermayer, Ludwig, 'Illuminaten in Bayern. Zu Geschichte, Fortwirken und Legende des Geheimbundes', in, *Krone und Verfassung* (Munich, 1992), 147–73.

'Journal du Bailli de la Tour du Pin', National Library of Malta, Valletta, Libr. MS. 1130.

Kayser, Christoph Albrecht, *Neuestes Gemählde von Malta* (Ronneburg–Leipzig, 1799).

Kleinschmidt, A., 'Der Vertrag von Gatschina', in, *Forschungen zur Geschichte Bayerns* vi (Ratisbon, 1898).

Litzenburger, Ludwig, 'Der bischöfliche Informativprozeß des Münchener Hofbibliothekars Casimir Haeffelin', *Römische Quartalschrift* 50 (1955), 230–47.

Loras, Charles Abel de, 'Observations sur la langue anglo-bavaroise', National Library of Malta, Libr. MS. 421, ff. 142r–5v.

Panzavecchia, Fortunato, *L'ultimo periodo della Storia di Malta* (Malta, 1835).

'Piano dell'erezzione della Lingua di Baviera nell'Ordine di Malta, 1782', Archives of the Grand Magistry, Palazzo di Malta, Rome, LABR, I.

Schermerhorn, Elizabeth, *Malta of the Knights* (Surrey, 1929).

Schüttler, H., *Die Mitglieder des Illuminatenordens 1776-1787/93* (n.pl., 1991) (= Deutsche Hochschuledition, vol. 18).

Van Dülmen, Richard *Der Geheimbund der Illuminaten* (Stuttgart–Bad Cannstadt, 1977).

Chapter 5 – A dangerous mission and the last days of Hospitaller Malta

Antier, Jean Jacques, *Marins de Provence et du Languedoc. Ving-cinq siecles d' histoire du littoral français mediteranéen* (Avignon, 1977).

Archive of the Rechberg family, Donzdorf, HA K 34 F 11 (correspondence between Joseph Maria and his brother Franz Xaver referring to the plans to take over the commandery of Mindelheim St Johannes from his brother Johann Nepomuk); F 14, F 15 (correspondence of Joseph Maria to his brothers concerning his voyage to Malta in the spring of 1798); RA A 623 (correspondence between Maximilian Emanuel von

Rechberg and his son Aloys referring to Joseph Maria's promotion to the post of castellan of the Anglo-Bavarian langue, November 1795).

Archive of the Order of Malta, Valletta, MS 275, f. 70r.; 277, ff. 5r–v (= report on the capture of a Tunisian pink near Gozo by the squadron of Lieutenant-General *Balí* Paul Julian Suffren de Saint Tropez on 29 April 1798).

Dauber, Robert L., *Die Marine des Johanniter-Malteser Ritter Ordens* (Graz–Gnas, 1989).

Gemeinder, Emil (ed.), *Joseph Maria von Rechberg: Kriegszug gegen Algier* (Schwäbisch Gmünd, 1971).

Hoppen, Alison, *The Fortification of Malta by the Order of St John 1530–1798* (Malta, 1999).

Hurter, Friedrich (ed.), *Denkwürdigkeiten aus den letzten Decennium des achtzehnten Jahrhunderts* (Schaffhausen, 1840).

'Journal du Bailli de la Tour du Pin', National Library of Malta, Valletta, Libr. MS. 1130.

Lavigerie, Olivier de, *L'Ordre de Malta depuis la Révolution Française* (Paris, 1889).

Meyer de Knonau, Charles Joseph, 'collection of letters and papers', National Library of Malta, Valletta, Libr. MSS 418–21.

Meyer de Knonau, Charles Joseph, *Révolution de Malte en 1798; gouvernement, principes, lois, status del'Ordre. Réponse au manifeste du Prieuré de Russie* (Trieste, 1799).

Mori Ubaldini, Ubaldo, *La Marina del Sovrano Militare Ordine di San Giovanni* (Rome, 1971).

Müller, Adolph, *Bayerische Politik und Bayerische Diplomaten zur Zeit Carl Theodors und Max Josephs* (Munich, 1954).

Panzavecchia, Fortunato, *L'ultimo periodo della Storia di Malta* (Malta, 1835).

'Précis de la prise de Malte', National Library of Malta, Valletta, Libr. MS. 420.

Spiteri, Stephen C., *Fortresses of the Cross. Hospitaller Military Architecture* (1136–1798) (Malta, 1994).

Testa, Carmel, *The French in Malta. 1798–1800* (Malta, 1997).

Wismayer, Joseph M., *The History of the King's Own Malta Regiment and the Armed Forces of the Order of St John* (Malta, 1989).

Chapter 6 – Fighting until the end

'Annales historiques', National Library of Malta, Valletta, Libr. MS. 269 (= comments on traitors who prevented the forts from being equipped with gunpowder and munitions).

Antier, Jean Jacques, *Marins de Provence et du Languedoc. Ving-cinq siecles d'histoire du littoral français mediteranéen* (Avignon, 1977).

Archive of the Rechberg family, Donzdorf, HA K 34 F 14 (collection of papers, reports and letters from Joseph Maria referring to the fall of Malta in June 1798 and his activities as commander of Fort Tigné).

Archivum Cathedralis Melitensis, Mdina, Malta, MS. 136 (= documents on the departure of Grand Master Hompesch and a list of knights who accompanied him).

Castillo, Dennis, *The Maltese Cross. A Strategic History of Malta* (Westport 2006).

Dauber, Robert L., *Die Marine des Johanniter-Malteser Ritter Ordens* (Graz–Gnas, 1989).

Freller, Thomas, *The Anglo-Bavarian Langue of the Order of Malta* (Malta, 2001).

Galea, Michael, *German Knights of Malta. A Gallery of Portraits* (Malta, 1986).

Gemeinder, Emil (ed.), *Joseph Maria von Rechberg: Kriegszug gegen Algier* (Schwäbisch Gmünd, 1971).

Hardman, William, *A History of Malta during the French and British Occupations, 1798–1800* (London, 1909).

Hoppen, Alison, *The Fortification of Malta by the Order of St John 1530–1798* (Malta, 1999).

Hurter, Friedrich (ed.), *Denkwürdigkeiten aus den letzten Decennium des achtzehnten Jahrhunderts* (Schaffhausen, 1840).

'Journal du Bailli de la Tour du Pin', National Library of Malta, Valletta, Libr. MS. 1130.

Lavigerie, Olivier de, *L'Ordre de Malta depuis la Révolution Française* (Paris, 1889).

Maisonneuve, Joseph de, *Annales Historiques de l'Ordre Souverain de St Jean de Jerusalem depuis l'année 1725 jusqu'au moment présent* (St Petersburg, 1799).

Meyer de Knonau, Charles Joseph, 'Collection of letters and papers', National Library of Malta, Valletta, Libr. MSS. 418–21.

Meyer de Knonau, Charles Joseph, *Révolution de Malte en 1798; gouvernement, principes, lois, status del'Ordre. Réponse au manifeste du Prieuré de Russie* (Trieste, 1799).

Mori Ubaldini, Ubaldo, *La Marina del Sovrano Militare Ordine di San Giovanni* (Rome, 1971).

Müller, Adolph, *Bayerische Politik und Bayerische Diplomaten zur Zeit Carl Theodors und Max Josephs* (Munich, 1954).

National Library of Malta, Valletta, Libr. MS. 421 (= documents on the departure of Hompesch and other knights of St John).

Panzavecchia, Fortunato, *L'ultimo periodo della Storia di Malta* (Malta, 1835).

'Précis de la prise de Malte', National Library of Malta, Valletta, Libr. MS. 420.

Spiteri, Stephen C., *Fortresses of the Cross. Hospitaller Military Architecture (1136–1798)* (Malta, 1994).

Terrinoni, G., *Memorie Storiche della resa di Malta ai Francesi nel 1798 e del S. M.*

Ordine Gerosolimitano dal detto anno ai nostri giorni (Rome, 1867).

Testa, Carmel, *The French in Malta. 1798–1800* (Malta, 1997).

Wismayer, Joseph M., *The History of the King's Own Malta Regiment and the Armed Forces of the Order of St John* (Malta, 1989).

Zammit, William, 'De Rohan's Reggimento di Malta: a source of religious unorthodoxy in late eighteenth-century Malta', *Sacra Militia*, iv (2005).

Chapter 7 – Immersed in the Order's struggle for survival

'*Acte d'Incorporation du Grand Prieuré de Russie dans l'ancienne Langue d'Angleterre actuellement Langue Anglo-Bavaro-Russe*' (4 January/7 August 1797), Archive of the Order of Malta, Valletta, MS. 2196, ff. 1r–5v, 72r–5v.

Archive of the Rechberg family, Donzdorf, HA K 34 F 11 / 14 (collection of papers and letters by Joseph Maria written in the summer and autumn of 1798 in Vienna to his brothers Aloys and Franz Xaver, referring to the situation and future of the Order of St John), ibid. F 5, F 14 (collection of letters from Joseph Maria referring to his participation in the French War of 1800 and 1801).

Artaud de Montor, A.F., *Histoire du Pape Pie VII*, i (Paris, 1839).

Distler, Uwe, *Franz Albert Leopold von Oberndorff. Die Politik Pfalzbayerns (1778–1795)* (Kaiserslautern, 2000).

Du Moulin-Eckart, Richard, *Bayern unter dem Ministerium Montgelas 1799–1817*, i (Munich, 1895).

Fichtl, Wilhelm, 'Aufklärung und Zensur', in *Krone und Verfassung* (Munich, 1992), 174–85.

Freller, Thomas, *The Anglo Bavarian Langue of the Order of Malta* (Malta, 2001).

Gemeinder, Emil (ed.), *Joseph Maria von Rechberg: Kriegszug gegen Algier* (Schwäbisch Gmünd, 1971).

Gumppenberg, Ludwig A., 'Das bayerische Gross-Priorat des Johanniter-Ordens', *Oberbayerisches Archiv für vaterländische Geschichte*, iv (1843).

Hardman, William, *A History of Malta during the period of the French and British Occupations, 1798–1815* (London, 1908).

Lavigerie, Olivier de, *L'Ordre de Malta depuis la Révolution Française* (Paris, 1889).

Maisonneuve, Joseph de, *Annales Historiques de l'Ordre Souverain de St Jean de Jerusalem depuis l'année 1725 jusqu'au moment présent* (St Petersburg, 1799).

National Library of Malta, Valletta, Libr. MS. 1130 (= documents on the departure of Grand Master Hompesch and a list of knights who accompanied him).

Kayser, Christoph Albrecht, *Neuestes Gemählde von Malta* (Ronneburg–Leipzig, 1799).

Mc Grew, R.E., *Paul I of Russia 1754–1801* (Oxford, 1992).

Meyer de Knonau, Charles Joseph, 'collection of letters and papers', National Library of Malta, Valletta, Libr. MSS. 418–21.

Panzavecchia, Fortunato, *L'ultimo periodo della Storia di Malta* (Malta, 1835).

Schermerhorn, Elizabeth, *Malta of the Knights* (Surrey, 1929).

Sherbowitz-Wetzor, Olgerd de; Toumanoff, Cyrill, *The Order of Malta and the Russian Empire* (Rome, 1969).

Sicherer, H. von, *Staat und Kirche in Bayern vom Regierungsantritt des Kurfürsten Maximilian Joseph IV. bis zur Erklärung von Tegernsee 1799–1821* (Munich, 1873).

Testa, Carmel, *The French in Malta. 1798–1800* (Malta, 1997).

Vivant Denon, Dominique, *Mit Napoleon in Ägypten. 1798–1799* (Tübingen, 1978).

Chapter 8 – Back in the Mediterranean – Bavarian envoy and spy in Catania

Archive of the Rechberg family, Donzdorf, HA K 34, F 5, F 14 (collection of letters and papers from Joseph Maria related to his mission in Catania).

Archives of the Grand Magistry, Palazzo di Malta, Rome, Conciliorum Status, I (1803–07), AGM. 'Russie', A) Sacré Conseil à Saint-Petersbourg, Grand-Prieurés de Russie, Correspondence, I–III Maisonneuve, IV Litta, V Serra Capriola; AGM 'Spoglio della Corrispondenza', Classe I a, No 4 / No 24; Classe II, No 6 / No 211 / No 215; Classe VI, No 222 / No 224 / No 244; Classe VII, No 782; Classe VIII, No 353.

Bayerisches Hauptstaatsarchiv, München, Kasten blau 428/5, Gr Fasz. 742, No. 86, 'Minutes of the provincial chapter of the Bavarian Grand Priory 1804–1809'; Kasten schwarz 398/35 (= Letters and reports sent by Rechberg from Catania to Munich).

Blondy, A., 'Malte et l'Ordre de Malte a l'epreuve des idees nouvelles (1740–1820)' unpublished habilitation thesis, University of Sorbonne (Paris IV) 1992/93, 4 vols.

Correspondence de Napoléon Ier publiée par ordre de l'empereur Napoléon III, xiii (Paris, 1863).

Doublet, P.J.L.O., *Memoires historiques sur l'invasion et l'occupation de Malte* (Paris, 1883).

Gemeinder, Emil (ed.), *Joseph Maria von Rechberg: Kriegszug gegen Algier* (Schwäbisch Gmünd, 1971).

Georgel, Jean François, *Mémoires pour servir á l'Histoire des Evènements de la fin du dixhuitième siècle, depuis 1760 jusqu'en 1806–1810* (Paris, 1818).

Graß, Karl Gotthard, *Sicilische Reise, oder Auszuege aus dem Tagebuche eines Landschaftsmalers*, 2 parts (Stuttgart, 1815).

Lavigerie, Olivier de, *L'Ordre de Malte depuis la Revolution Française* (Paris, 1889).

Panzac, Daniel, *Les corsaires barbaresques. La fin d'une épopée (1800–1820)* (Paris, 1999).

Panzavecchia, F., *L'ultimo periodo della Storia di Malta* (Malta, 1835).

Pierredon, Michel de, *Histoire politique de l'Ordre souverain de Saint Jean de Jérusalem (Ordre de Malte) de 1789 à 1955*, 2 vols. (Paris, 1956–63).

Rechberg, Joseph Maria von, 'Letters from Catania to Munich', Bayerisches Hauptstaatsarhiv München, Kasten schwarz 398/35.

Saul, E., *Russia and the Mediterranean 1796–1807* (Chicago, 1970).

Sherbowitz-Wetzor, Olgerd de, Cyrill Toumanoff, *The Order of Malta and the Russian Empire* (Rome, 1969).

Terrinoni, G., *Memorie Storiche della resa di Malta ai Francesi nel 1798 e del S.M. Ordine Gerosolimitano dal detto anno ai nostri giorni* (Rome, 1867).

Chapter 9 – A hero of the Napoleonic Wars and the closing of a circle

Archive of the Rechberg family, Donzdorf, HA K 34, F 11 (collection of letters and papers from Joseph Maria related to his participation in Napoleon's Russian campaign 1812/13.), ibid. F 14 (collection of letters and papers from Joseph Maria related to the running of the former commandery of Mindelheim St Johannes, 1819–23); RA A 245 (inventory of books which were in the legacy of Joseph Maria).

Archives of the Grand Magistry, Palazzo di Malta, Rome, Conciliorum Status, 1 (= Minutes of the chapter of the Anglo-Bavaro-Russo langue from June 1806).

Badisches Generallandesarchiv, Karlsruhe, 'Johanniter-Orden, Urkundenarchiv des Großpriorats Heitersheim', 20/176.

'Bayr. Großpriorat des Johanniterordens, Zentralkasse des aufgehobenen Johanniter-ordens bei Zentraladministration der ehemaligen Johanniterordens-Güter, 1809–1812', Bayerisches Hauptstaatsarchiv, München, Gr Fasz. 742, No 81 (= documentation of the income from the sequestrated property of the Bavarian grand priory).

Bayerisches Hauptstaatsarchiv, München, Kasten blau 428/5, Gr Fasz. 742, No. 86, 'Minutes of the provincial chapter of the Bavarian Grand Priory 1804–1809'.

Breycha-Vauthier de Baillamont, A.K., 'Das Großpriorat Böhmen-Österreich', in Adam Wienand, Karl Wilhelm von Ballestrem, Christoph von Imhof (eds.), *Der Johanniter-Orden. Der Malteser-Orden. Der ritterliche Orden des hl. Johannes vom Spital zu Jerusalem. Seine Geschichte, seine Aufgaben* (Cologne, 1988).

Castagnino Berlinghieri, Umberto, *Congresso di Vienna e principio di legittimità. La questione del Sovrano Militare Ordine di San Giovanni Gerosolimitano, detto di Malta* (Milan, 2006).

Chroust, A. (ed.), *Gesandtschaftsberichte aus München 1814-1848. Die Berichte der preußischen Gesandten*, 2 vols. (Munich, 1949/50) (= Schriftenreihe zur bayerischen Landesgeschichte vols. 39, 40).

Clark, Robert M., *The Evangelical Knights of Saint John. A history of the Bailiwick of Brandenburg* (Dallas, 2003).

Correspondence de Napoléon Ier publiée par ordre de l'empereur Napoléon III, xiii (Paris, 1863).

Die Stiftsmäßigkeit des gegenwärtig in Bayern immatrikulierten Adels in Bezug auf das Hochstift Würzburg. Reprint of the edition of 1871. (Wiesbaden, 1981) (= Genealogy of the Barons and Counts of Rechberg).

Du Moulin-Eckart, Richard, *Bayern unter dem Ministerium Montgelas 1799–1817*, i (Munich, 1895).

Freller, Thomas, *The Anglo-Bavarian Langue of the Order of Malta* (Malta, 2001).

Gemeinder, Emil (ed.), *Joseph Maria von Rechberg: Kriegszug gegen Algier* (Schwäbisch Gmünd, 1971).

Herrmann, Friedrich, *Über die Seeräuber im Mittelmeer und ihre Vertilgung. Ein Völkerwunsch an den erlauchten Kongreß in Wien. Mit den nöthigen historischen und statistischen Erläuterungen* (Lübeck, 1815).

Kayser, Albrecht Christoph, *Kurzgefasste Nachricht von Sr. Russisch Kaiserlichen Majestaet Paul I. Gelangung zur Wuerde eines Grossmeisters des Ordens St Johann von Jerusalem. Ein Auszug aus den Annales historique de l'Ordre Souverain de St Jean* (n.pl., 1802).

Kayser, Albrecht Christoph, *Nachricht von Kaiser Paul I. Gelangung zur Wuerde eines Grossmeisters des Malteserordens* (n.pl., 1799).

Klemm, Liselotte, *Aloys von Rechberg als bayerischer Politiker (1766–1849)* (Munich, 1975).

Lavigerie, Olivier de, *L'Ordre de Malta depuis la Révolution Française* (Paris, 1889).

Montgelas, M. von, *Denkwürdigkeiten des Bayerischen Staatsministers Maximilian Grafen von Montgelas (1799–1817). From the French original translated by Max Freiherr von Freyberg-Eisenberg*. Ed. by Ludwig Count of Montgelas. (Stuttgart, 1887).

Müller, Adolph, *Bayerische Politik und Bayerische Diplomaten zur Zeit Carl Theodors und Max Josephs* (Munich, 1954).

Pierredon, M. de, *Histoire politique de l'Ordre souverain de Saint Jean de Jérusalem (Ordre de Malte) de 1789 à 1955*, 2 vols. (Paris, 1956–63).

Sauter, Johann Anton, *Über den Maltheserorden* (Frankfurt a. M., 1804).

Sherbowitz-Wetzor, Olgerd de, Cyrill Toumanoff, *The Order of Malta and the Russian Empire* (Rome, 1969).

Völderndorff und Maradein, Eduard von, *Kriegsgeschichte von Bayern unter König Maximilian Joseph I*, i (Munich, 1826).

Waldstein-Wartenberg, Berthold, 'Entwicklung des Malteser-Ordens nach dem Fall von Malta bis zur Gegenwart', in Adam Wienand (ed.), *Der Johanniter-Orden. Der Malteser-Orden. Der ritterliche Orden des hl. Johannes vom Spital zu Jerusalem. Seine Aufgaben, seine Geschichte* (Cologne, 1970), 233–9.

Weis, Eberhard, *Montgelas. Der Architekt des modernen Bayerischen Staates 1799–1838*, ii (Munich, 2005).

BIBLIOGRAPHY

1) Archival-Manuscript Sources

Archive of the Rechberg family, Donzdorf:

HA K 34, F 5 (correspondence between Joseph Maria and his brother Aloys during the latter's sojourn in Malta in 1785, also including letters and papers from Joseph Maria related to his mission in Catania in 1804/5).

HA K 34, F 11 (letters from Joseph Maria to his brothers during his military service in Munich in the late 1780s and early 1790s, and during his campaigns against the French in the mid-1790s; also including the exchange between Joseph Maria with his brother Franz Xaver referring to the plans to take over the commandery of Mindelheim St Johannes from his brother Johann Nepomuk; also including a collection of papers and letters from Joseph Maria written in the summer and autumn 1798 in Vienna to his brothers Aloys and Franz Xaver, referring to the situation and future of the Order of St John, also including letters and papers from Joseph Maria related to his participation in Napoleon's Russian campaign of 1812/13).

HA K 34, F 14 (collection of papers, reports and letters from Joseph Maria referring to the fall of Malta in June 1798 and his activities as commander of Fort Tigné; also including a collection of letters from Joseph Maria referring to his participation in the French War of 1800 and 1801, also including letters and papers from Joseph Maria related to his mission in Catania 1804/5, also including letters and papers from Joseph Maria related to the running of the former commandery of Mindelheim St Johannes, 1819–23).

HA K 34, F 14 and F 15 (documents referring to the nomination of Johann Nepomuk von Rechberg as candidate of the commandery of Mindelheim St. Johannes, also including a collection of papers and letters by Joseph Maria written in the summer and autumn of 1798 in Vienna to his brothers Aloys and Franz Xaver, referring to the situation and future of the Order of St John, F 15 also including correspondence of Joseph Maria with his brothers concerning his voyage to Malta in spring 1798).

RA A 245 (inventory of books which were in the legacy of Joseph Maria).

RA A 422 (documents and receipts of Joseph Maria's expenditure in Malta between August 1783 and May 1787).

RA A 623 (correspondence of Maximilian Emanuel von Rechberg with his sons, referring to the exploits of Joseph Maria in the campaigns against the French in the mid-1790s; also including correspondence between Maximilian Emanuel von Rechberg with his son Aloys referring to Joseph Maria's promotion to the post of castellan of the Anglo-Bavarian langue, November 1795).

RA A 625 (correspondence between Maximilian Emanuel von Rechberg and Joseph Maria).

RA A 630 (correspondence between Maximilian Emanuel von Rechberg with Priest-Commander Johann Felix Eisele in May 1786).

RA A 692 (diary of Joseph Maria during his caravans in 1784).

Archives of the Grand Magistry, Palazzo di Malta, Rome:
AGM. Conciliorum Status, I (1803–07).
AGM. LABR, I 'Piano dell'erezzione della Lingua di Baviera nell'Ordine di Malta, 1782'.
AGM. 'Russie', A) Sacré Conseil à Saint-Petersbourg, B) Grand-Prieurés de Russie, C) Correspondence, I–III Maisonneuve, IV Litta, V Serra Capriola.
AGM. 'Spoglio della Corrispondenza', Classe I a, Nos. 4, 24, Classe II, Nos. 6, 211, 215, Classe VI, Nos. 222, 224, 244, Classe VII, No 782, Classe VIII, No 353.

Archive of the Order of Malta, Valletta:
(documents with relevance to Joseph Maria von Rechberg, his service in the Order, the commandery of Mindelheim and the Bavarian Grand Priory)
AOM. MSS. 136, 162, 163, 164, 203, 204, 205, 206, 260, 270, 273, 274, 275, 276, 277, 463, 575, 582, 583, 584, 585, 586, 589, 617, 861, 1237, 1526, 1534, 1535, 1536, 1537, 1538, 1539, 1540, 1581, 1582, 2195, 2196, 6406, 6425.

Archivum Cathedralis Melitensis, Mdina, Malta:
ACM., MS. 136 (= documents on the departure of Grand Master Hompesch and a list of knights who accompanied him).

Badisches Generallandesarchiv, Karlsruhe, Baden-Württemberg:
'Johanniter-Orden, Urkundenarchiv des Großpriorats Heitersheim', 20/176.

Bayerisches Hauptstaatsarchiv, München, Bavaria:

BHStAM. Kasten schwarz, 10132, I and II.
BHStAM. Kasten schwarz, 11935.
BHStAM. Kasten blau, 427/4.
BHStAM. Kasten blau 428/5 (= former based in 'Königliches Kreisarchiv', Munich, Serie A, General Registratur, Fasc. 742, 44 ecclesiastical affairs, Nos. 73–87).
Gr Fasz. 742, No 76, Bavarian Grand Priory of the Order of St John, 1798.
Gr Fasz. 742, No 77, Bavarian Grand Priory of the Order of St John.
Gr Fasz. 742, No 78, Bavarian Grand Priory of the Order of St John, 1795.
Gr Fasz. 742, No 79, Bavarian Grand Priory of the Order of St John, 1795-1798.
Gr Fasz. 742, No 80/1, Bavarian Grand Priory of the Order of St John, provincial chapter, 1784–94.
Gr Fasz. 742, No 82, Bavarian Grand Priory of the Order of St John, provincial chapter, 1781–1802.
Gr Fasz. 742, No 83, Bavarian Grand Priory of the Order of St John, 1786–1804.
Gr Fasz. 742, No 84, Bavarian Grand Priory of the Order of St John, 1796–97.
Gr Fasz. 742, No 85, Bavarian Grand Priory of the Order of St John, provincial chapter, no date.
Gr Fasz. 742, No 87, Bavarian Grand Priory of the Order of St John, provincial chapter, 1783–87.
BHStAM. Cod. Germ. 4282 ('Aus den Statuten des Ordens St Johann von Jerusalem zu Malta. Denen Brüdern der Englisch-Baierischen Zunge zum besseren Verständniß der üblichen Wörter und richtigen Wissenschaft mitgeteilt').
BHStAM. MA. 9385/7.

National Library of Malta, Valletta:
(documents with relevance to Joseph Maria von Rechberg, his service in the Order, the commandery of Mindelheim and the Bavarian Grand Priory)
NLM. Libr. MSS. 418–21 (papers and letters of the collection of Charles Joseph Meyer de Knonau), 1130, 1259.

2) **Single manuscript sources**
'*Acte d'Incorporation du Grand Prieuré de Russie dans l'ancienne Langue d'Angleterre actuellement Langue Anglo-Bavaro-Russe*' (4 January/7 August 1797), Archive of the Order of Malta, Valletta, MS 2196, ff. 1r–15v, 72r–5v.
'Bayr. Großpriorat des Johanniterordens, Zentralkasse des aufgehobenen

Johanniter-ordens bei Zentraladministration der ehemaligen Johanniterordens-Güter, 1809–1812', Bayerisches Hauptstaatsarchiv, München, Gr Fasz. 742, No 81 (= documentation of the income from the sequestrated property of the Bavarian grand priory).

De Bray, Fr. G., Mémoire sur l'mportance de conserver l'Isle de Malte dans les mains de ses Souverains actuels' (1794), National Library of Malta, Valletta, Libr. MS. 1259, ff. 1–27.

'Etablissement de la Langue de Bavière', National Library of Malta, Valletta, MS. 421, ff. 49r–53v, ff. 203r–9v.

Flachslanden, J.B., 'Examen de la Motion relativement à l'Ordre de Malte et Réponse sommaire par un Citoyen de l'Ancien Ordre du Tiers Etat' (February 1790), Archive of the Order of Malta, Valletta, MS. 6406.

Haeffelin, C., 'Aus den Statuten des Ordens St Johann von Jerusalem zu Malta. Denen Brüdern der Englisch-Baierischen Zunge zum besseren Verständniß der üblichen Wörter und richtigen Wissenschaft mitgeteilt. Anno 1793', Bayerisches Hauptstaatsarchiv, München, Cod. Germ. 4282).

Haeffelin, C., 'Travel diary Malta 1796/97', Bayerisches Hauptstaatsarchiv, München, GR fasc. 742/79.

'Journal du Bailli de la Tour du Pin', National Library of Malta, Valletta, Libr. MS 1130.

Loras, Charles Abel de, 'Observations sur la langue anglo-bavaroise', National Library of Malta, Valletta, Libr. MS 421, ff. 142r–5v.

Meyer de Knonau, Charles Joseph, 'collection of letters and papers', National Library of Malta, Valletta, Libr. MSS 418–21.

'Note des Commandeurs et Chevaliers aspirant dans l'Ordre de Malte' (1781), Bayerisches Hauptstaatsarchiv, München, Kasten schwarz, 10132, I, f. 244r–v.

'Note des Prieurs Commandeurs et Chevaliers designés par S.A.S.E. pour former la nouvelle Langue Anglo Bavaroise' (1783), Bayerisches Hauptstaatsarchiv, München, Kasten schwarz 10132, II, ff. 801r–2r.

'Précis de la prise de Malte', National Library of Malta, Valletta, Libr. MS. 420.

Rechberg, Joseph Maria von, 'Letters from Catania to Munich', Bayerisches Hauptstaatsarchiv, München, Kasten schwarz 398/35.

'Spoglio della Corrispondenza attiva e passiva S.A. Ema. Il Gran Maestro Hompesch e di altre scritture e documenti restituiti dalla famiglia del fu Gran Maestro', Classe XXII, 'Relazione del Bombardamento di Algere dalla flotta Spagnola, Napoletana, Portoghesa, e Maltese in Luglio 1784', Archives of the Grand Magistry, Palazzo di Malta, Rome.

'Verzeichnis der Commenthuren', 'Verzeichnis der Ritter', Bayerisches Hauptstaatsarchiv München, Kasten schwarz, 10132, II, ff. ibid. 870r–5r.

3 Printed works

a) Sources

Almanach de l'Ordre Souverain de Saint-Jean de Jérusalem (St Petersburg, 1800).

Anon., *Povsednenniya Zapiski Putyeshestviya v Sitsiliyu i Maltu v 1782 godu* (St Petersburg, 1784).

Barruel, A., *Nachrichten zur Erörterung der Geschichte der Entstehung, der Fortschritte und Folgen der Jakobiner in und außer Frankreich* (London, 1802).

Beschreibung der Feierlichkeiten, welche bei Ablegung der Gelübde in dem hohen Malteser-Orden beobachtet zu werden pflegen (Munich, 1783).

Beschreibung des feyerlichen Sterbegedächtnisses des durchlauchtigen Fürsten Rohan, welche zu München in der Prioratskirche des Malteserordens am 20. Dezember 1797 gefeyert wurde (Munich, 1798).

Bienemann, F. (ed.), *Aus den den Tagen Kaiser Pauls. Aufzeichnungen eines kurländischen Edelmanns* (Leipzig, 1886).

Boisgelin, L. de, *Ancient and Modern Malta*, 3 vols. (London, 1805).

Bosredon de Ransijat, I. F., *Journal du siège et blocus de Malta, depuis le 16 fructidor an 6 jusqu'au 22 fructidor an 8, jour de l'évacuation de cette place par la garnison française* (Paris, 1802).

Cherenkov, I., *Istoriya Ordena Svyatago Ioanna Ierusalimskago* (Woronesch, 1803).

Chroust, A. (ed.), *Gesandtschaftsberichte aus München 1814–1848. Die Berichte der preußischen Gesandten*, 2 vols. (Munich, 1949/50) (= Schriftenreihe zur bayerischen Landesgeschichte, vols. 39, 40).

Churbaierisches Intelligenz-Blatt, Munich, 24 May 1800, 12 April 1802.

Correspondence de Napoléon Ier publiée par ordre de l'empereur Napoléon III, xiii (Paris, 1863).

Czermack, H., *Kurzgefaßter Begriff von dem hohen Orden der Johanniter- oder Malteser-Ritter* (Munich, 1782).

De Bray, F.G., *Aus dem Leben eines Diplomaten alter Schule. Aufzeichnungen und Denkwürdigkeiten des Grafen François Gabriel de Bray* (Leipzig, 1901).

De Bray, F.G., 'Un témoin de la Révolution française à l'étranger, d'après la correspondance inédite du Chevalier de Bray', *Revue d'histoire diplomatique*, Year 23 (1909), 354–597; Year 25 (1911), 559–90.

Derzhavnii Orden Svyatago Ioanna, 4 vols. (St Petersburg, 1799–1804).

Développement de la motion de M. Camus relativement a l'Ordre de Malte (Paris, 1790).

Doublet, P.J.L.O., *Memoires historiques sur l'invasion et l'occupation de Malte* (Paris, 1883).

Ein Wort an die Stände Baierns (Frankfurt a. M., 1799).

Flachslanden, A.J.B., *Protestation contre le décret de l'Assemblée prétendue nationale* (Paris, 1790).

Flachslanden, A.J.B., *Réflexions sommaires et impartiales sur l'utilité de l'Ordre de S. Jean de Jérusalem et sur les dangers de sa suppression en France* (Paris, 1790).

223

Gemeinder, Emil (ed.), *Joseph Maria von Rechberg: Kriegszug gegen Algier* (Schwäbisch Gmünd, 1971).

Georgel, J.F., *Mémoires pour servir á l'Histoire des Evènements de la fin du dixhuitième siècle, depuis 1760 jusqu'en 1806–1810* (Paris, 1818).

Georgel, J.F., *Voyage à Saint Pétersbourg, en 1799-1800, fait avec l'ambassade des Chevaliers de l'Ordre de St. Jean de Jérusalem, allant offrir à l'Empereur Paul premier la grand Maîtraise de l'Ordre* (Paris, 1818).

Hurter, Fr. (ed.), *Denkwürdigkeiten aus dem letzten Decennium des achtzehnten Jahrhunderts* (Schaffhausen, 1840).

Istoricheskoye Sokrasheniye Derzhaynago Ordena Svyatago Ioanna Ierusalemskago (St Petersburg, 1800).

Ittner, J.A. von, *Kurzgefaßte Nachricht von Kaiser Pauls I. Erlangung zur Würde eines Großmeisters des Johanniterordens* (n.pl., 1802).

Ittner, J.A. von, *Paul der Erste, russischer Kaiser, als Großmeister des Malteserordens* (Aarau, 1808).

Journal politique ou gazette des gazettes (Bouilon), 1783, Janvier 2me quinzaine.

Kayser, A.C., *Neuestes Gemälde von Malta* 3 vols. (Ronneburg–Leipzig, 1799–1800).

Krayevski, G., *Kratkoye Tipograficheskoye, Istoricheskoye i Politicheskoye Opisaniye Ostrova Malti*, 2 vols. (St Petersburg, 1800–01).

Kurzgefasste Nachricht von Sr. Russisch-Kaiserl. Majestät Paul I. Gelangung zur Würde eines Grossmeisters des Ordens St Johann von Jerusalem und von Höchstgedacht Sr. Kaiserl. Majestät neuen Johanniterritterordensstiftung (n.pl., 1799, re-published 1802).

Längenfeld, J.N., *Kurzgefaßte pragmatische Geschichte des hohen Malteserordens.* (Munich, 1783).

Lang, K.H.R. von, *Memoiren. Skizzen aus meinem Leben und Wirken, meinen Reisen und meiner Zeit* (Braunschweig, 1842).

Lipowsky, E., *Leben und Thaten Kurfürst Karl Theodors* (Sulzbach, 1828).

Maisonneuve, J. de, *Annales Historiques de l'Ordre Souverain de St Jean de Jerusalem depuis l'année 1725 jusqu'au moment présent* (St Petersburg, 1799).

Mayr, G.K. (ed.), *Sammlung der neuest- und merkwürdigsten Churbaierischen Generalien und Landesverordnungen*, 6 vols. (Munich, 1784–99).

Meyer de Knonau, J.C., *Révolution de Malte en 1798; gouvernement, principes, lois, statuts de l'Ordre. Réponse au manifeste du Prieuré de Russie* (Trieste, 1799).

Montgelas, M. von, *Denkwürdigkeiten des Bayerischen Staatsministers Maximilian Grafen von Montgelas (1799–1817).* From the French original translated by Max Freiherr von Freyberg-Eisenberg. Ed. by Ludwig Count of Montgelas (Stuttgart, 1887).

Münter, F., *Aus dem Briefwechsel Friedrich Münters. Europäische Beziehungen eines Dänischen Gelehrten. 1780–1830.* Ed. by Ojvind Andreasen, 3 parts (Copenhagen–Leipzig, 1944).

Sauter, J.A., *Über den Maltheserorden* (Frankfurt a. M., 1804).

Stengel, St von, *Denkwürdigkeiten*. Ed. by Günther Ebersold (Mannheim, 1993).

Theiner, A. (ed.), *Clementis XIV pontificis maximi epistolae et brevia selectiora ac nonnulla alia acta pontificatum eius illustrantia* (Paris, 1852).

Vivant Denon, Dominique, *Mit Napoleon in Ägypten. 1798–1799* (Tübingen, 1978).

Westenrieder, L. von, *Beyträge zur vaterländischen Historie, Geographie, Statistik und Landwirtschaft, samt einer Uebersicht der schönen Literatur*, 10 vols. (Munich, 1788–1807).

'Zu der neuesten Geschichte des Malteser-Ordens', in *Europäische Annalen*, iv (Tübingen, 1808).

b) Literature

Antier, J.J., *Marins de Provence et du Languedoc. Ving-cinq siecles d'histoire du littoral français mediteranéen* (Avignon, 1977).

Antochevsky, J.K., *L'Ordre Souverain de Saint-Jean de Jérusalem, dit Ordre de Malte* (St. Petersburg, 1914).

Aretin, H. von, 'Die Bayerische Zunge des Souverainen Ordens vom H. Johannes zu Jerusalem (Malteser Orden) 1782–1808', *RSMOM*, ii, 16 (July 1938), 32–41.

Artaud de Montor, A. F., *Histoire du Pape Pie VII* (Paris, 1839).

Ay, K. L., *Land und Fürst im alten Bayern. 16.-18. Jahrhundert* (Ratisbon, n.y.).

Barz, W.-D., 'Die letzte Karawane des Johanniterordens von 1784. Betrachtet im Zusammenhang mit seinem Niedergang auf Malta', *Militärgeschichtliche Mitteilungen*, No. 44 (1988), 41–9.

Bastgen, B., *Bayern und der Heilige Stuhl in der ersten Hälfte des 19. Jahrhunderts* (Munich, 1940).

Bauer, R., *Der kurfürstliche geistliche Rat und die bayerische Kirchenpolitik 1768–1802* (Munich, 1971) (= Miscellanea bavarica monacensia, xxxii).

Bauer, R., 'Kasimir von Häffelin und die kurbayerischen Landes- und Hofbistumsbestrebungen zwischen 1781 und 1789', in *Zeitschrift für bayerische Landesgeschichte*, xxxiv, 3 (1972), 733–67.

Bauerreis, R., *Kirchengeschichte Bayerns*, vii '1600–1803' (Augsburg, 1970).

Benhadda, Abderrehim, *Le Maroc et la Sublime Porte (XVIe-XVIIIe siècles)* (Zaghouan, 1998).

Blondy, A., 'Malte et l'Ordre de Malte a l'epreuve des idees nouvelles (1740–1820)' unpublished habilitation thesis, University of Sorbonne (Paris IV) 1992/93, 4 vols.

Bono, Salvatore, *I corsari barbareschi* (Turin, 1964).

Broadley, A.M., *History of Freemasonry ... in Malta from 1800* (London, 1880).

Castagnino Berlinghieri, U., *Congresso di Vienna e principio di legittimità. La questione del Sovrano Militare Ordine di San Giovanni Gerosolimitano, detto di Malta* (Milan, 2006).

Castillo, D., *The Maltese Cross. A Strategic History of Malta* (Westport 2006).

Cavaliero, R., 'The Decline of the Maltese Corso in the XVIIIth Century. A Study in Maritime History', *Melita Historica* ii, 4 (1959), 224–38.

Cavaliero, R., *The last of the Crusaders. The knights of St John and Malta in the eighteenth century* (London, 1960).

Caywood, D., 'Freemasonry and the Knights of Malta', *Ars Quatuor Coronatorum*, lxxxiii (1970), 71–95.

Cervera y Jácome, J., *El Panteón de Marinos Ilustres* (Madrid, 1926), 1

Ciappara, F., 'Gio. Nicolò Muscat: Church-State Relations in Hospitaller Malta during the Enlightenment, 1786–1798', in Victor Mallia-Milanes (ed.), *Hospitaller Malta 1530–1798. Studies on Early Modern Malta and the Order of St John of Jerusalem* (Malta, 1993), 605–58.

Clark, R.M., *The Evangelical Knights of Saint John. A history of the Bailiwick of Brandenburg* (Dallas, 2003).

Cook, Weston F. *The hundred years war for Morocco: gunpowder and the military revolution in the early modern Muslim world* (Boulder, 1994).

Darmanin Demajo, G., 'La lingue Angla Bavara e la sua albergia', *Archivio Storico di Malta* Anno VII, xiv, Fasc. II (28 January 1936), 224–36.

Dauber, Robert L., *Die Marine des Johanniter-Malteser Ritter Ordens* (Graz-Gnas, 1989).

Du Moulin-Eckart, R., *Bayern unter dem Ministerium Montgelas 1799–1817*, i (Munich, 1877).

Earle, P., *Corsairs of Malta and Barbary* (London, 1970).

Ebersold, G., *Rokoko, Reform und Revolution - ein politisches Lebensbild des Kurfürsten Karl Theodor* (Frankfurt a. M., 1985).

Engel, L., *Geschichte des Illuminaten-Ordens. Ein Beitrag zur Geschichte Bayerns* (Berlin, 1906).

Fendler, R., *Johann Casimir von Haeffelin. 1737-1827. Historiker – Kirchenpolitiker – Diplomat und Kardinal* (Mainz, 1980) (= Quellen und Abhandlungen zur Mittelrheinischen Kirchengeschichte, xxxv).

Fernán-Núñez, Conde de, *Vida de Carlos III* (Madrid, 1898).

Fernández Duro, C., *La Armada Española, desde la unión de los reinos de Castilla y Aragón* viii (Madrid, 1973).

Fichtl, W., 'Aufklrung und Zensur', in *Krone und Verfassung* (Munich, 1992), 174–85.

Fontenay, M., 'Corsaires de la foi ou rentiers du sol? Les chevaliers de Malte dans le corso méditerranéen au XVIIe siècle', *Revue d'Histoire Moderne et Contemporaine*, xxxv (July–September 1988), 361–84.

Fontenay, M., 'Les missions des galères de Malte, 1530–1798', in *Guerre et commerce en Méditerranée, IXe-XXe siècles*, ed. M. Verge Franceschi (Paris, 1991).

Fontenay, M., 'The Mediterranean World, 1500–1800: Social and Economic Perspectives', in *Hospitaller Malta 1530–1798. Studies on Early*

Modern Malta and the Order of St John of Jerusalem, ed. V. Mallia–Milanes (Malta, 1993), 43–110.

Fontenay, M., Tenenti, A., 'Course et piraterie méditerranéennes de la fin du Moyen Age au début du XIXe siècle', in *Course et Piraterie. 18e Colloque International d'Histoire maritime* (San Francisco, 1975, Paris, 1975), 78–131.

Förch, A., 'Die letzte Hofhaltung zu Neuburg a.d', *Collektaneen-Blatt für die Geschichte Bayerns*, Year 35 (1869), 1–41.

Franz-Willing, G., *Die Bayerische Vatikangesandtschaft. 1803–1934* (Munich, 1965).

Freller, T., 'Die "Malteserkrise". Anmerkungen zum bayerisch-russischen Verhältnis am Beginn der Regierungszeit Max' IV. Joseph', *Zeitschrift für bayerische Landesgeschichte*, lxix, 2 (2006), 595–643.

Freller, T., 'Korsarenjäger, General und Gesandter – Joseph Maria von Rechberg und Rothenlöwen (1769–1833)', *Militärgeschichtliche Zeitschrift* lxv, 2 (2006), 485–504.

Freller, T., *The Anglo-Bavarian Langue of the Order of Malta* (Malta, 2001).

Freller, T., '"The Shining of the Moon" – The Mediterranean Tour of Muhammad Ibn Uthmān, envoy of Morocco, in 1782', *Journal of Mediterranean Studies*, xii, 2 (2002), 307–26.

Galea, M., *Die deutschen Ordensritter von Malta* (Malta, 1996).

Galea, M., *Grand Master Emanuel de Rohan. 1775–1797* (Malta, 1996)

Geschichte des Bayerischen Heeres. Im Auftrage des Kriegs-Ministeriums herausgegeben vom Königlich Bayerischen Kriegsarchiv, iii (Munich, 1909).

Golovkine, F., *La cour et le règne de Paul I* (Paris, 1905).

Gomez Vizcaino, J. A., *Antonio Barceló y Pont de la Terra. De Patron de jabeque – correo a Tenente General de la Real Armada* (Madrid, 2007).

Gregory, D., *Malta, Britain, and the European Powers, 1793-1815* (London, 1996).

Gumppenberg, L.A., 'Das bayerische Gross-Priorat des Johanniter-Ordens', *Oberbayerisches Archiv für vaterländische Geschichte*, iv (1843), 68–91.

Habel, H., *Landkreis Mindelheim* (Munich, 1971).

Hammermayer, L., 'Illuminaten in Bayern. Zu Geschichte, Fortwirken und Legende des Geheimbundes', in *Krone und Verfassung* (Munich, 1992), 147–73.

Hardman, William, *A History of Malta during the French and British Occupations, 1798–1800* (London, 1909).

Heigel, K.T. von, 'Neue Denkwürdigkeiten vom pfalzbayerischen Hof unter Karl Theodor', in K.T. von Heigel, *Quellen und Abhandlungen zur neueren Geschichte Bayerns*, ii (Munich, 1890).

Hoppen, Alison, *The Fortification of Malta by the Order of St John 1530–1798* (Malta, 1999).

Kleinschmidt, A., 'Der Vertrag von Gatschina', *Forschungen zur Geschichte*

Bayerns, vi (1898), 213–16.

Klemm, L., *Aloys von Rechberg als bayerischer Politiker (1766–1849)* (Munich, 1975).

Krone und Verfassung. König Max I. Joseph und der neue Staat. Beiträge zur Bayerischen Geschichte und Kunst 1799–1825 (Munich, 1992).

Lacroix, A. (ed.), *Deodat Dolomieu*, 2 vols. (Paris, 1921).

Lavigerie, O. de, *L'Ordre de Malte depuis la Revolution Française* (Paris, 1889).

Le Chevalier des soirées de St Petersbourg par l'Abbé Jules Loth (Rouen, 1885).

Litzenburger, L., 'Der bischöfliche Informativprozeß des Münchener Hofbibliothekars Casimir Haeffelin', *Römische Quartalschrift*, 1 (1955), 230–47.

Lourido-Díaz, Ramón, *Marruecos en la Segunda mitad del siglo XVIII* (Madrid, 1978).

Lurz, G., 'Zur Geschichte der bayerischen Schulreformation in der Aufklärungsepoche', *Mitteilungen der Gesellschaft für deutsche Erziehungs- und Schulgeschichte*, xiii (Berlin, 1903).

Lynch, J., *Bourbon Spain 1700–1808* (Oxford, 1993).

Mallia-Milanes, V. (ed.), *Hospitaller Malta 1530–1798. Studies on Early Modern Malta and the Order of St John of Jerusalem* (Malta, 1993).

Miège, L., *Histoire de Malte*, 2 vols. (Paris, 1840).

Morane, P., *Paul 1er de Russie avant l'avènement (1754–1796)* (Paris, 1907).

Müller, A., *Bayerische Politik und Bayerische Diplomaten zur Zeit Carl Theodors und Max Josephs* (Munich, 1954).

Moreno, J., *Viage á Constantinopla en el año de 1784* (Madrid, 1790).

Mori Ubaldini, U., *La Marina del Sovrano Militare Ordine di San Giovanni* (Rome, 1971).

Muscat, J., *Naval Activities of the Knights of St John 1530–1798* (Malta, 2002).

Muscat, J., *The Maltese Vaxxell. The Third Rates of the Order of St John. 1700–1798* (Malta, 1999).

Panzac, D., *Les corsaires barbaresques. La fin d'une épopée (1800–1830)* (Paris, 1999).

Panzavecchia, F., *L'ultimo periodo della Storia di Malta* (Malta, 1835).

Pierredon, M. de, *Histoire politique de l'Ordre souverain de Saint Jean de Jérusalem (Ordre de Malte) de 1789 à 1955*, 2 vols. (Paris, 1956–63).

Rall, H., *Kurfürst Karl Theodor, Regierender Herr in sieben Ländern* (Mannheim–Leipzig–Vienna–Zurich, 1993).

Rodriguez Casado, V., *Política marroquí de Carlos III* (Madrid, 1946).

Rossi, E., 'Corrispondenza fra i Pascia di Tripoli ed i Gran Maestri dell'Ordine a Malta dal 1711 al 1760', *Rivista degli Studi Orientali*, 10 (1923–25), 414–32.

Rossi, E., 'Il dominio dei cavalieri di Malta a Tripoli 1530–1551, e i rapporti dell'Ordine con Tripoli nei secoli seguenti 1551–1798', *Archivum Melitense*, vi, 2 (1924), 43–85.

Rossi, E., 'Manoscritti e documenti orientali nelle Biblioteche e negli Archivi di Malta.', *Archivio Storico di Malta*, Anno 2, 2, fasc. I (October–December 1930), 1–10.

Rossi, E., *Storia della Marina dell'Ordine di S. Giovanni di Gerusalemme di Rodi e di Malta* (Rome, 1926).

Rouet de Journel, M.J., *Nonciatures de Russie d'après les documents authentiques*, ii, 'Nonciature de Litta 1797–1799', (Vatican City, 1943) (Studie e Testi, clxvii).

Rouet de Journel, M.J., 'Malte et Russie', *Annales de l'O.S.M. de Malte* (July/September 1961), 84–97.

Ryan, F.R., *The House of the Temple: A Study of Malta and its Knights in the French Revolution* (London, 1930).

Saul, E., *Russia and the Mediterranean 1796–1807* (Chicago, 1970).

Schembri, G., *The Malta and Russia Connection* (Malta, 1990).

Schermerhorn, E., *Malta of the Knights* (Surrey, 1929).

Schottenloher, K., 'Der bayerische Gesandte Kasimir Haeffelin in Malta, Rom und Neapel (1796–1827)', *Zeitschrift für bayerische Landesgeschichte* v (1932), 378–415.

Schüttler, H., *Die Mitglieder des Illuminatenordens 1776–1787/93* (n.y., 1991) (= Deutsche Hochschuledition, xviii).

Shaler, W., *Algiers, political, historical, and civil…* (Boston, 1826).

Sherbowitz-Wetzor, O. de, C. Toumanoff, *The Order of Malta and the Russian Empire* (Rome, 1969).

Sicherer, H. von, *Staat und Kirche in Bayern vom Regierungsantritt des Kurfürsten Maximilian Joseph IV. bis zur Erklärung von Tegernsee 1799–1821* (Munich, 1873).

Spiteri, S., *Fortresses of the Cross. Hospitaller Military Architecture (1136–1798)* (Malta, 1994).

Steinberger, L., *Die Gründung der baierischen Zunge des Malteserordens* (Berlin, 1911).

Terrinoni, G., *Memorie Storiche della resa di Malta ai Francesi nel 1798 e del S. M. Ordine Gerosolimitano dal detto anno ai nostri giorni* (Rome, 1867).

Testa, C., *The French in Malta. 1798–1800* (Malta, 1997).

Valensi, L., 'Esclaves Chrétiens et Esclaves Noirs à Tunis au XVIIIe Siècle', *Annales É.S.C.* xxii, 6 (1967), 1267–88.

Van Dülmen, R., *Der Geheimbund der Illuminaten* (Stuttgart–Bad Cannstadt, 1977).

Van Dülmen, R., *Der Geheimbund der Illuminaten. Darstellung, Analyse, Dokumentation* (Stuttgart, 1975).

Vella, A.P., *Malta and the Czars. Diplomatic relations between the Order of St John and Russia, 1697–1802* (Malta, 1972).

Völderndorff und Maradein, Eduard von, *Kriegsgeschichte von Bayern unter König Maximilian Joseph I*, i (Munich, 1826).

Waldstein-Wartenberg, B., 'Entwicklung des Malteser-Ordens nach dem Fall von Malta bis zur Gegenwart', in, Adam Wienand (ed.), *Der Johanniter-Orden. Der Malteser-Orden. Der ritterliche Orden des hl. Johannes vom Spital zu Jerusalem. Seine Aufgaben, seine Geschichte* (Cologne, 1970), 233–9.

Walishewski, K., *Paul the First of Russia, the Son of Catherine the Great* (London, 1913, French version published in 1903).

Weis, E., *Montgelas. 1759–1799. Zwischen Revolution und Reform* (Munich, 1972).

Wettinger, G., *Slavery in the Islands of Malta and Gozo (ca. 1000–1812)* (Malta, 2002).

Wismayer, J.M., *The Fleet of the Order of St John 1530–1798* (Malta, 1997).

Wismayer, J.M., *The History of the King's Own Malta Regiment and the Armed Forces of the Order of St John* (Malta, 1989).

Zammit, William, 'De Rohan's Reggimento di Malta: a source of religious unorthodoxy in late eighteenth-century Malta', *Sacra Militia*, iv (2005).